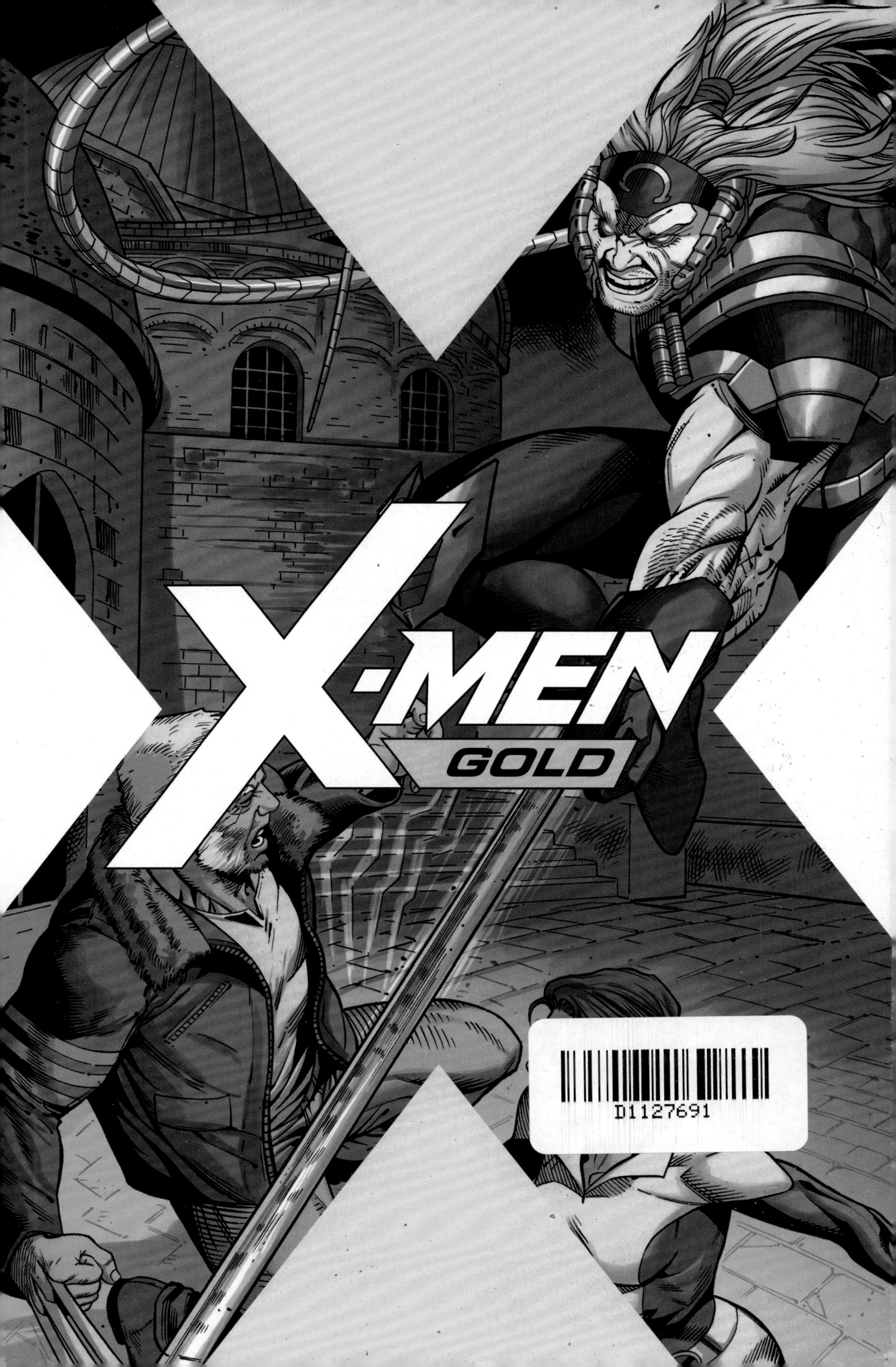
X-MEN
GOLD

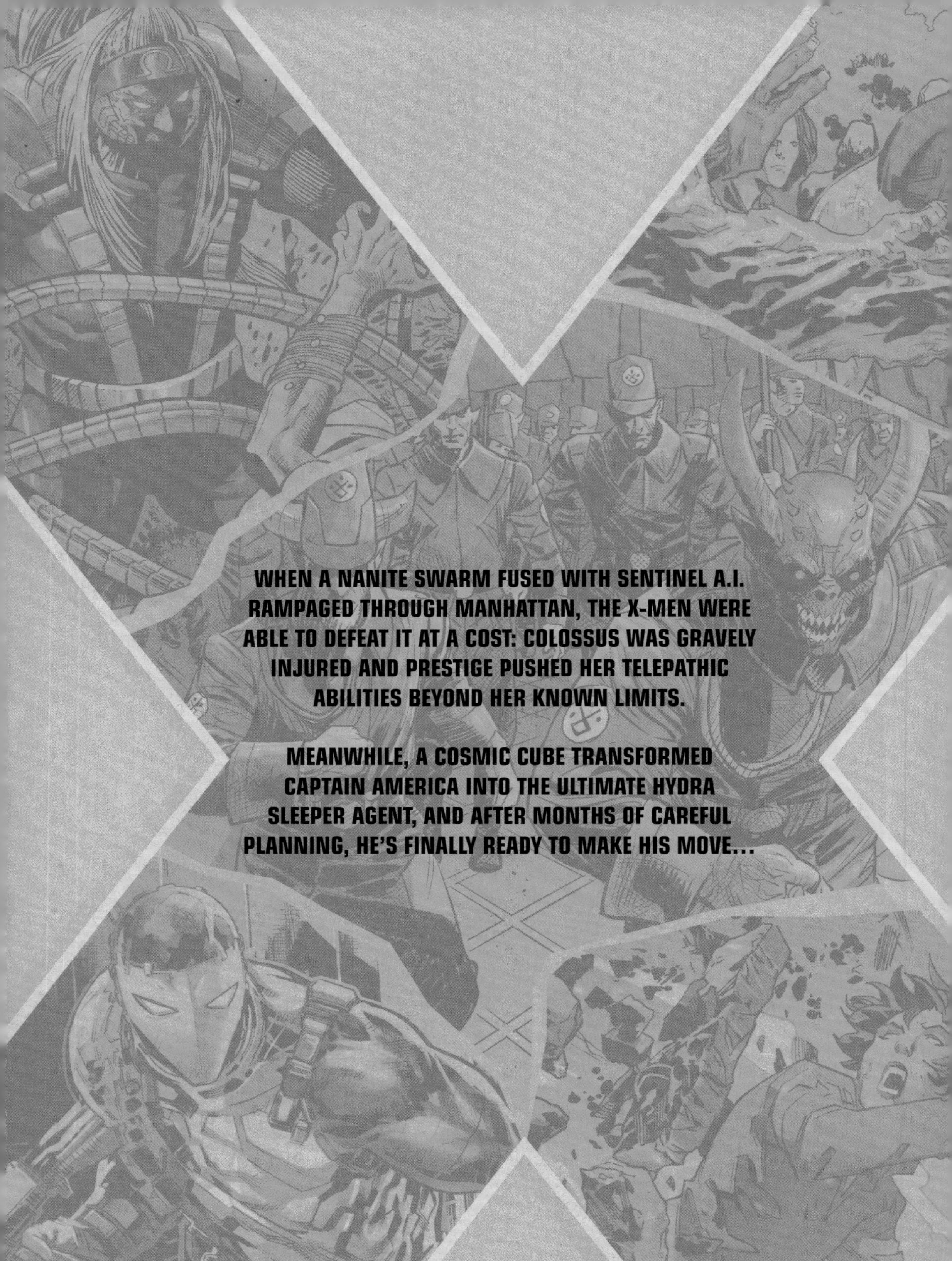

WHEN A NANITE SWARM FUSED WITH SENTINEL A.I.
RAMPAGED THROUGH MANHATTAN, THE X-MEN WERE
ABLE TO DEFEAT IT AT A COST: COLOSSUS WAS GRAVELY
INJURED AND PRESTIGE PUSHED HER TELEPATHIC
ABILITIES BEYOND HER KNOWN LIMITS.

MEANWHILE, A COSMIC CUBE TRANSFORMED
CAPTAIN AMERICA INTO THE ULTIMATE HYDRA
SLEEPER AGENT, AND AFTER MONTHS OF CAREFUL
PLANNING, HE'S FINALLY READY TO MAKE HIS MOVE...

X-MEN GOLD VOL. 2: EVIL EMPIRES. Contains material originally published in magazine form as X-MEN GOLD #7-12. First printing 2017. ISBN# 978-1-302-90731-0. Published by MARVEL WORLDWIDE, INC., a subsidiary of MARVEL ENTERTAINMENT, LLC. OFFICE OF PUBLICATION: 135 West 50th Street, New York, NY 10020. Copyright © 2017 MARVEL No similarity between any of the names, characters, persons, and/or institutions in this magazine with those of any living or dead person or institution is intended, and any such similarity which may exist is purely coincidental. **Printed in Canada.** DAN BUCKLEY, President, Marvel Entertainment; JOE QUESADA, Chief Creative Officer; TOM BREVOORT, SVP of Publishing; DAVID BOGART, SVP of Business Affairs & Operations, Publishing & Partnership; C.B. CEBULSKI, VP of Brand Management & Development, Asia; DAVID GABRIEL, SVP of Sales & Marketing, Publishing; JEFF YOUNGQUIST, VP of Production & Special Projects; DAN CARR, Executive Director of Publishing Technology; ALEX MORALES, Director of Publishing Operations; SUSAN CRESPI, Production Manager; STAN LEE, Chairman Emeritus. For information regarding advertising in Marvel Comics or on Marvel.com, please contact Vit DeBellis, Integrated Sales Manager, at vdebellis@marvel.com. For Marvel subscription inquiries, please call 888-511-5480. **Manufactured between 9/22/2017 and 10/24/2017 by SOLISCO PRINTERS, SCOTT, QC, CANADA.**

X-MEN GOLD

EVIL EMPIRES

Writer/**MARC GUGGENHEIM**

ISSUES #7-9
Artist/**KEN LASHLEY**
Colorists/**FRANK MARTIN** (#7-9)
& **ANDREW CROSSLEY** (#8-9)
Cover Art/**KEN LASHLEY** & **DAVID CURIEL**

ISSUES #10-11
Penciler/**LAN MEDINA**
Inkers/**JAY LEISTEN** (#10) & **CRAIG YEUNG** (#11)
Colorist/**FRANK MARTIN**
Cover Art/**KEN LASHLEY** & **DAVID CURIEL** (#10)
and **DAN MORA** & **DAVID CURIEL** (#11)

ISSUE #12
Artist/**LUKE ROSS**
Colorist/**FRANK MARTIN**
Cover Art/**KEN LASHLEY** & **NOLAN WOODARD**

Letterers/**VC'S JOE SABINO** (#7) & **CORY PETIT** (#8-12)

Assistant Editor/**CHRIS ROBINSON**
Editor/**DANIEL KETCHUM**
X-Men Group Editor/**MARK PANICCIA**

X-MEN CREATED BY **STAN LEE** & **JACK KIRBY**

Collection Editor/**JENNIFER GRÜNWALD** · Assistant Editor/**CAITLIN O'CONNELL**
Associate Managing Editor/**KATERI WOODY** · Editor, Special Projects/**MARK D. BEAZLEY**
VP Production & Special Projects/**JEFF YOUNGQUIST** · SVP Print, Sales & Marketing/**DAVID GABRIEL**
Book Designer/**JAY BOWEN**

Editor in Chief/**AXEL ALONSO** · Chief Creative Officer/**JOE QUESADA**
President/**DAN BUCKLEY** · Executive Producer/**ALAN FINE**

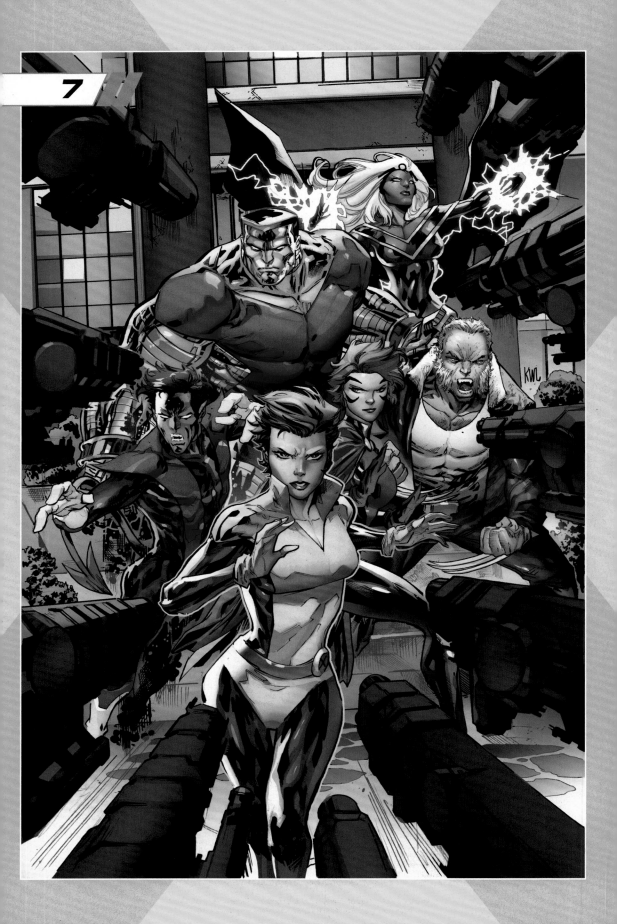

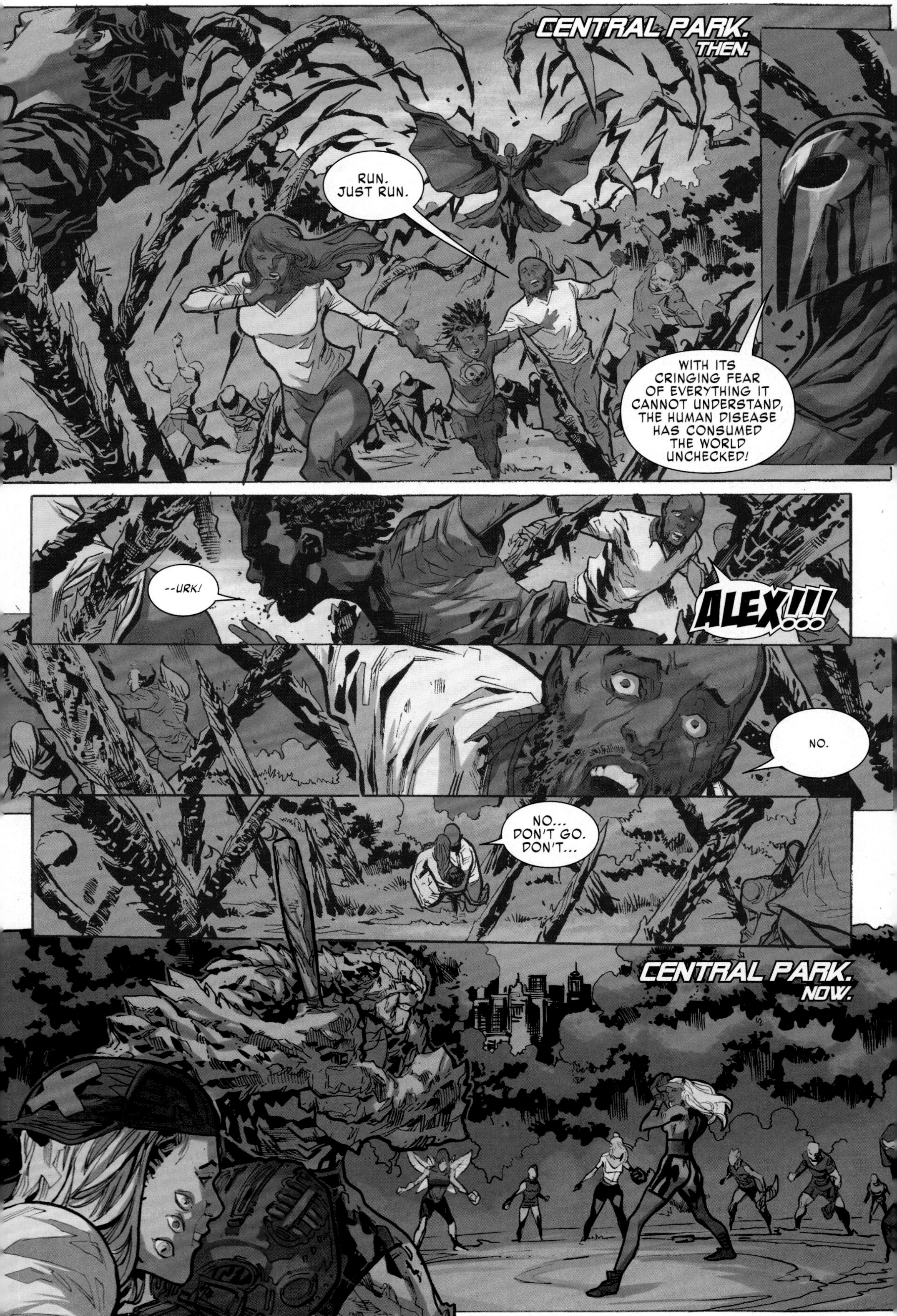
CENTRAL PARK. THEN.
RUN. JUST RUN.
WITH ITS CRINGING FEAR OF EVERYTHING IT CANNOT UNDERSTAND, THE HUMAN DISEASE HAS CONSUMED THE WORLD UNCHECKED!
--URK!
ALEX!!!
NO.
NO... DON'T GO. DON'T...
CENTRAL PARK. NOW.

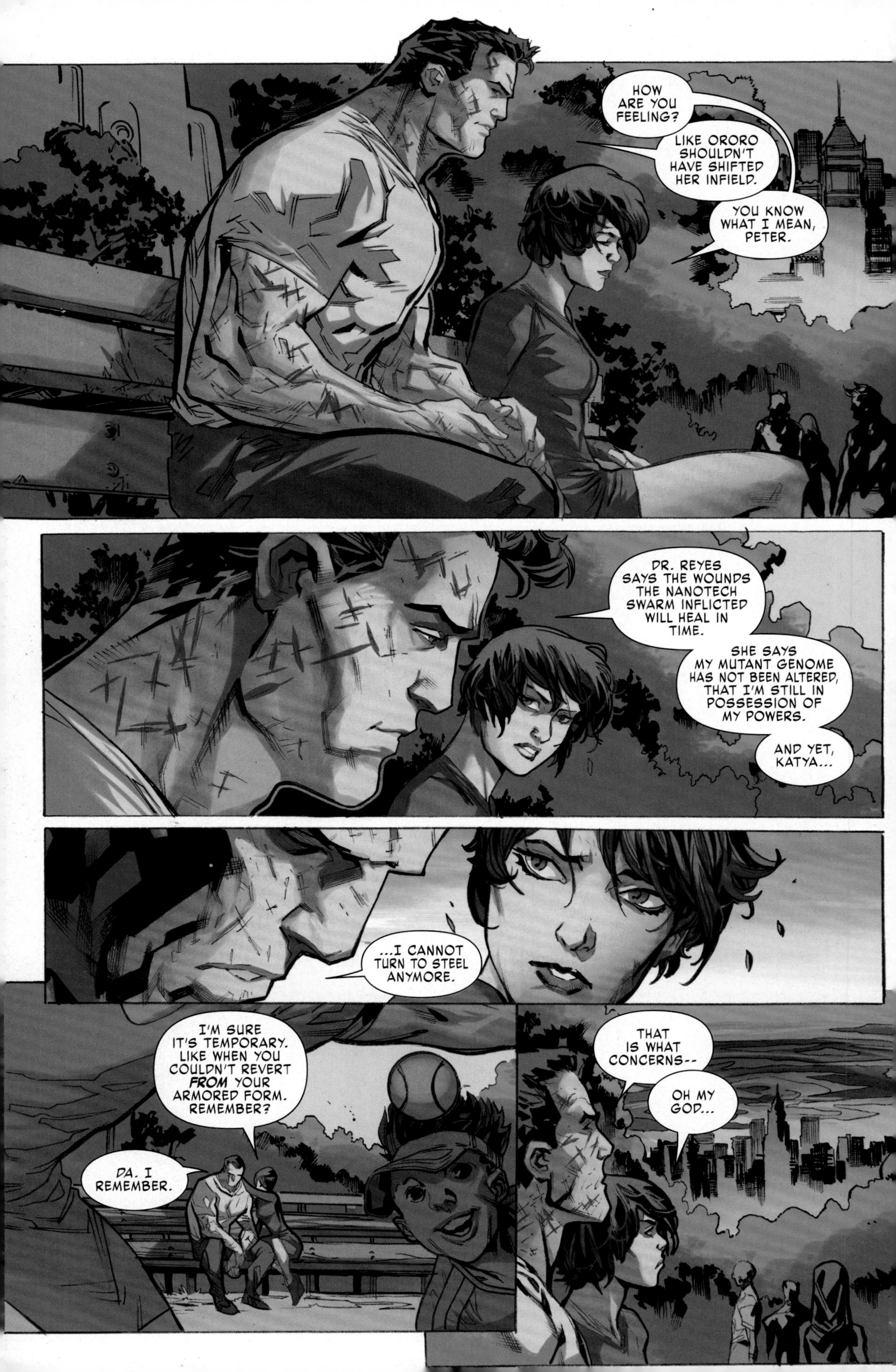
HOW ARE YOU FEELING?
LIKE ORORO SHOULDN'T HAVE SHIFTED HER INFIELD.
YOU KNOW WHAT I MEAN, PETER.
DR. REYES SAYS THE WOUNDS THE NANOTECH SWARM INFLICTED WILL HEAL IN TIME.
SHE SAYS MY MUTANT GENOME HAS NOT BEEN ALTERED, THAT I'M STILL IN POSSESSION OF MY POWERS.
AND YET, KATYA...
...I CANNOT TURN TO STEEL ANYMORE.
I'M SURE IT'S TEMPORARY. LIKE WHEN YOU COULDN'T REVERT FROM YOUR ARMORED FORM. REMEMBER?
DA. I REMEMBER.
THAT IS WHAT CONCERNS--
OH MY GOD...

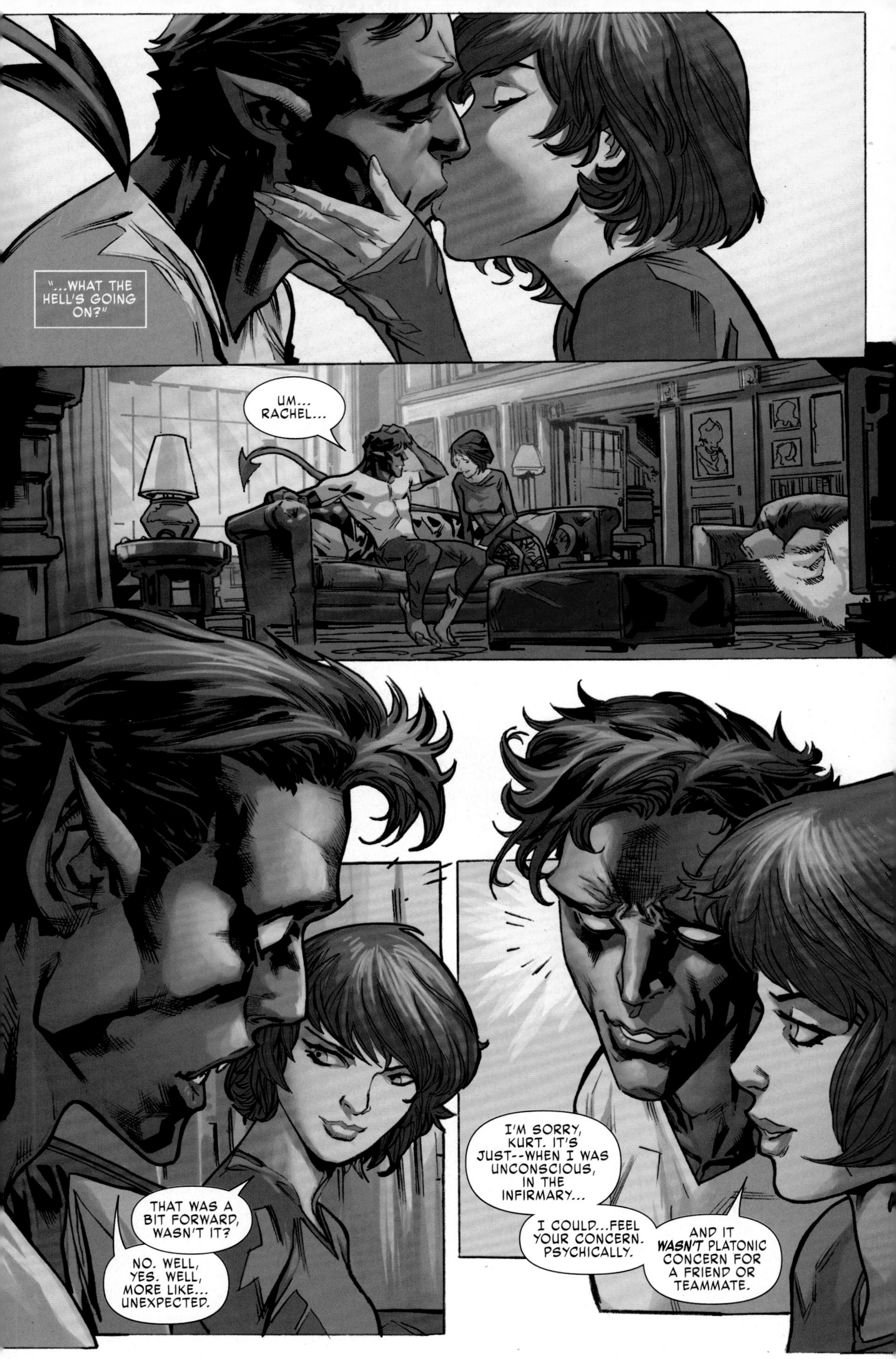
"...WHAT THE HELL'S GOING ON?"
UM... RACHEL...
THAT WAS A BIT FORWARD, WASN'T IT?
NO. WELL, YES. WELL, MORE LIKE... UNEXPECTED.
I'M SORRY, KURT. IT'S JUST--WHEN I WAS UNCONSCIOUS, IN THE INFIRMARY...
I COULD...FEEL YOUR CONCERN. PSYCHICALLY.
AND IT WASN'T PLATONIC CONCERN FOR A FRIEND OR TEAMMATE.

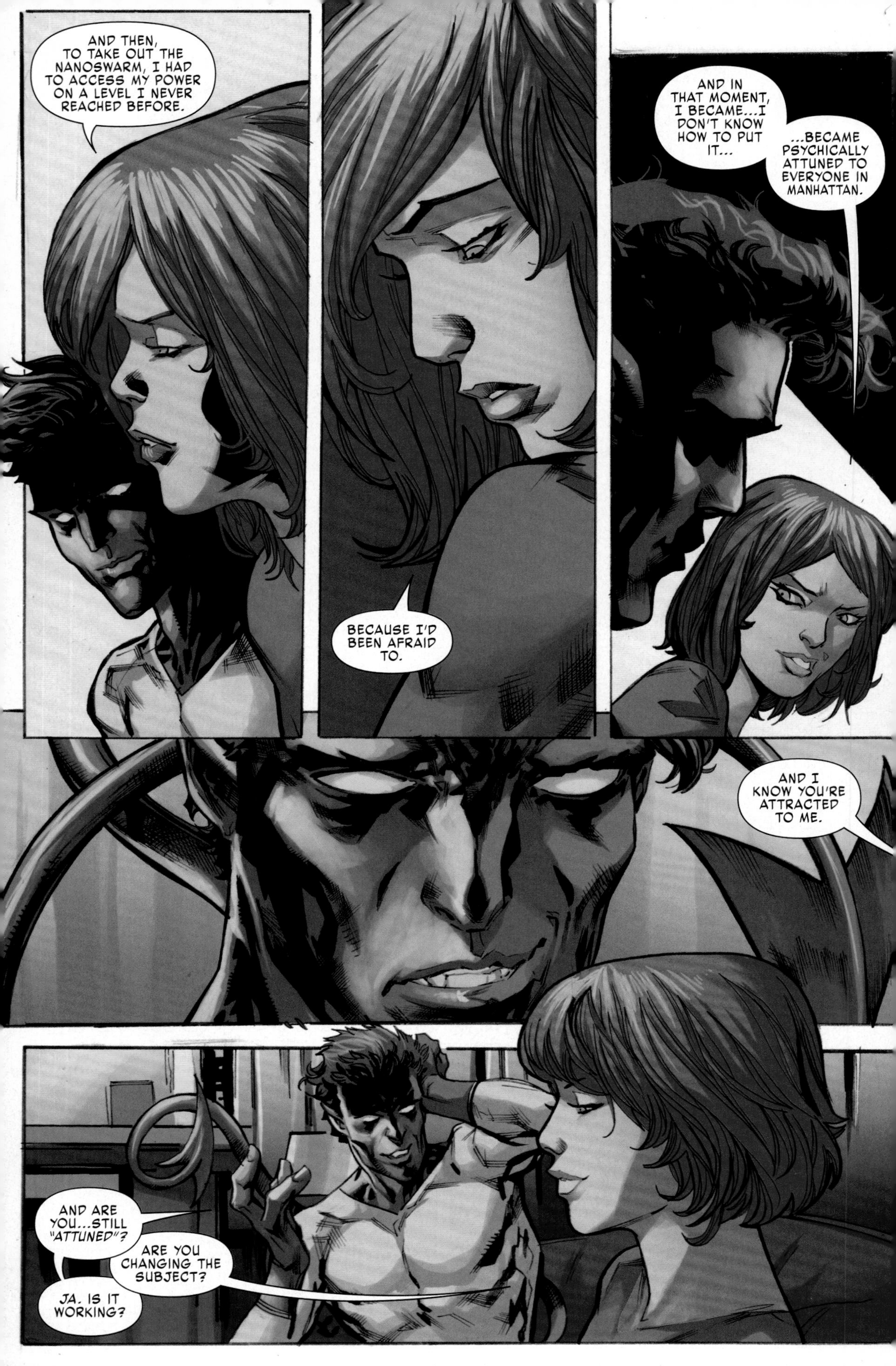

AND THEN, TO TAKE OUT THE NANOSWARM, I HAD TO ACCESS MY POWER ON A LEVEL I NEVER REACHED BEFORE.
BECAUSE I'D BEEN AFRAID TO.
AND IN THAT MOMENT, I BECAME...I DON'T KNOW HOW TO PUT IT...
...BECAME PSYCHICALLY ATTUNED TO EVERYONE IN MANHATTAN.
AND I KNOW YOU'RE ATTRACTED TO ME.
AND ARE YOU...STILL "ATTUNED"?
ARE YOU CHANGING THE SUBJECT?
JA. IS IT WORKING?

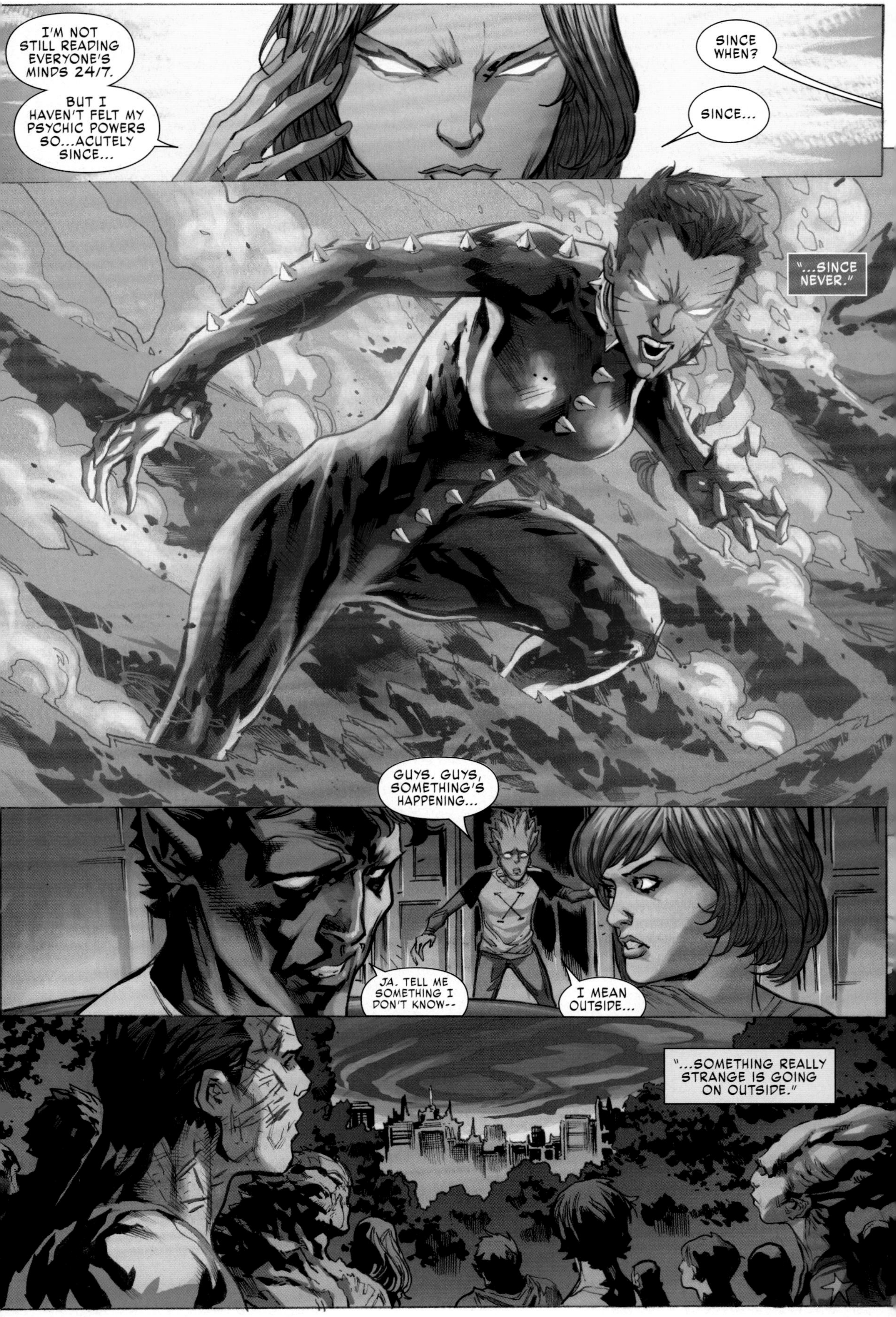

I'M NOT STILL READING EVERYONE'S MINDS 24/7.
BUT I HAVEN'T FELT MY PSYCHIC POWERS SO...ACUTELY SINCE...
SINCE WHEN?
SINCE...
"...SINCE NEVER."
GUYS. GUYS, SOMETHING'S HAPPENING...
JA. TELL ME SOMETHING I DON'T KNOW--
I MEAN OUTSIDE...
"...SOMETHING REALLY STRANGE IS GOING ON OUTSIDE."

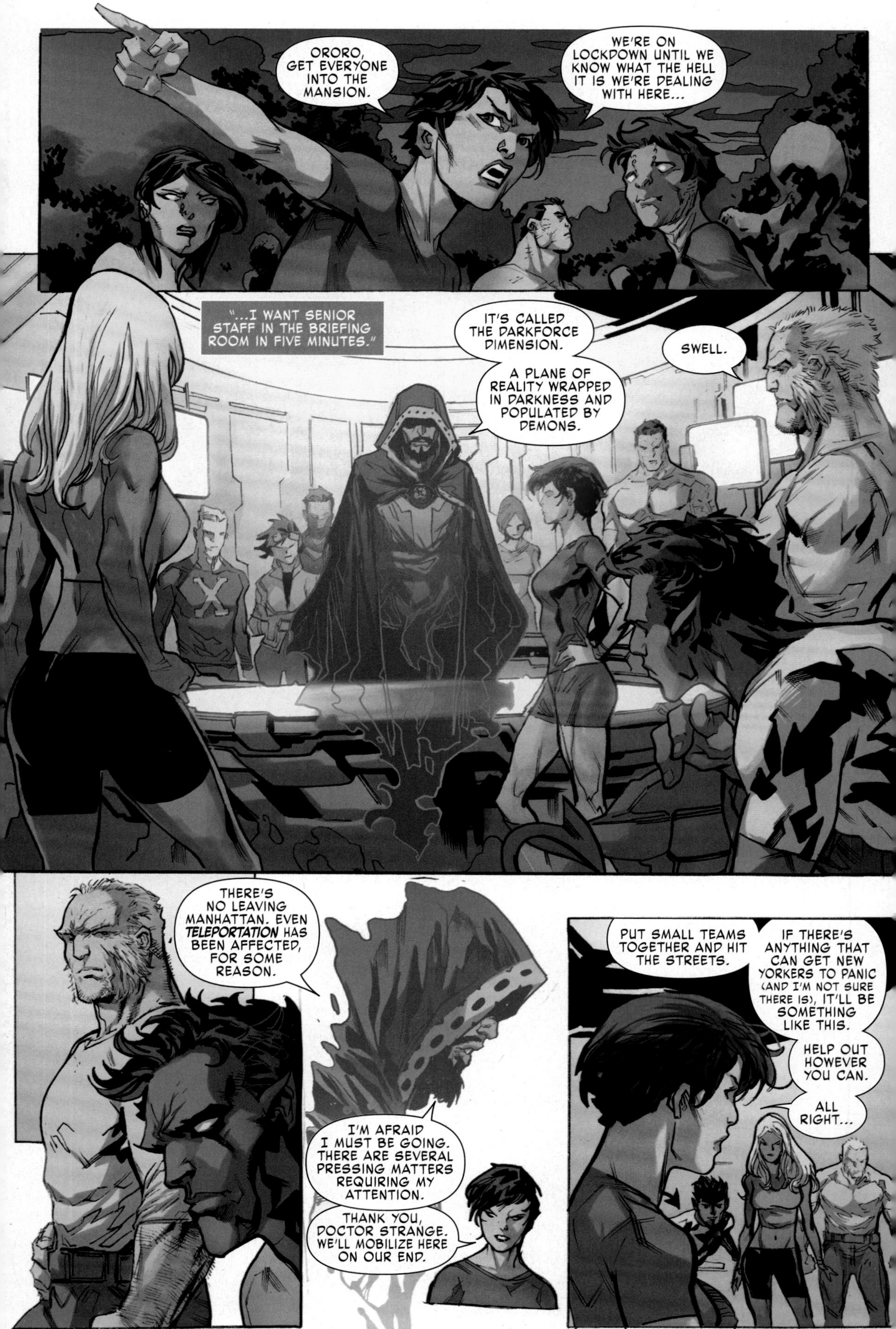
ORORO, GET EVERYONE INTO THE MANSION.
WE'RE ON LOCKDOWN UNTIL WE KNOW WHAT THE HELL IT IS WE'RE DEALING WITH HERE...
"...I WANT SENIOR STAFF IN THE BRIEFING ROOM IN FIVE MINUTES."
IT'S CALLED THE DARKFORCE DIMENSION.
A PLANE OF REALITY WRAPPED IN DARKNESS AND POPULATED BY DEMONS.
SWELL.
THERE'S NO LEAVING MANHATTAN. EVEN *TELEPORTATION* HAS BEEN AFFECTED, FOR SOME REASON.
I'M AFRAID I MUST BE GOING. THERE ARE SEVERAL PRESSING MATTERS REQUIRING MY ATTENTION.
THANK YOU, DOCTOR STRANGE. WE'LL MOBILIZE HERE ON OUR END.
PUT SMALL TEAMS TOGETHER AND HIT THE STREETS.
IF THERE'S ANYTHING THAT CAN GET NEW YORKERS TO PANIC (AND I'M NOT SURE THERE IS), IT'LL BE SOMETHING LIKE THIS.
HELP OUT HOWEVER YOU CAN.
ALL RIGHT...

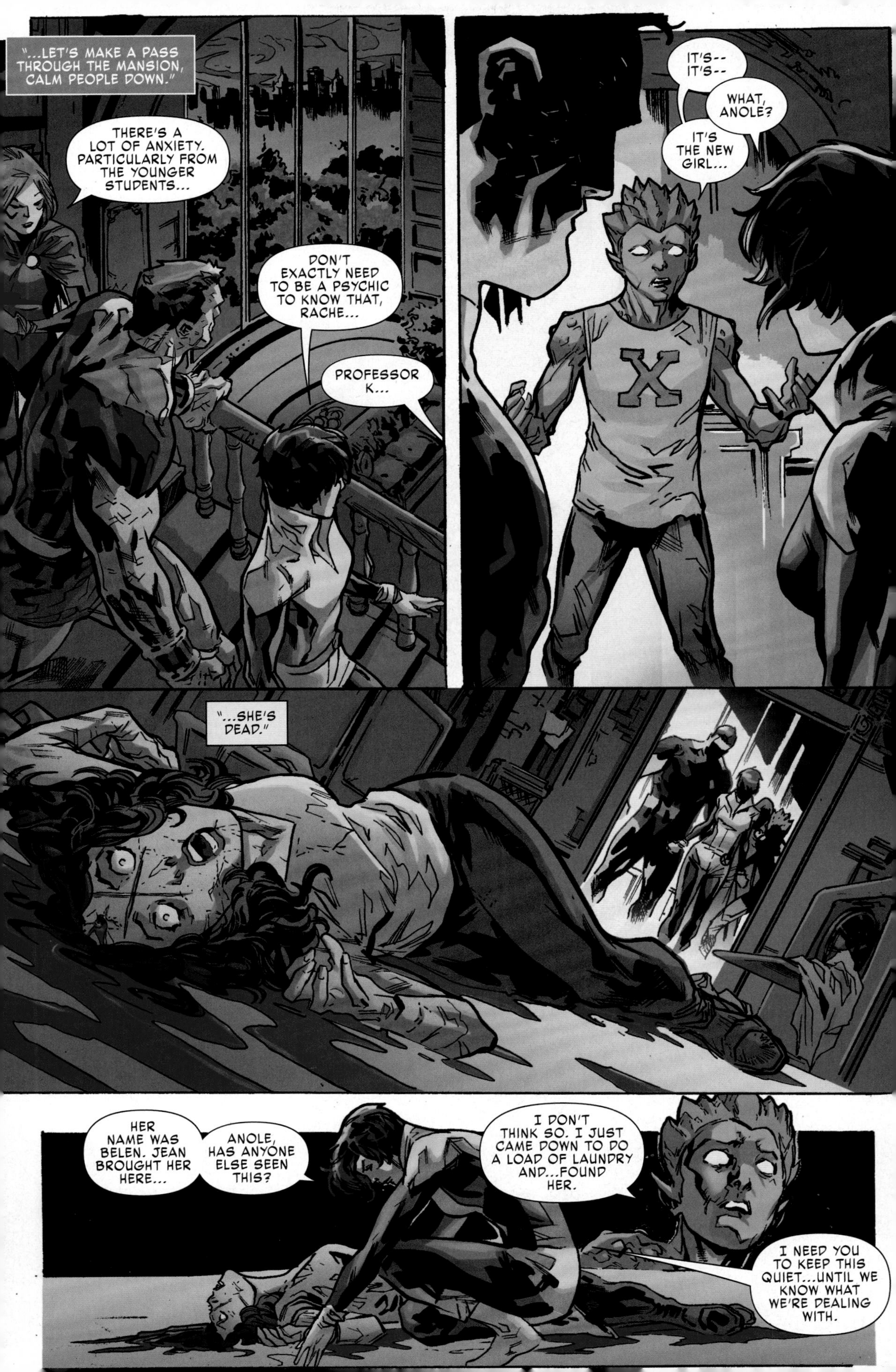
"...LET'S MAKE A PASS THROUGH THE MANSION, CALM PEOPLE DOWN."
THERE'S A LOT OF ANXIETY. PARTICULARLY FROM THE YOUNGER STUDENTS...
DON'T EXACTLY NEED TO BE A PSYCHIC TO KNOW THAT, RACHE...
PROFESSOR K...
IT'S-- IT'S--
WHAT, ANOLE?
IT'S THE NEW GIRL...
"...SHE'S DEAD."
HER NAME WAS BELEN. JEAN BROUGHT HER HERE...
ANOLE, HAS ANYONE ELSE SEEN THIS?
I DON'T THINK SO. I JUST CAME DOWN TO DO A LOAD OF LAUNDRY AND...FOUND HER.
I NEED YOU TO KEEP THIS QUIET...UNTIL WE KNOW WHAT WE'RE DEALING WITH.

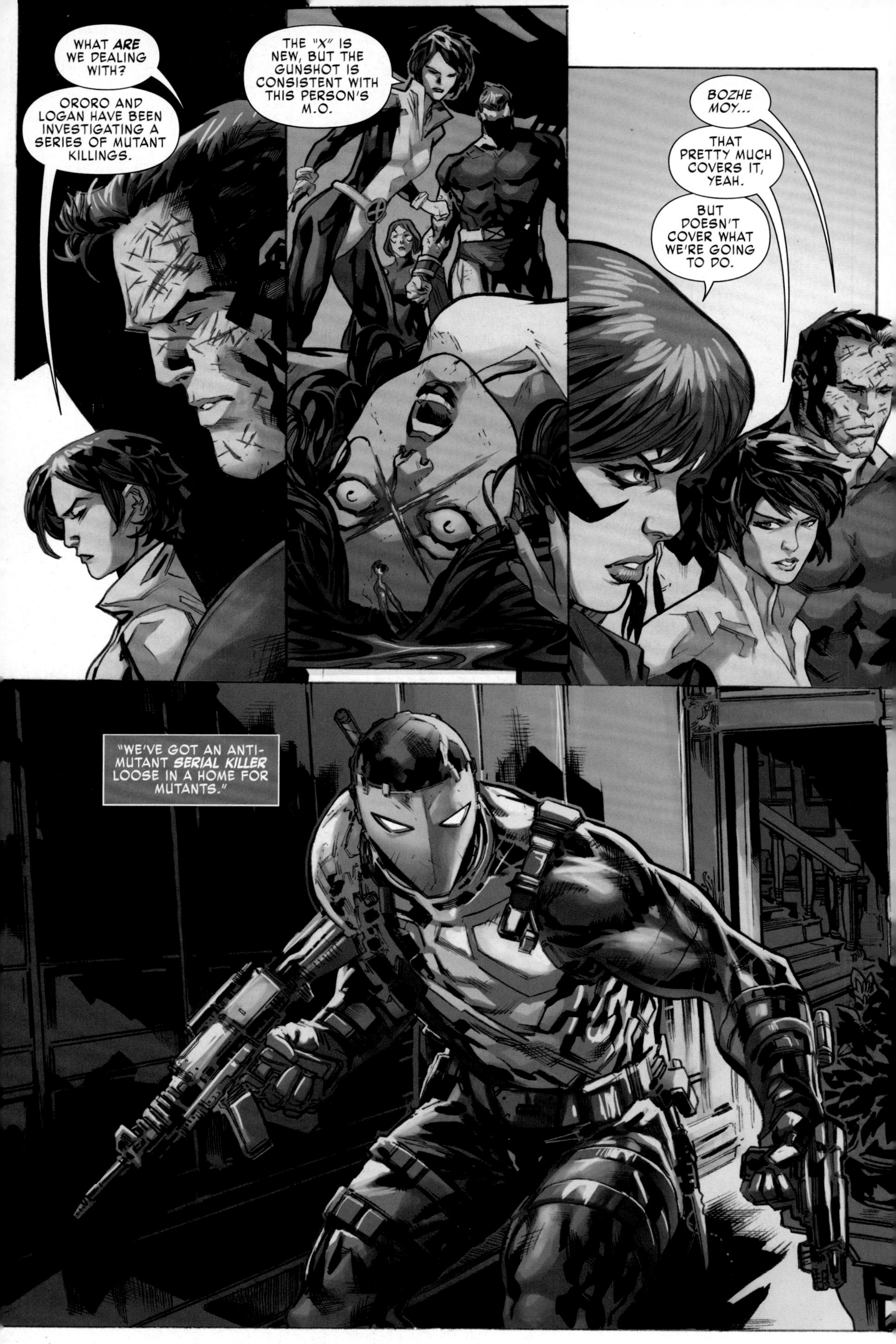

WHAT *ARE* WE DEALING WITH?
ORORO AND LOGAN HAVE BEEN INVESTIGATING A SERIES OF MUTANT KILLINGS.
THE "X" IS NEW, BUT THE GUNSHOT IS CONSISTENT WITH THIS PERSON'S M.O.
BOZHE MOY...
THAT PRETTY MUCH COVERS IT, YEAH.
BUT DOESN'T COVER WHAT WE'RE GOING TO DO.
"WE'VE GOT AN ANTI-MUTANT *SERIAL KILLER* LOOSE IN A HOME FOR MUTANTS."

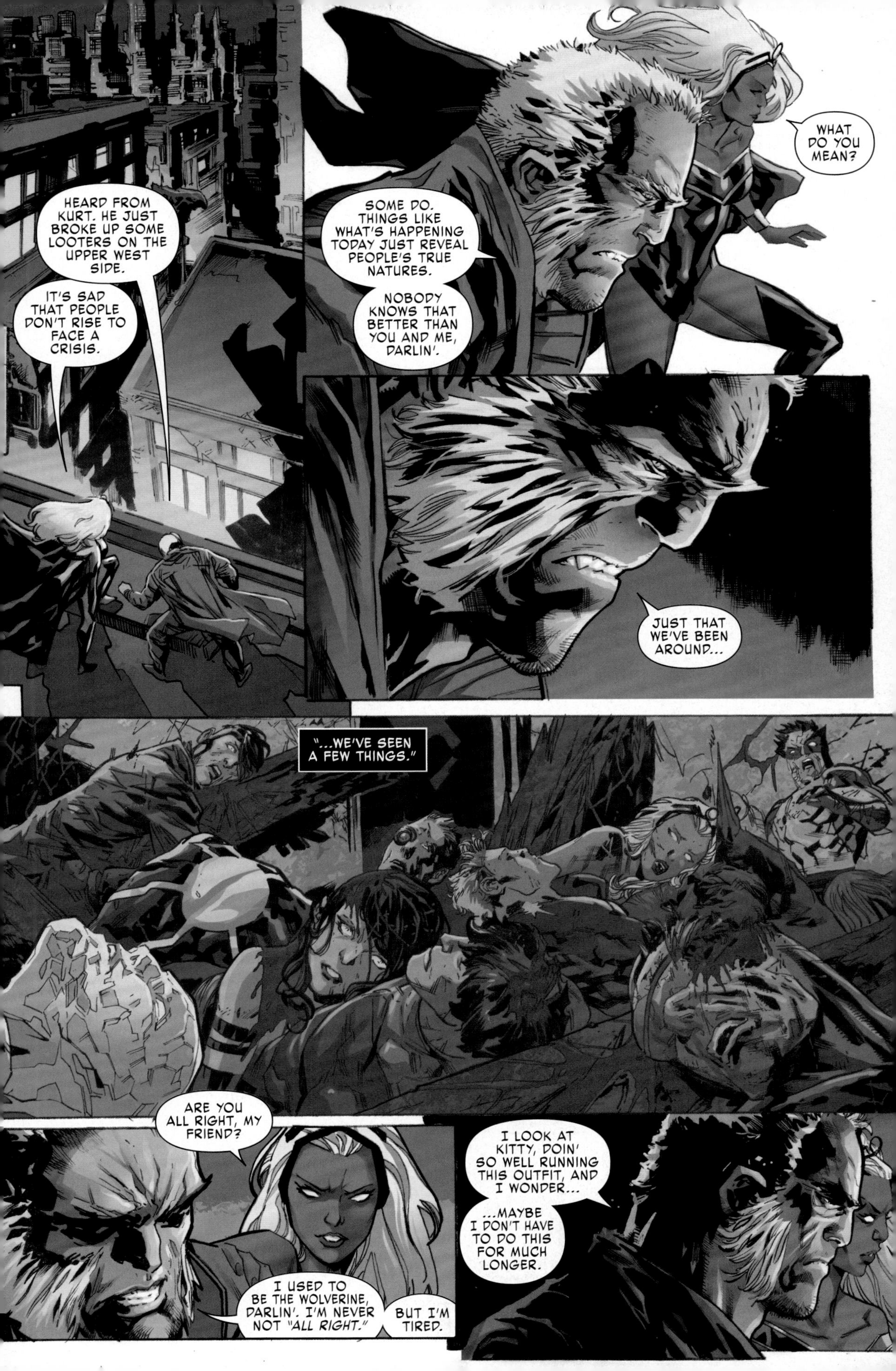
HEARD FROM KURT. HE JUST BROKE UP SOME LOOTERS ON THE UPPER WEST SIDE.
IT'S SAD THAT PEOPLE DON'T RISE TO FACE A CRISIS.
SOME DO. THINGS LIKE WHAT'S HAPPENING TODAY JUST REVEAL PEOPLE'S TRUE NATURES.
NOBODY KNOWS THAT BETTER THAN YOU AND ME, DARLIN'.
WHAT DO YOU MEAN?
JUST THAT WE'VE BEEN AROUND...
"...WE'VE SEEN A FEW THINGS."
ARE YOU ALL RIGHT, MY FRIEND?
I USED TO BE THE WOLVERINE, DARLIN'. I'M NEVER NOT "ALL RIGHT."
BUT I'M TIRED.
I LOOK AT KITTY, DOIN' SO WELL RUNNING THIS OUTFIT, AND I WONDER...
...MAYBE I DON'T HAVE TO DO THIS FOR MUCH LONGER.

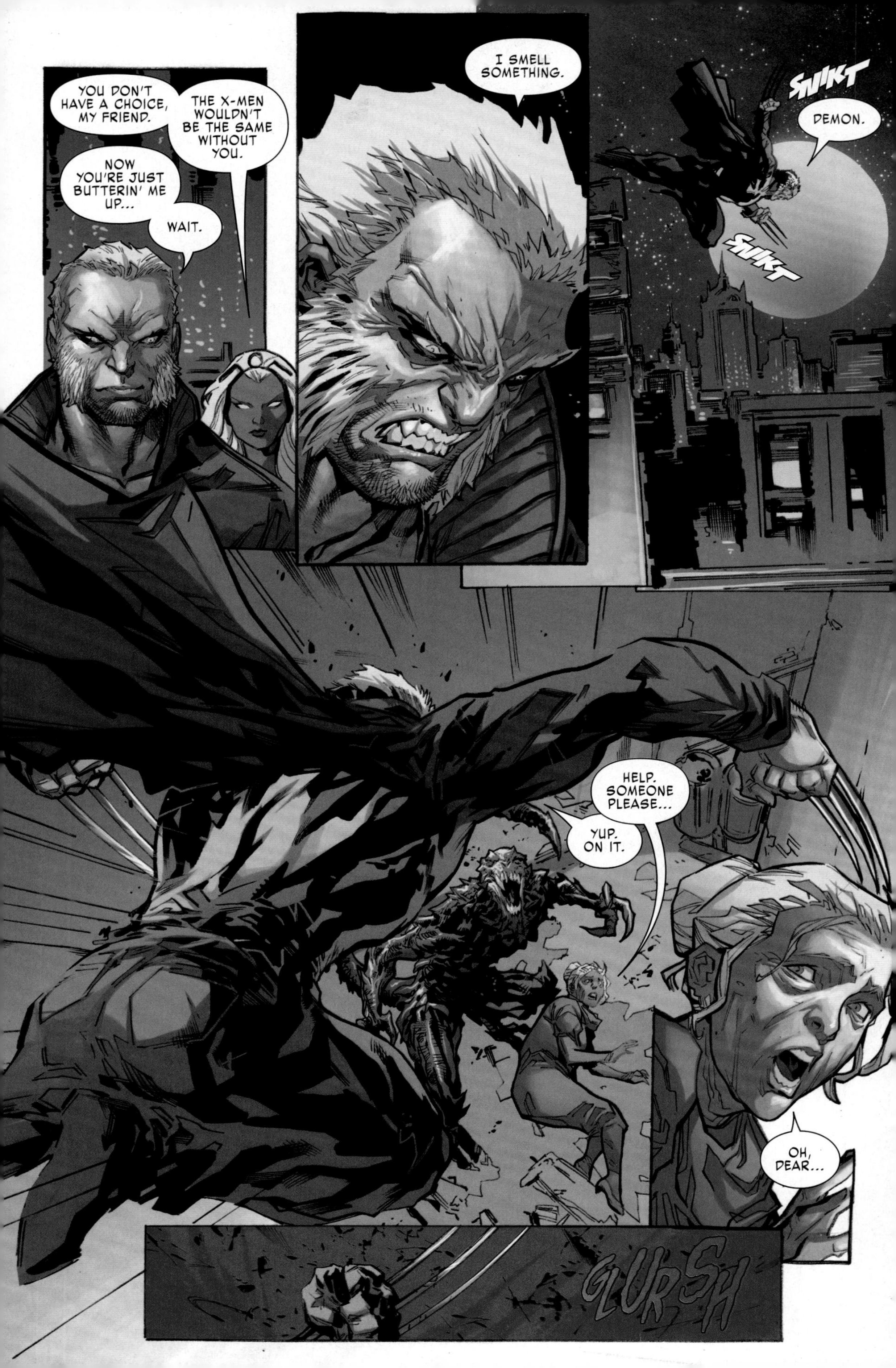
YOU DON'T HAVE A CHOICE, MY FRIEND.
THE X-MEN WOULDN'T BE THE SAME WITHOUT YOU.
NOW YOU'RE JUST BUTTERIN' ME UP...
WAIT.
I SMELL SOMETHING.
SNIKT
DEMON.
SNIKT
HELP. SOMEONE PLEASE...
YUP. ON IT.
OH, DEAR...
GLURSH

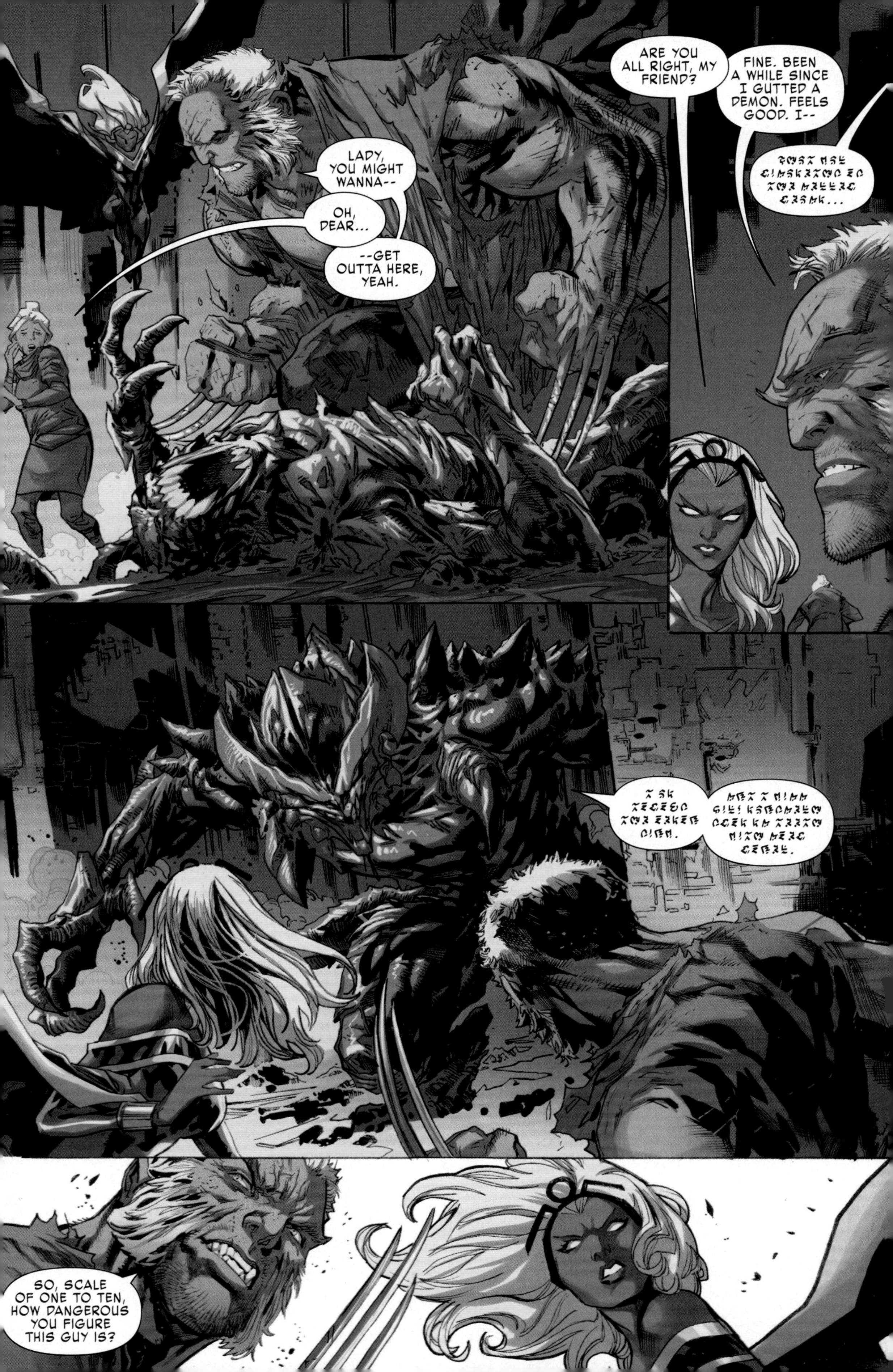
LADY, YOU MIGHT WANNA--
OH, DEAR...
--GET OUTTA HERE, YEAH.
ARE YOU ALL RIGHT, MY FRIEND?
FINE. BEEN A WHILE SINCE I GUTTED A DEMON. FEELS GOOD. I--
SO, SCALE OF ONE TO TEN, HOW DANGEROUS YOU FIGURE THIS GUY IS?

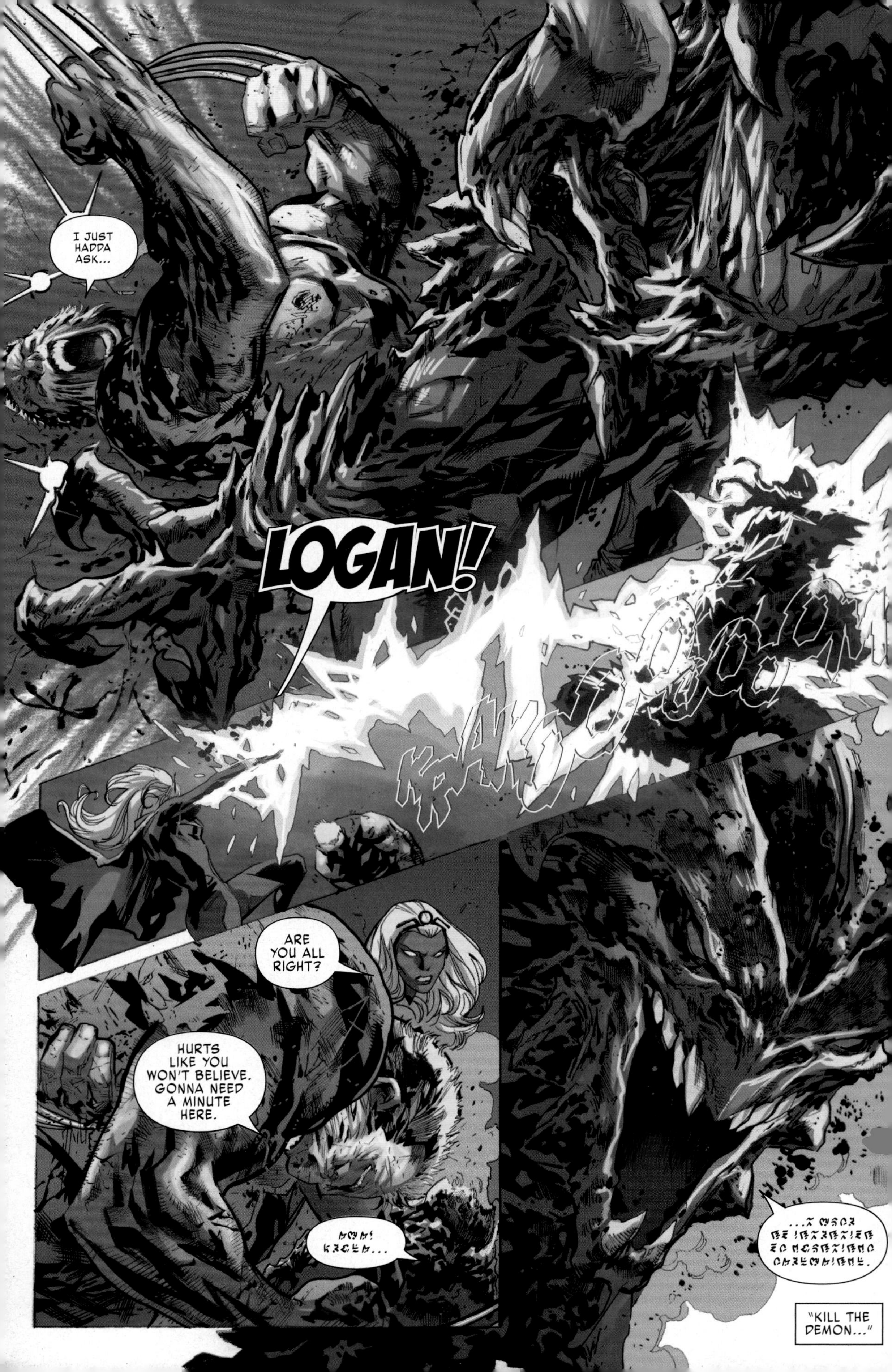
I JUST HADDA ASK...
LOGAN!
KRAKOOOOOM
ARE YOU ALL RIGHT?
HURTS LIKE YOU WON'T BELIEVE. GONNA NEED A MINUTE HERE.
"KILL THE DEMON..."

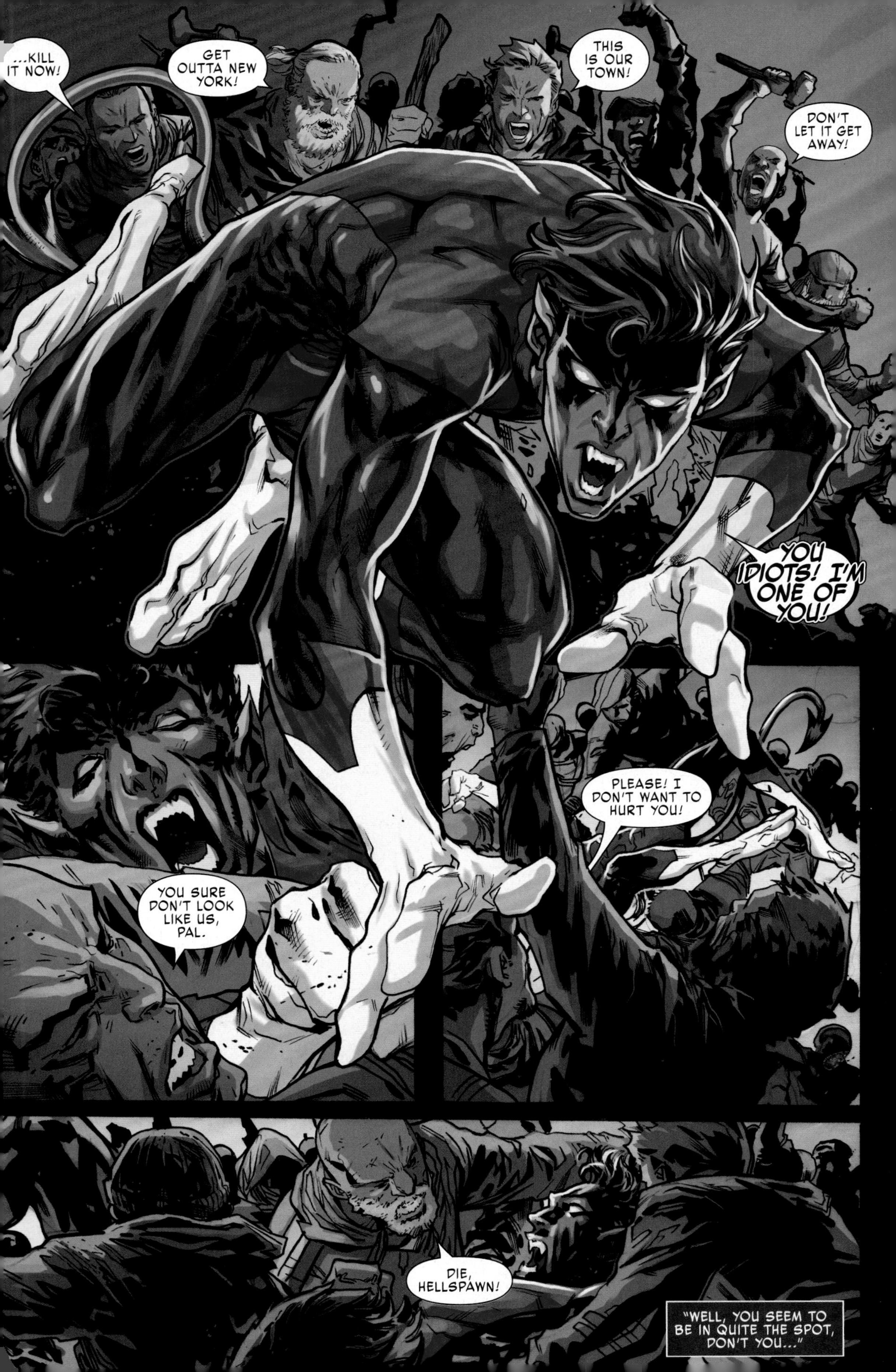
...KILL IT NOW!
GET OUTTA NEW YORK!
THIS IS OUR TOWN!
DON'T LET IT GET AWAY!
YOU IDIOTS! I'M ONE OF YOU!
PLEASE! I DON'T WANT TO HURT YOU!
YOU SURE DON'T LOOK LIKE US, PAL.
DIE, HELLSPAWN!
"WELL, YOU SEEM TO BE IN QUITE THE SPOT, DON'T YOU..."

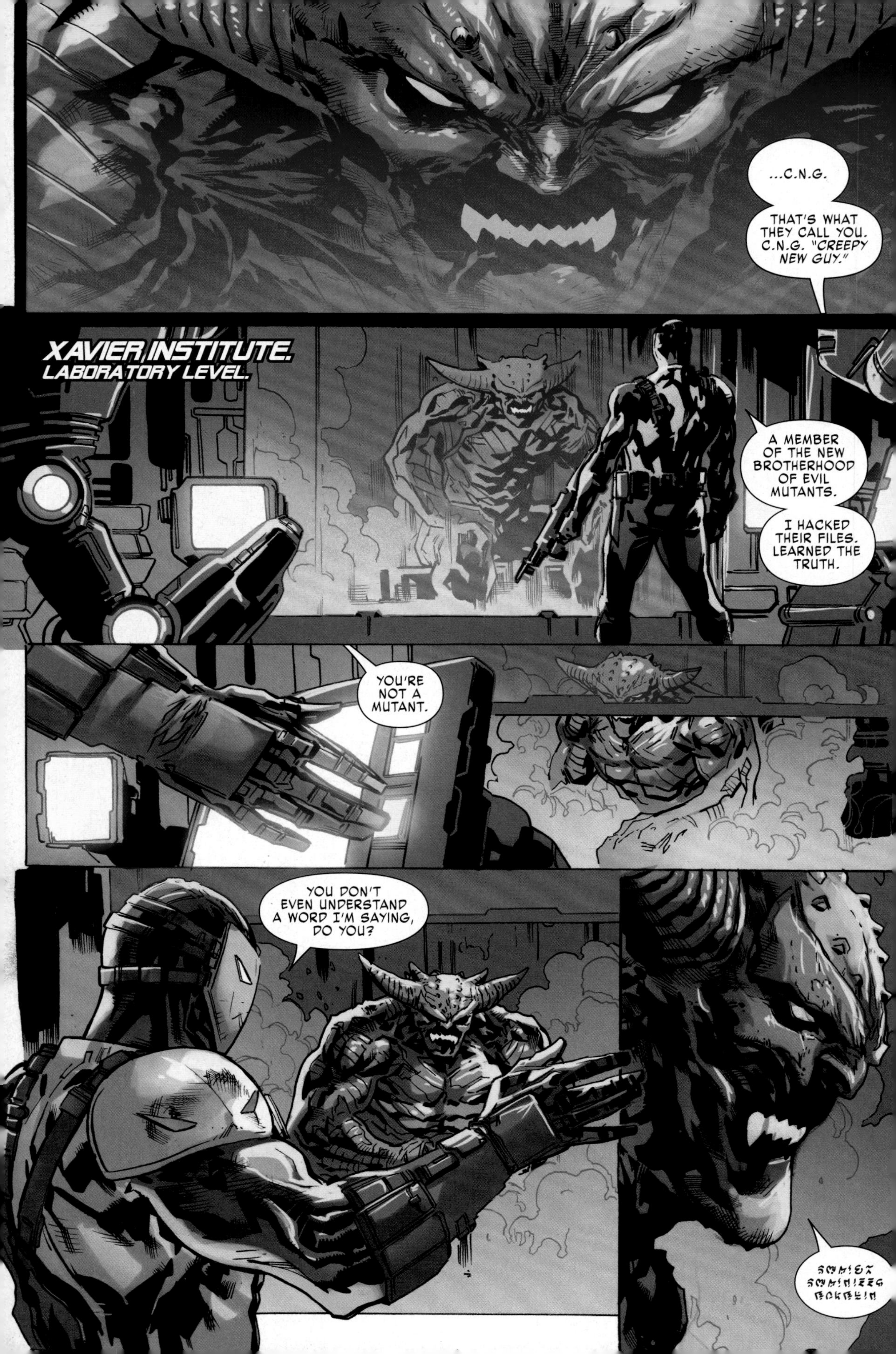
...C.N.G.
THAT'S WHAT THEY CALL YOU. C.N.G. "CREEPY NEW GUY."
XAVIER INSTITUTE. LABORATORY LEVEL.
A MEMBER OF THE NEW BROTHERHOOD OF EVIL MUTANTS.
I HACKED THEIR FILES. LEARNED THE TRUTH.
YOU'RE NOT A MUTANT.
YOU DON'T EVEN UNDERSTAND A WORD I'M SAYING, DO YOU?

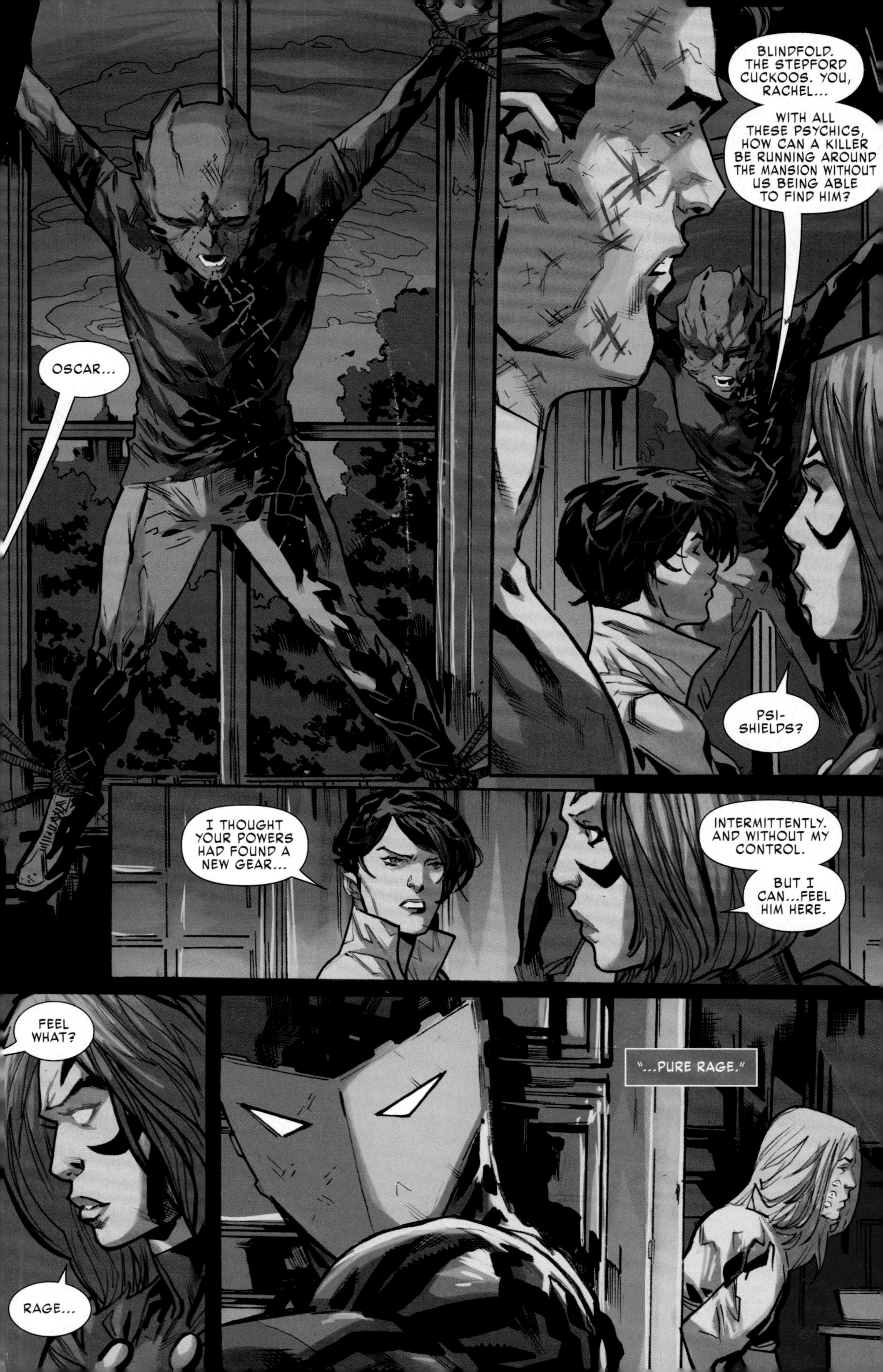
BLINDFOLD. THE STEPFORD CUCKOOS. YOU, RACHEL...
WITH ALL THESE PSYCHICS, HOW CAN A KILLER BE RUNNING AROUND THE MANSION WITHOUT US BEING ABLE TO FIND HIM?
OSCAR...
PSI-SHIELDS?
I THOUGHT YOUR POWERS HAD FOUND A NEW GEAR...
INTERMITTENTLY. AND WITHOUT MY CONTROL.
BUT I CAN...FEEL HIM HERE.
FEEL WHAT?
RAGE...
"...PURE RAGE."

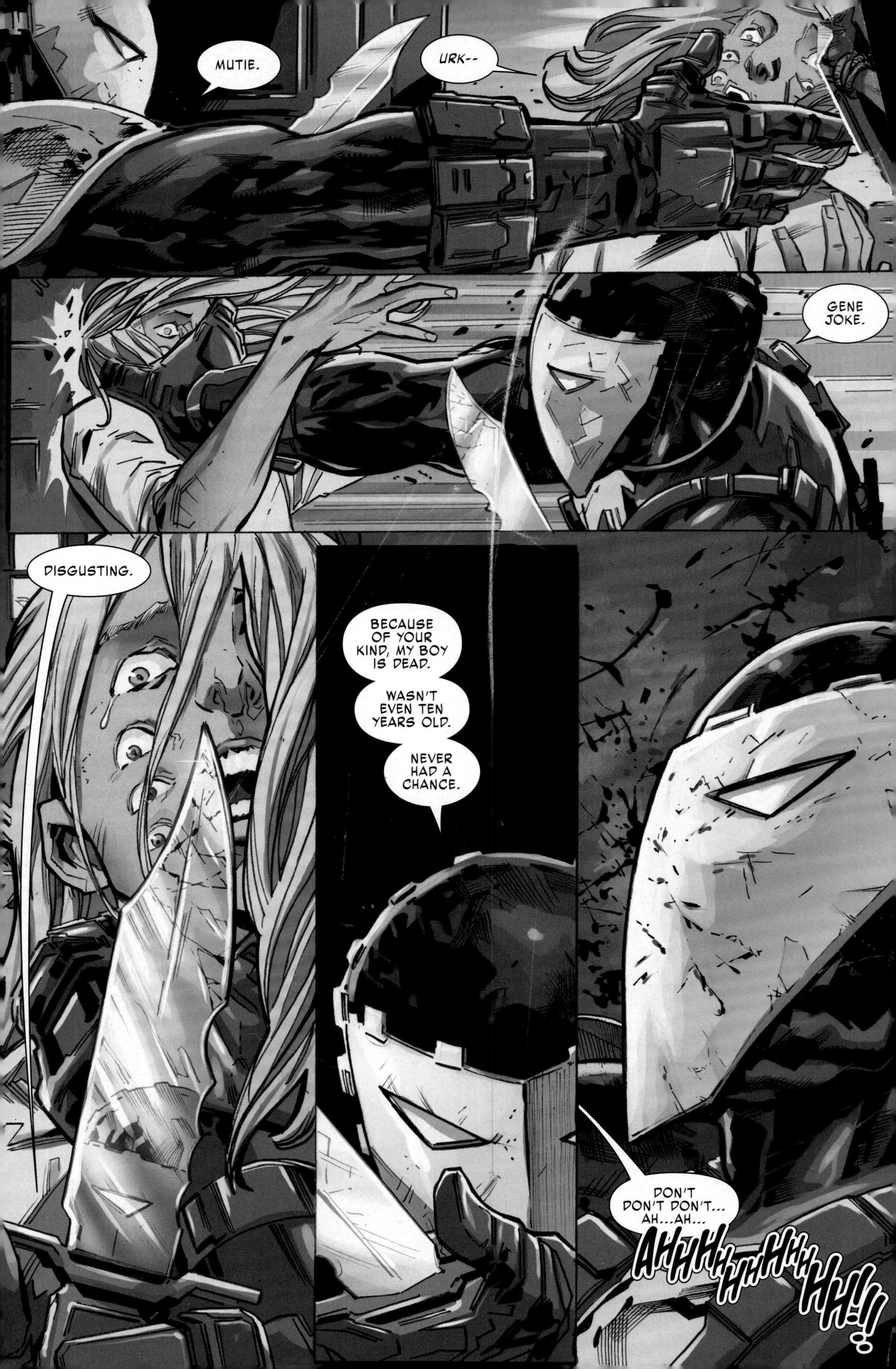
MUTIE.
URK--
GENE JOKE.
DISGUSTING.
BECAUSE OF YOUR KIND, MY BOY IS DEAD.
WASN'T EVEN TEN YEARS OLD.
NEVER HAD A CHANCE.
DON'T DON'T DON'T... AH...AH...
AHHHHHHHHHHHHHH!!!

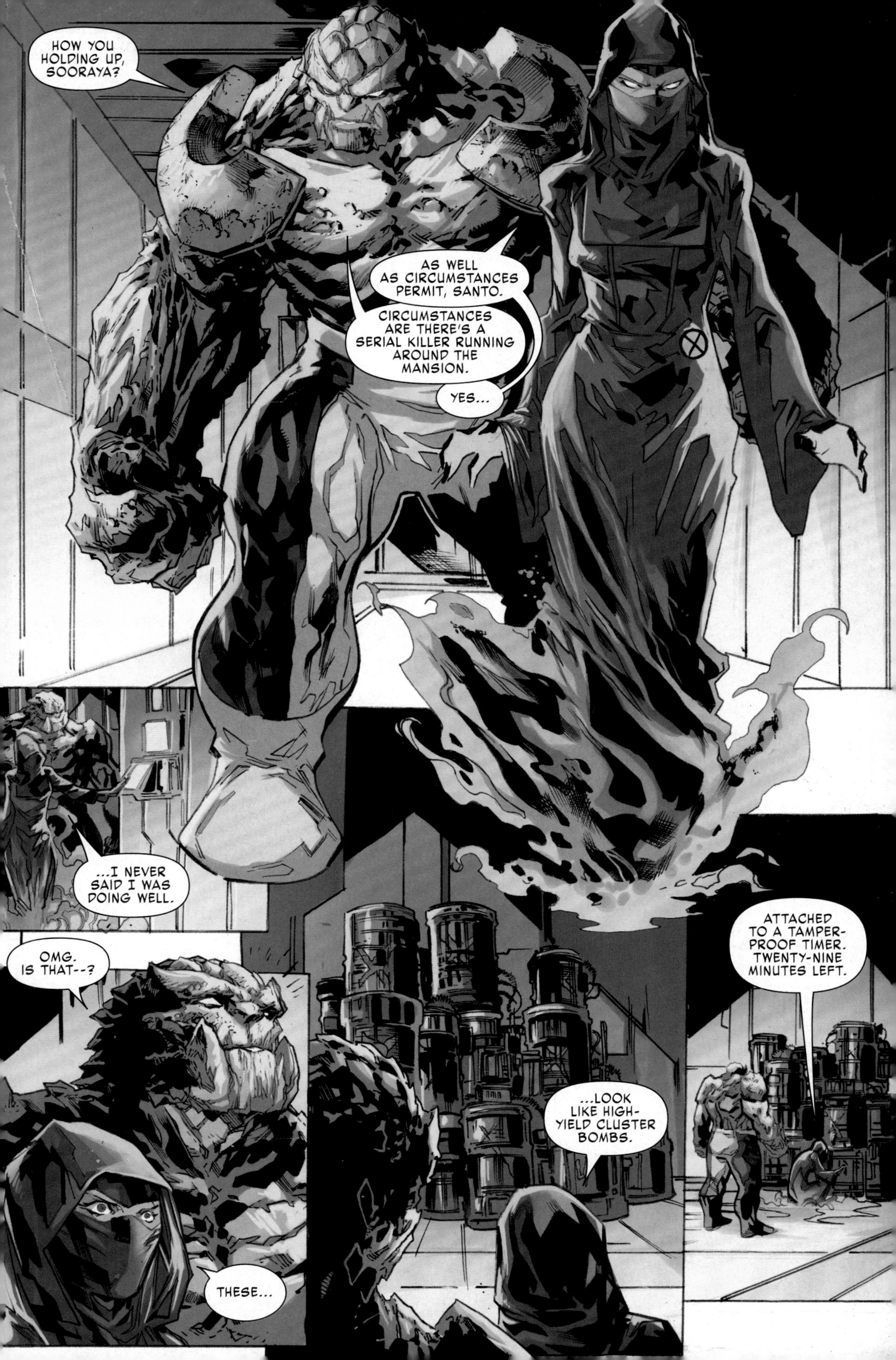
HOW YOU HOLDING UP, SOORAYA?
AS WELL AS CIRCUMSTANCES PERMIT, SANTO.
CIRCUMSTANCES ARE THERE'S A SERIAL KILLER RUNNING AROUND THE MANSION.
YES...
...I NEVER SAID I WAS DOING WELL.
OMG. IS THAT--?
THESE...
...LOOK LIKE HIGH-YIELD CLUSTER BOMBS.
ATTACHED TO A TAMPER-PROOF TIMER. TWENTY-NINE MINUTES LEFT.

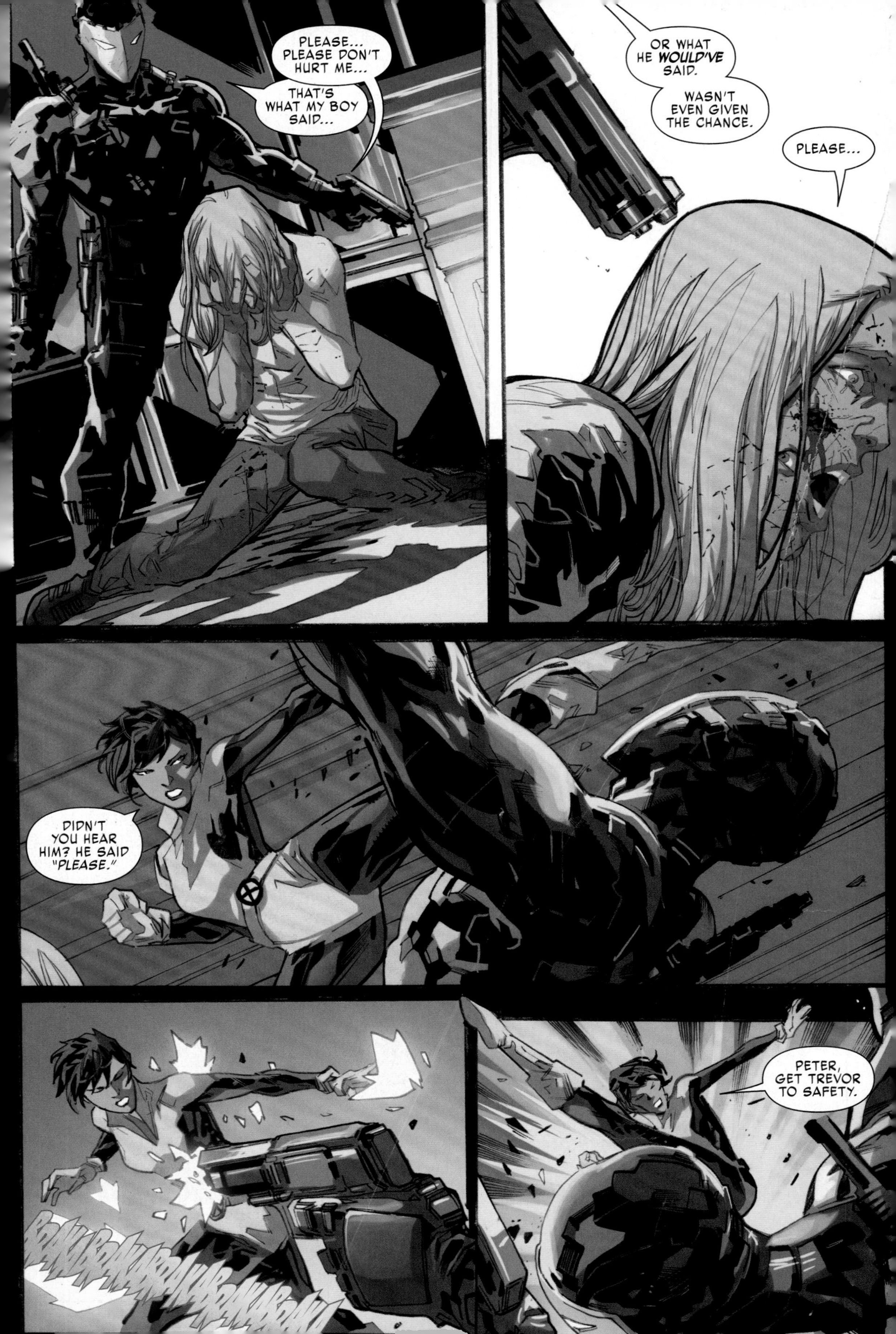
PLEASE... PLEASE DON'T HURT ME...
THAT'S WHAT MY BOY SAID...
OR WHAT HE WOULD'VE SAID.
WASN'T EVEN GIVEN THE CHANCE.
PLEASE...
DIDN'T YOU HEAR HIM? HE SAID "PLEASE."
PETER, GET TREVOR TO SAFETY.

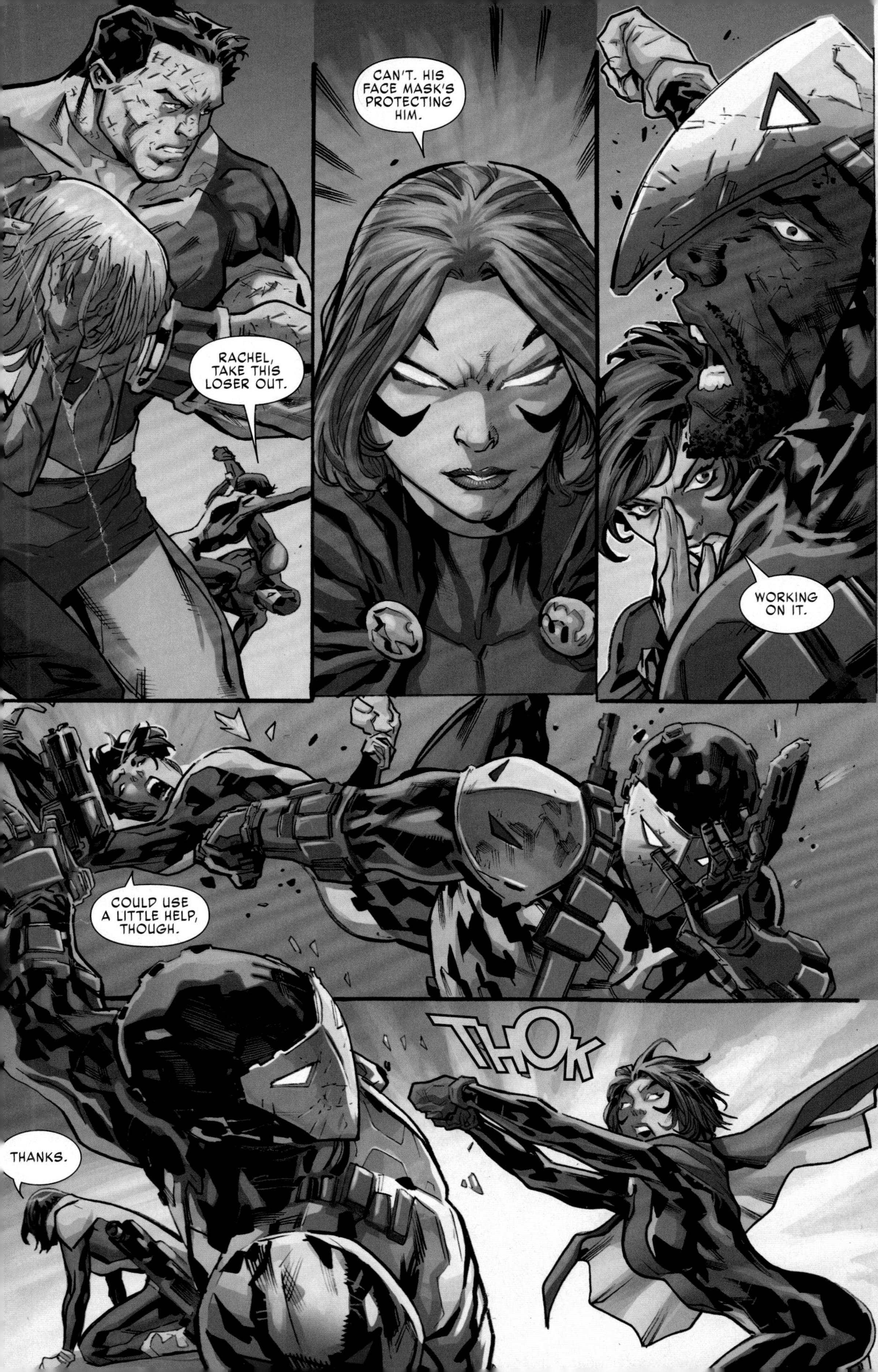
RACHEL, TAKE THIS LOSER OUT.
CAN'T. HIS FACE MASK'S PROTECTING HIM.
WORKING ON IT.
COULD USE A LITTLE HELP, THOUGH.
THOK
THANKS.

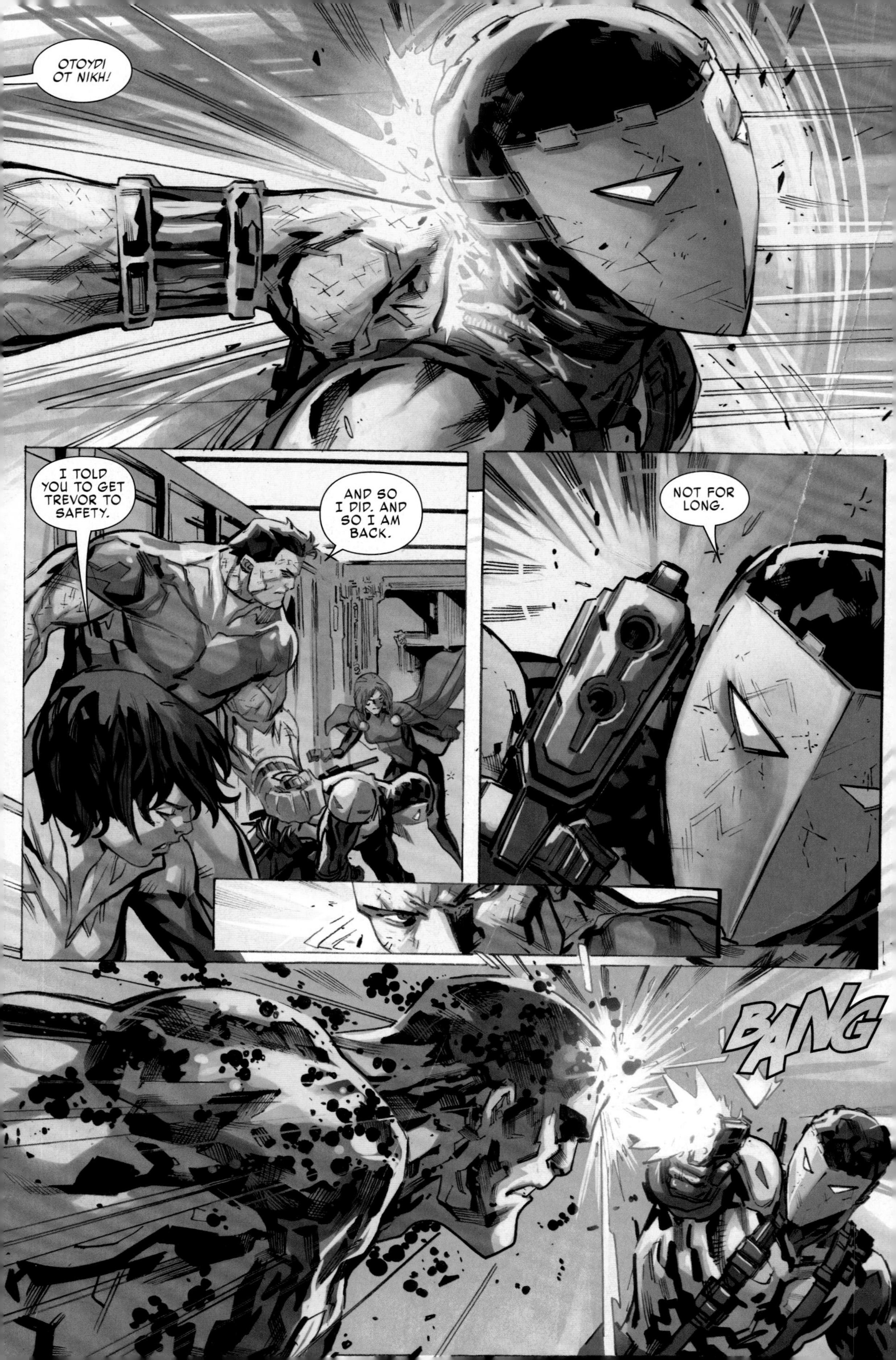
OTOYDI OT NIKH!
I TOLD YOU TO GET TREVOR TO SAFETY.
AND SO I DID. AND SO I AM BACK.
NOT FOR LONG.
BANG

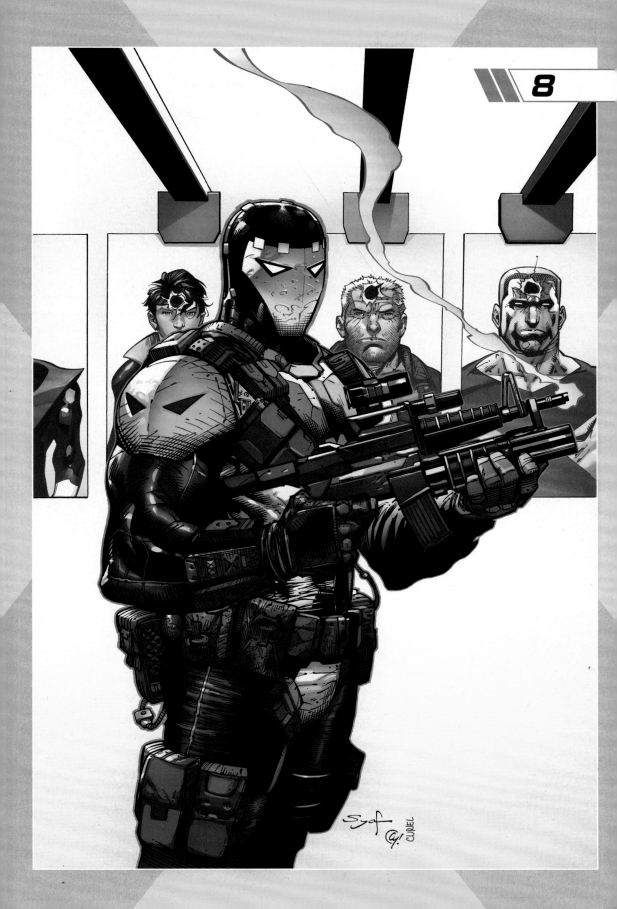

PETER!

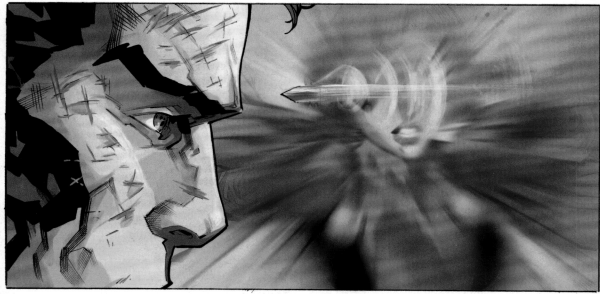

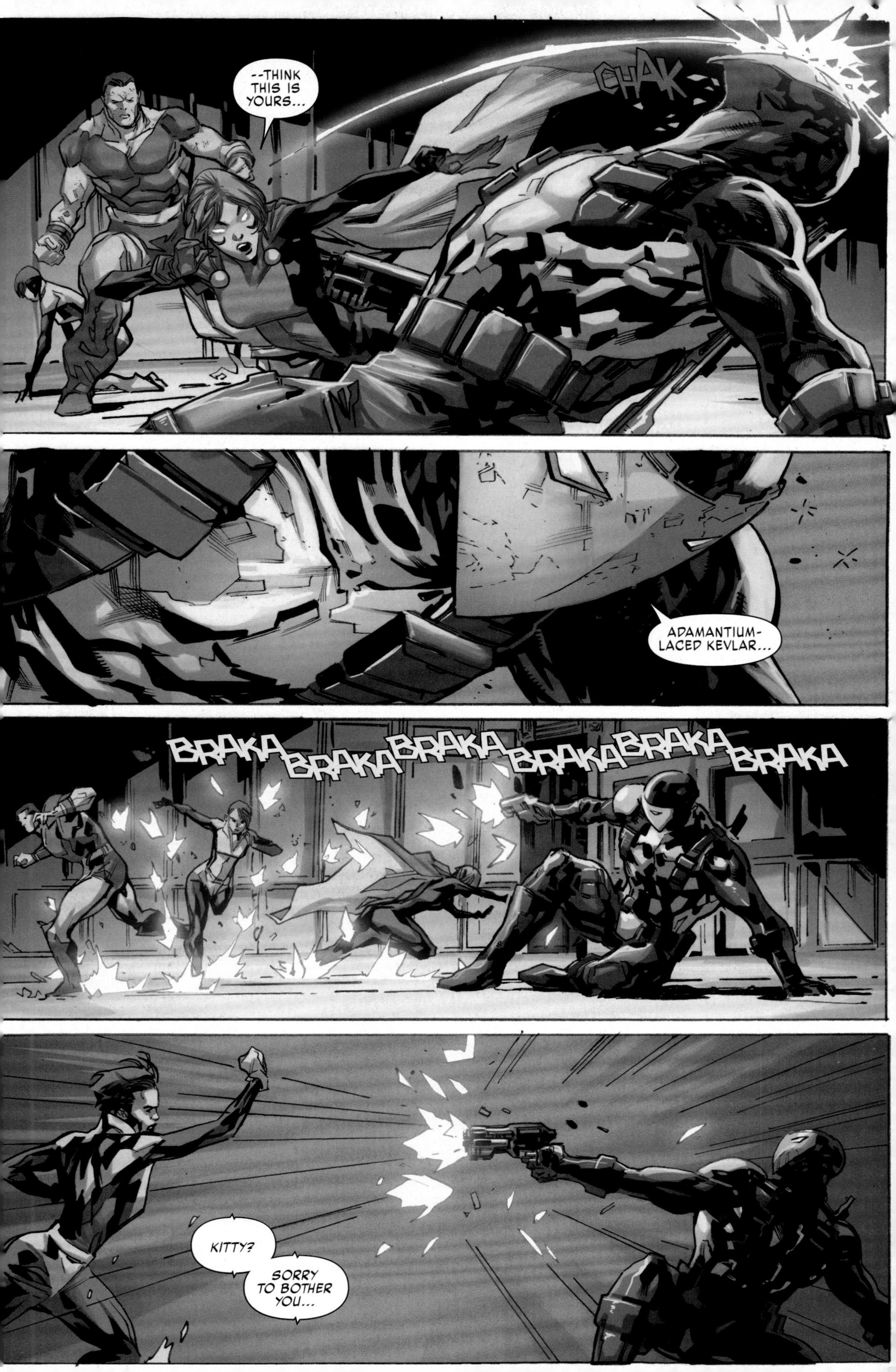
--THINK THIS IS YOURS...
CHAK
ADAMANTIUM-LACED KEVLAR...
BRAKA BRAKA BRAKA BRAKA BRAKA BRAKA
KITTY?
SORRY TO BOTHER YOU...

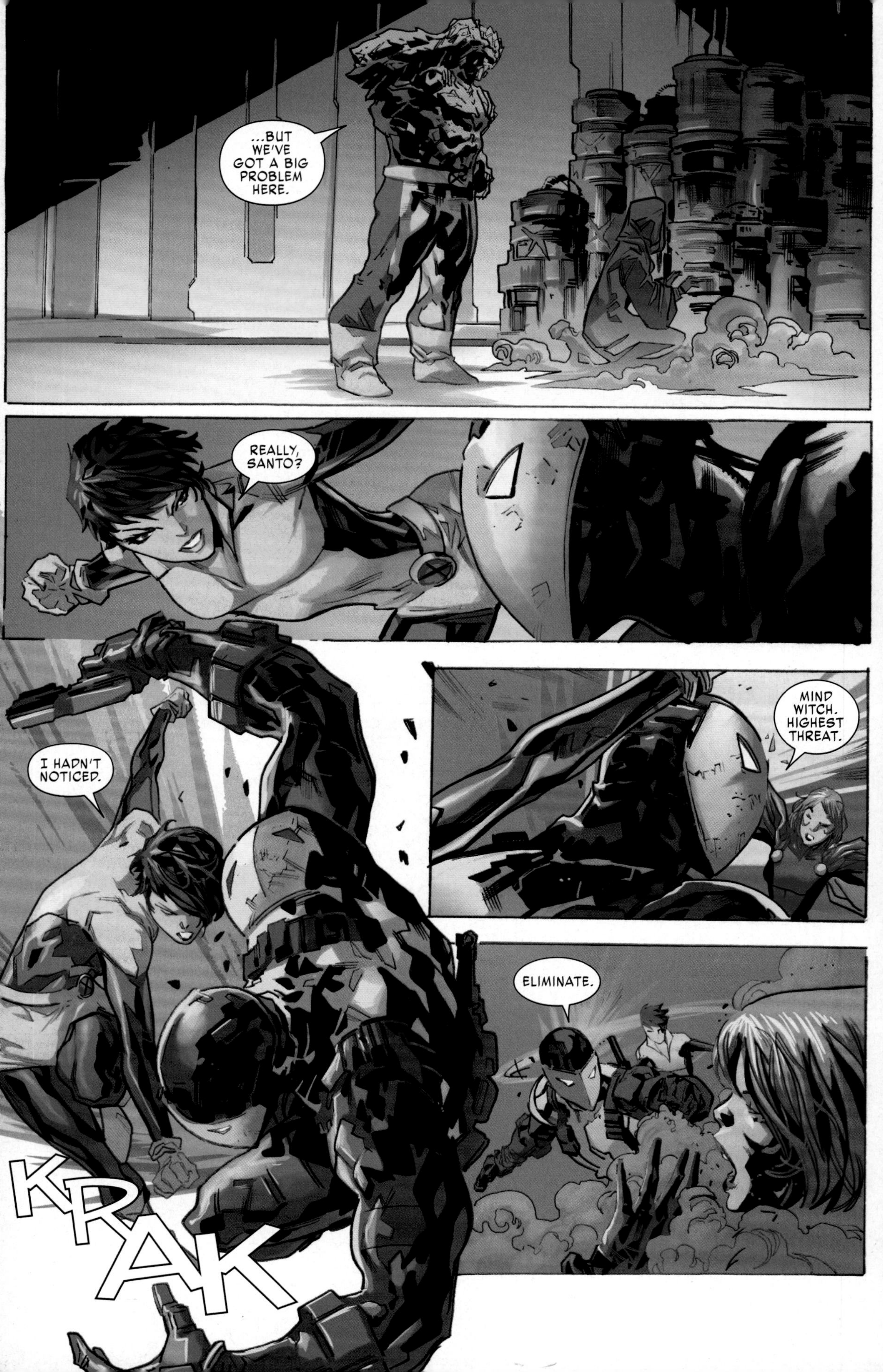
...BUT WE'VE GOT A BIG PROBLEM HERE.
REALLY, SANTO?
I HADN'T NOTICED.
MIND WITCH. HIGHEST THREAT.
ELIMINATE.
KRAK

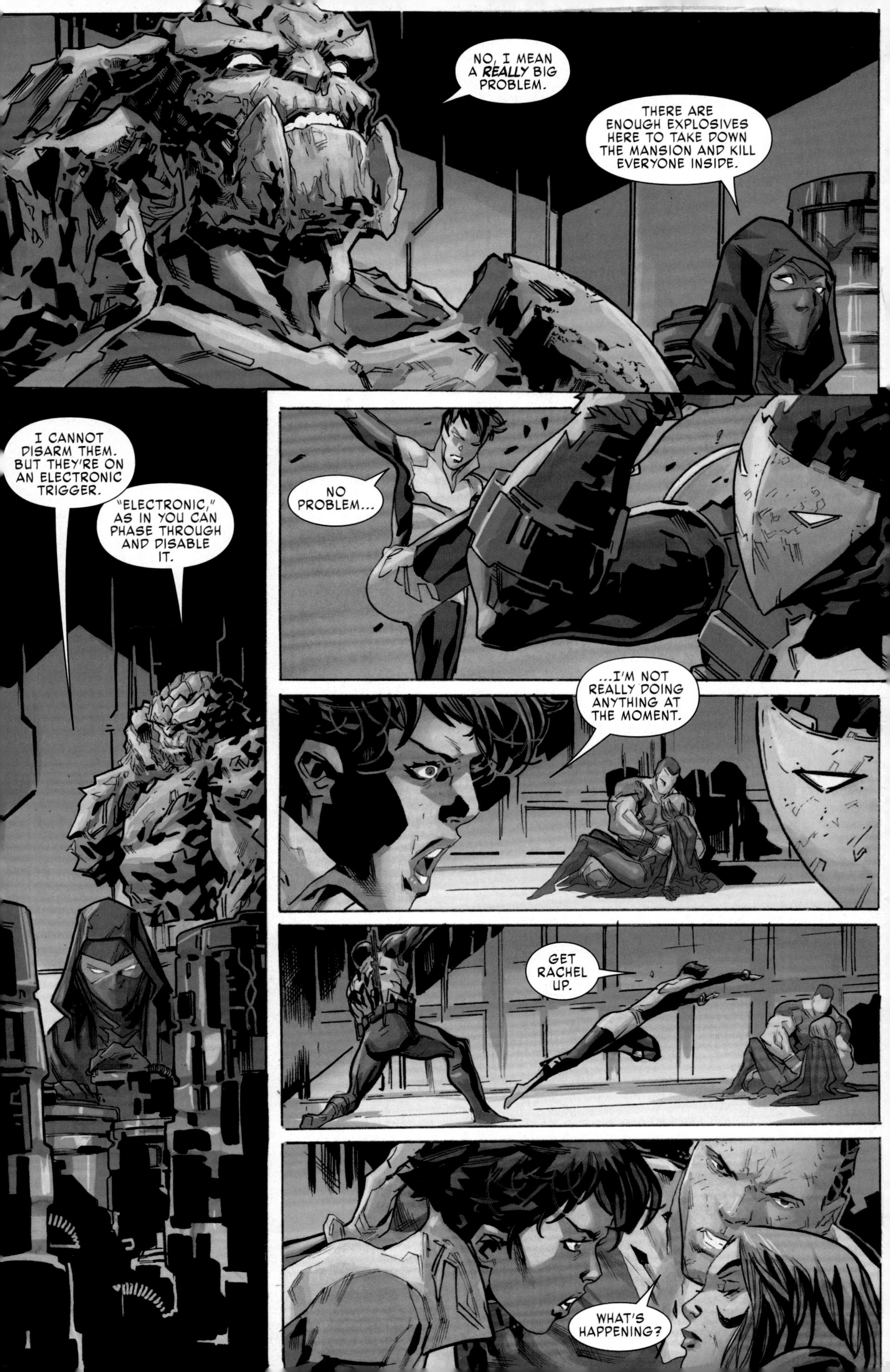
NO, I MEAN A *REALLY* BIG PROBLEM.
THERE ARE ENOUGH EXPLOSIVES HERE TO TAKE DOWN THE MANSION AND KILL EVERYONE INSIDE.
I CANNOT DISARM THEM. BUT THEY'RE ON AN ELECTRONIC TRIGGER.
"ELECTRONIC," AS IN YOU CAN PHASE THROUGH AND DISABLE IT.
NO PROBLEM...
...I'M NOT REALLY DOING ANYTHING AT THE MOMENT.
GET RACHEL UP.
WHAT'S HAPPENING?

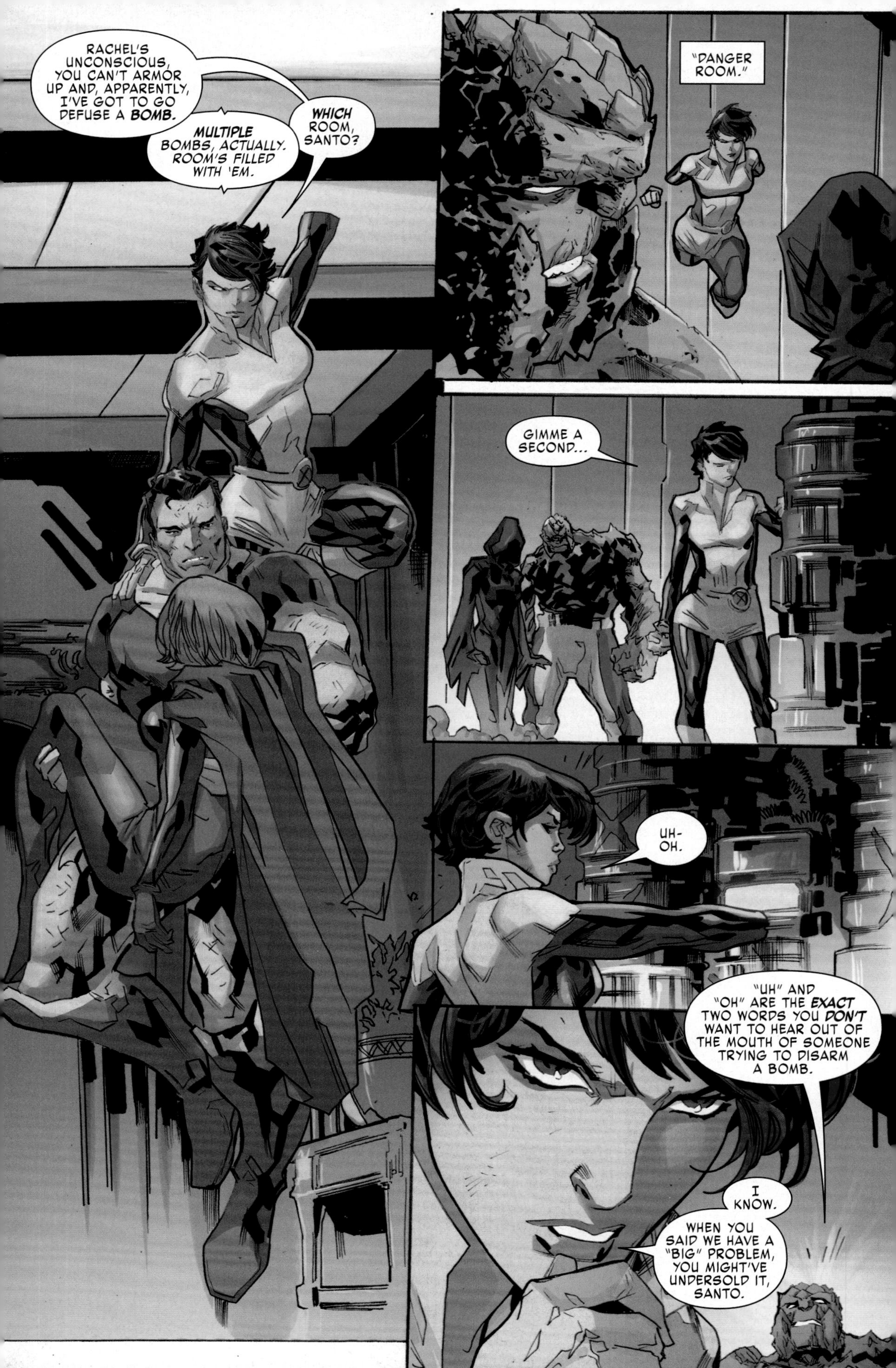
RACHEL'S UNCONSCIOUS, YOU CAN'T ARMOR UP AND, APPARENTLY, I'VE GOT TO GO DEFUSE A **BOMB.**
MULTIPLE BOMBS, ACTUALLY. ROOM'S FILLED WITH 'EM.
WHICH ROOM, SANTO?
"DANGER ROOM."
GIMME A SECOND...
UH-OH.
"UH" AND "OH" ARE THE ***EXACT*** TWO WORDS YOU ***DON'T*** WANT TO HEAR OUT OF THE MOUTH OF SOMEONE TRYING TO DISARM A BOMB.
I KNOW.
WHEN YOU SAID WE HAVE A "BIG" PROBLEM, YOU MIGHT'VE UNDERSOLD IT, SANTO.

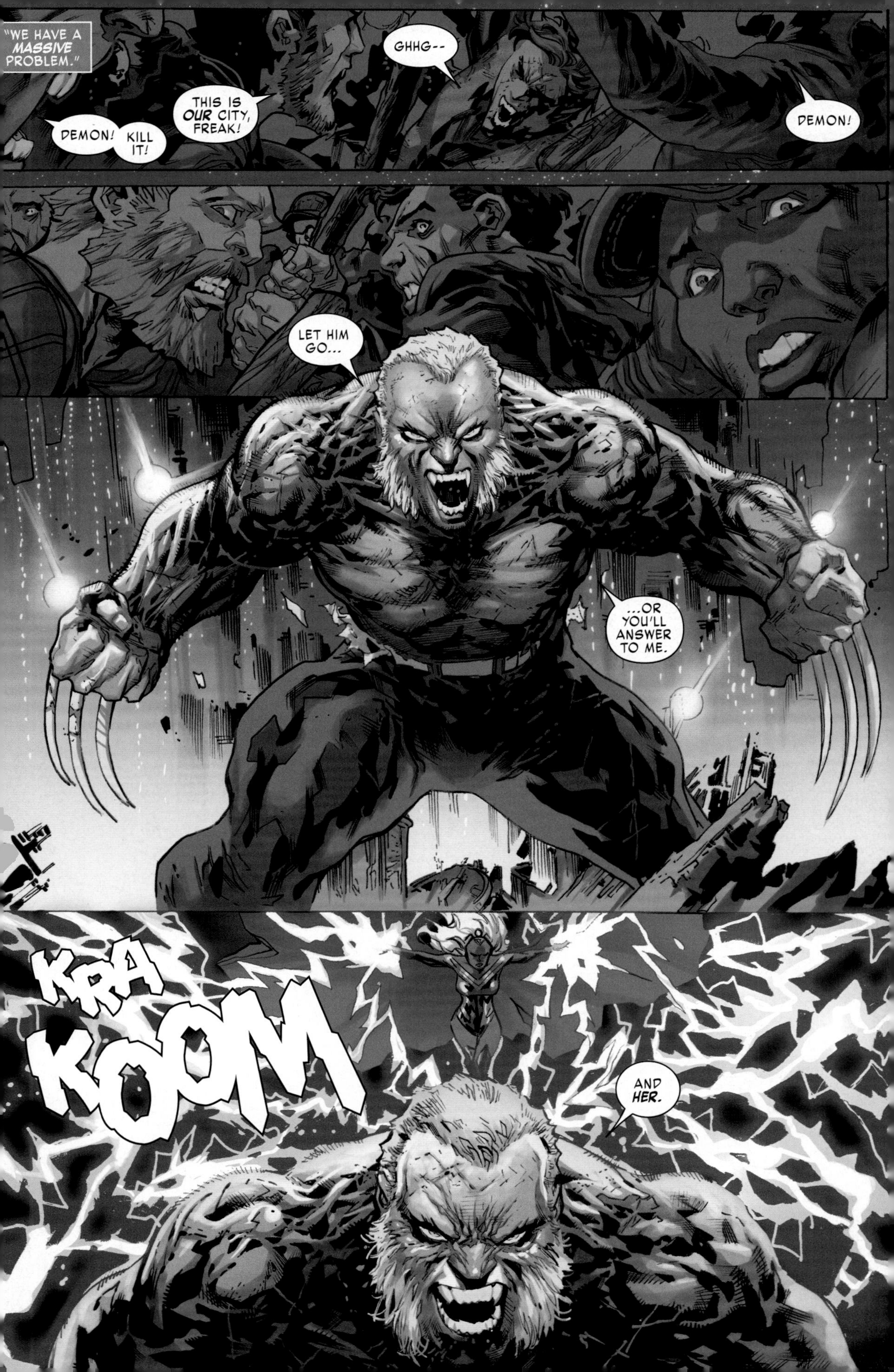
"WE HAVE A MASSIVE PROBLEM."
GHHG--
THIS IS OUR CITY, FREAK!
DEMON!
KILL IT!
DEMON!
LET HIM GO...
...OR YOU'LL ANSWER TO ME.
KRA KOOM
AND HER.

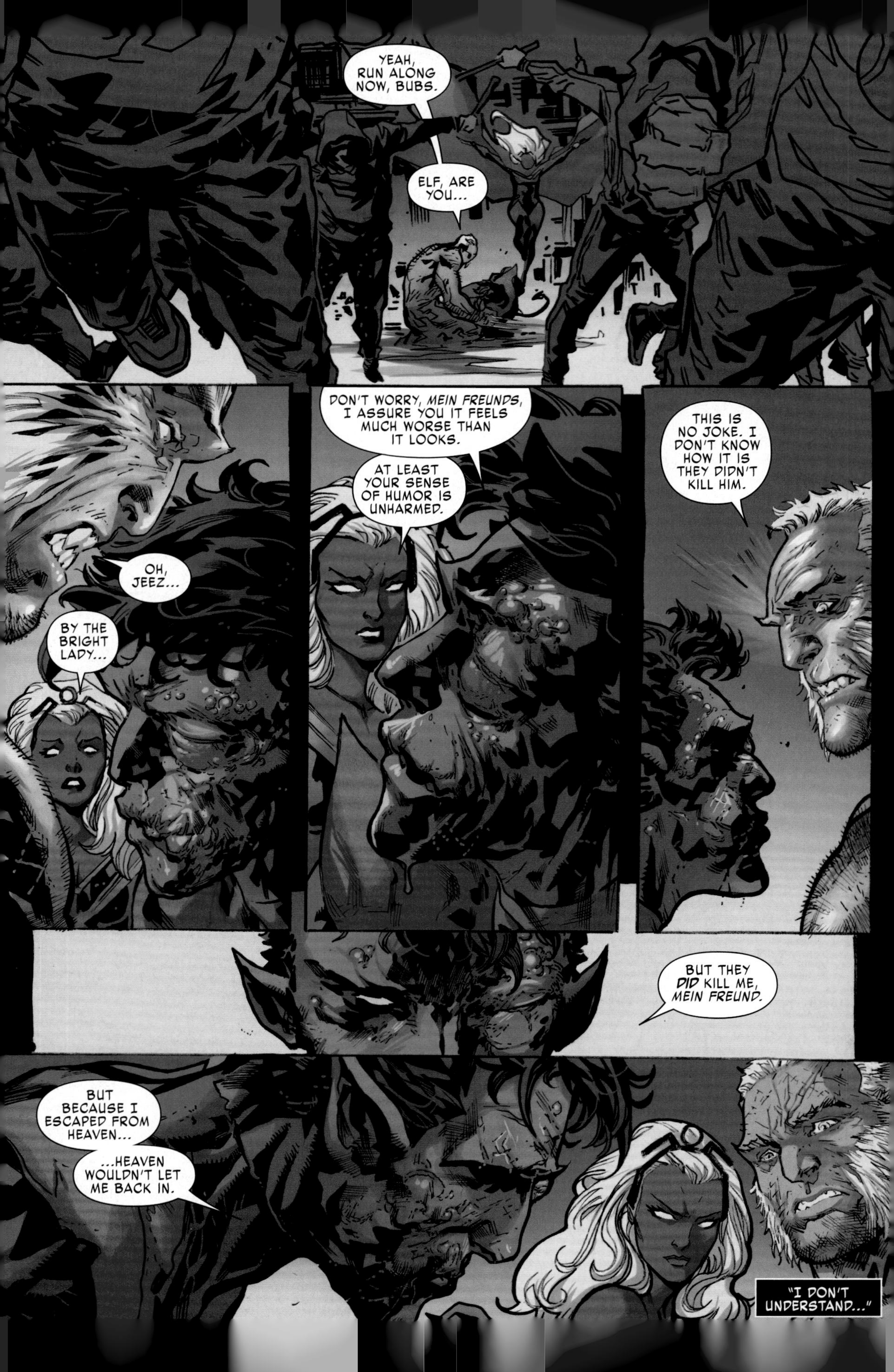
YEAH, RUN ALONG NOW, BUBS.
ELF, ARE YOU...
OH, JEEZ...
BY THE BRIGHT LADY...
DON'T WORRY, *MEIN FREUNDS*, I ASSURE YOU IT FEELS MUCH WORSE THAN IT LOOKS.
AT LEAST YOUR SENSE OF HUMOR IS UNHARMED.
THIS IS NO JOKE. I DON'T KNOW HOW IT IS THEY DIDN'T KILL HIM.
BUT THEY ***DID*** KILL ME, *MEIN FREUND*.
BUT BECAUSE I ESCAPED FROM HEAVEN...
...HEAVEN WOULDN'T LET ME BACK IN.
"I DON'T UNDERSTAND..."

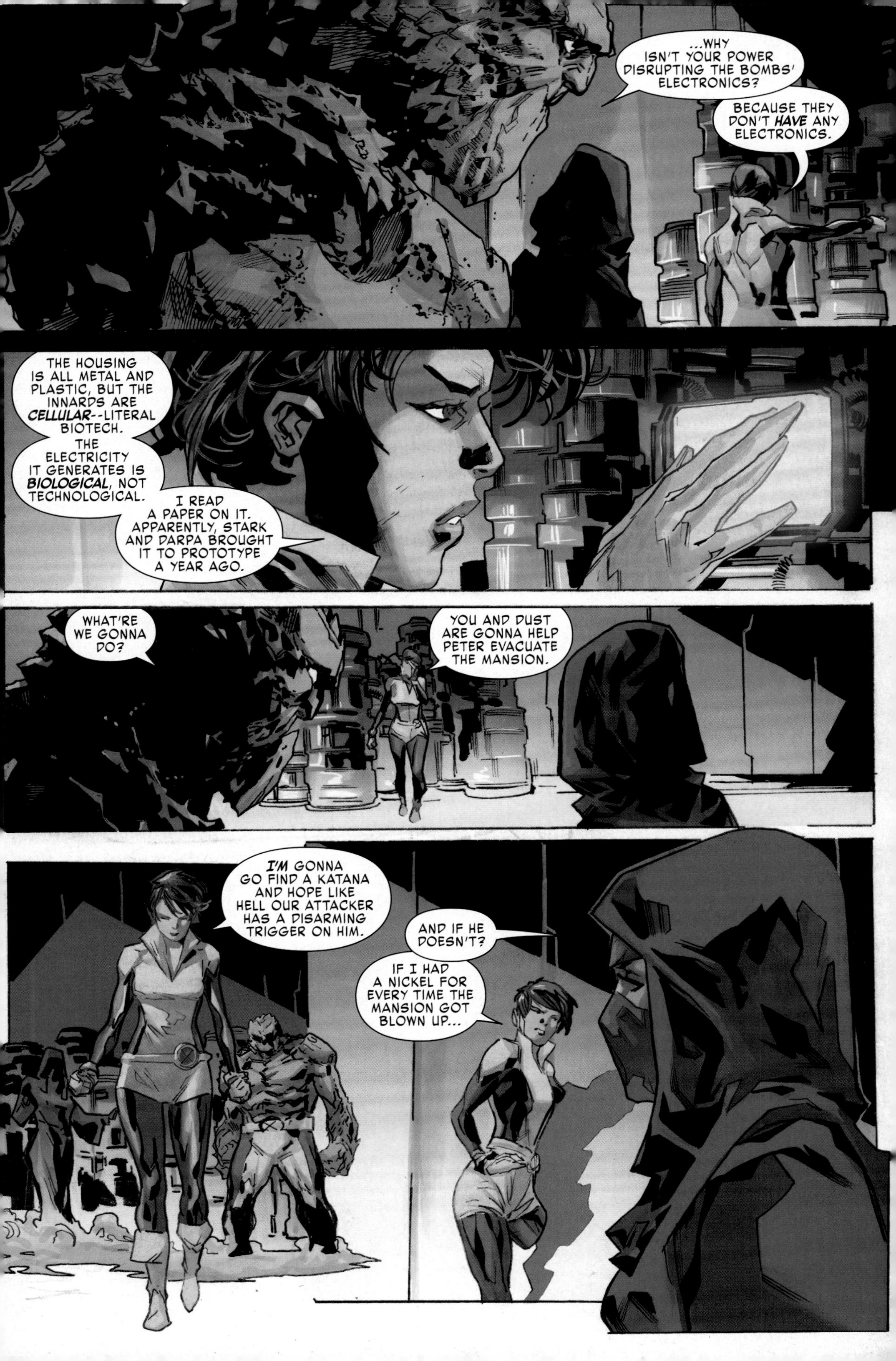
...WHY ISN'T YOUR POWER DISRUPTING THE BOMBS' ELECTRONICS?
BECAUSE THEY DON'T HAVE ANY ELECTRONICS.
THE HOUSING IS ALL METAL AND PLASTIC, BUT THE INNARDS ARE CELLULAR--LITERAL BIOTECH.
THE ELECTRICITY IT GENERATES IS BIOLOGICAL, NOT TECHNOLOGICAL.
I READ A PAPER ON IT. APPARENTLY, STARK AND DARPA BROUGHT IT TO PROTOTYPE A YEAR AGO.
WHAT'RE WE GONNA DO?
YOU AND DUST ARE GONNA HELP PETER EVACUATE THE MANSION.
I'M GONNA GO FIND A KATANA AND HOPE LIKE HELL OUR ATTACKER HAS A DISARMING TRIGGER ON HIM.
AND IF HE DOESN'T?
IF I HAD A NICKEL FOR EVERY TIME THE MANSION GOT BLOWN UP...

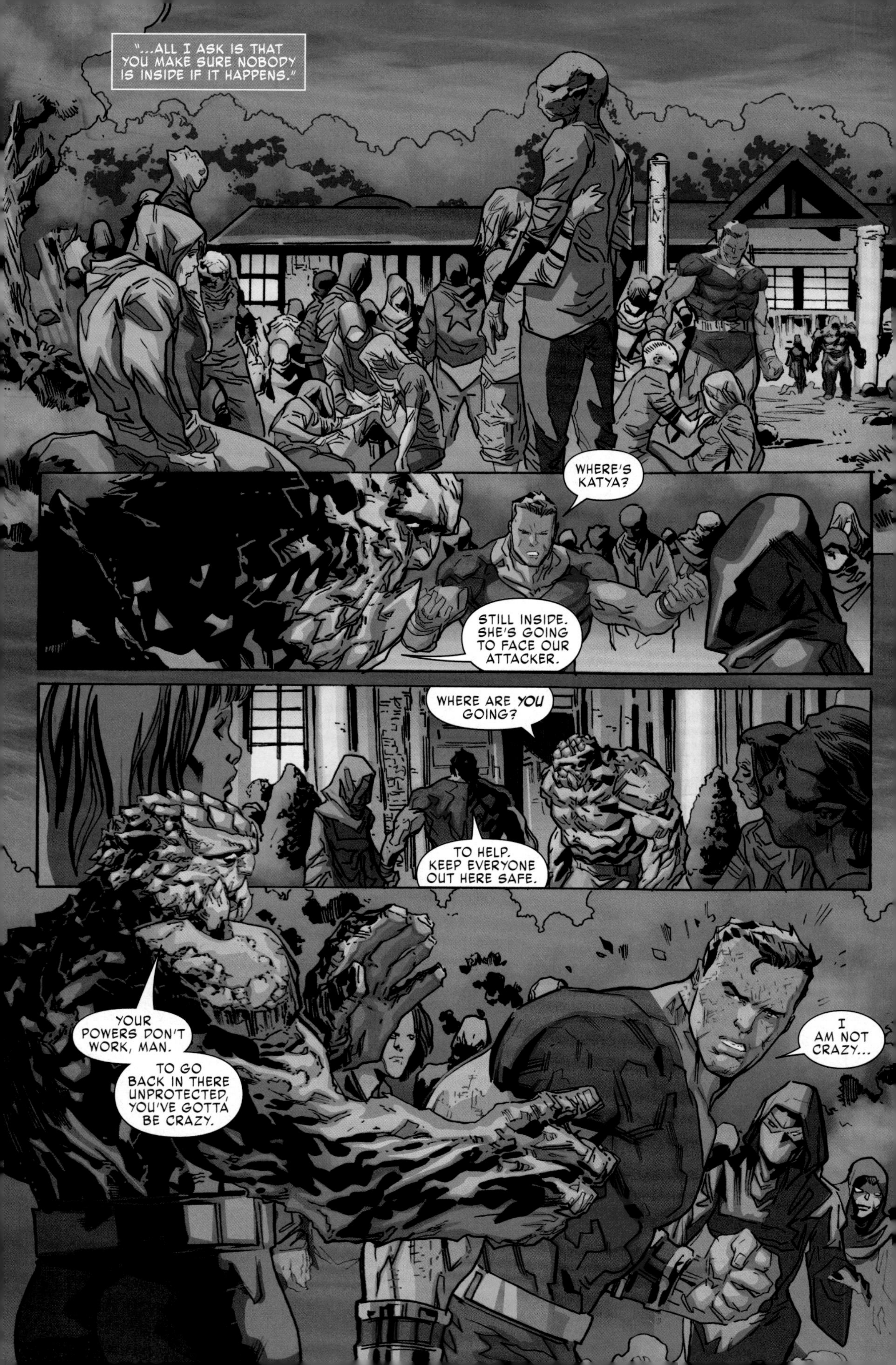
"...ALL I ASK IS THAT YOU MAKE SURE NOBODY IS INSIDE IF IT HAPPENS."
WHERE'S KATYA?
STILL INSIDE. SHE'S GOING TO FACE OUR ATTACKER.
WHERE ARE YOU GOING?
TO HELP. KEEP EVERYONE OUT HERE SAFE.
YOUR POWERS DON'T WORK, MAN.
TO GO BACK IN THERE UNPROTECTED, YOU'VE GOTTA BE CRAZY.
I AM NOT CRAZY...

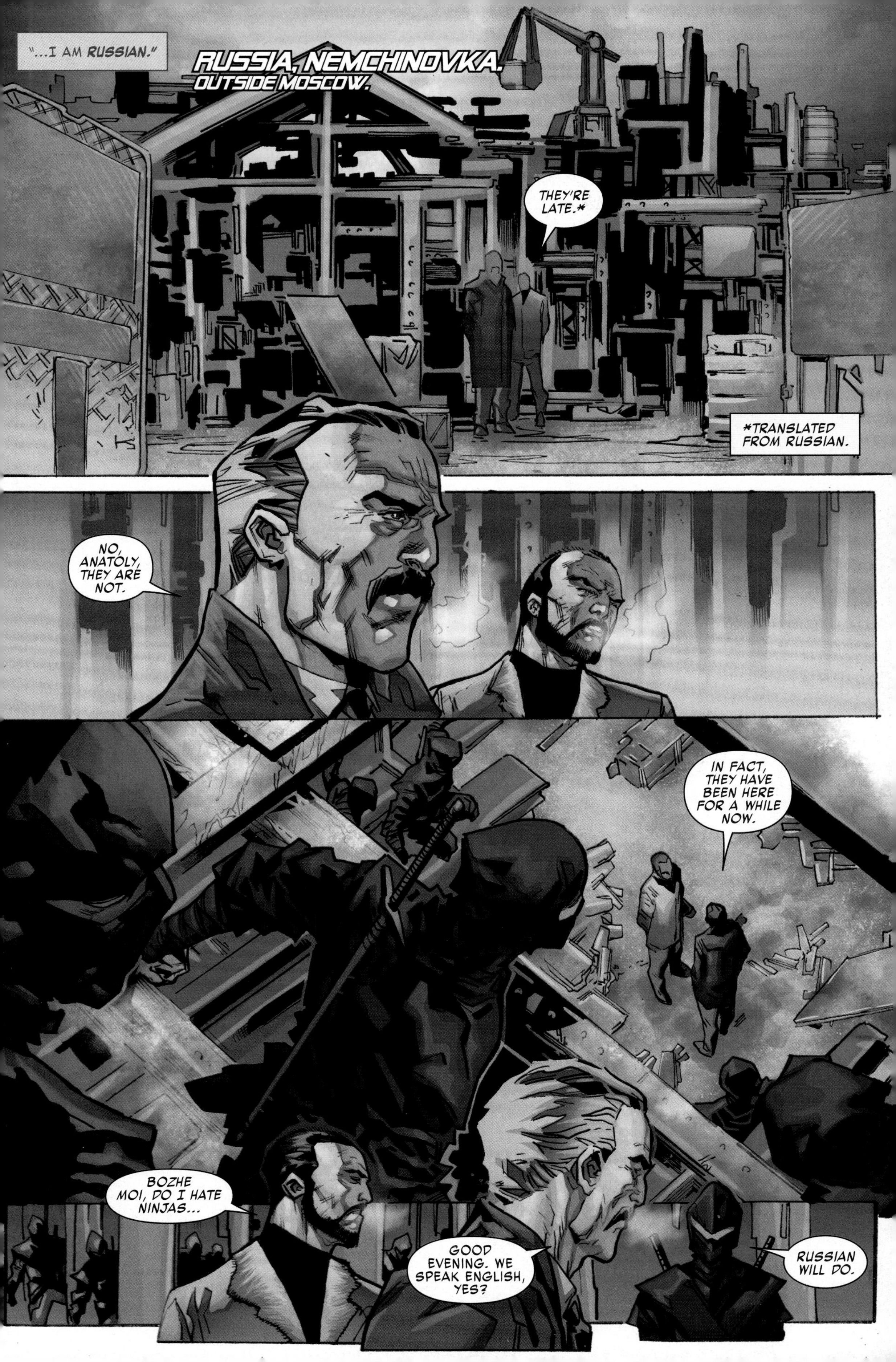

"...I AM RUSSIAN."
RUSSIA, NEMCHINOVKA. OUTSIDE MOSCOW.
THEY'RE LATE.*
*TRANSLATED FROM RUSSIAN.
NO, ANATOLY, THEY ARE NOT.
IN FACT, THEY HAVE BEEN HERE FOR A WHILE NOW.
BOZHE MOI, DO I HATE NINJAS...
GOOD EVENING. WE SPEAK ENGLISH, YES?
RUSSIAN WILL DO.

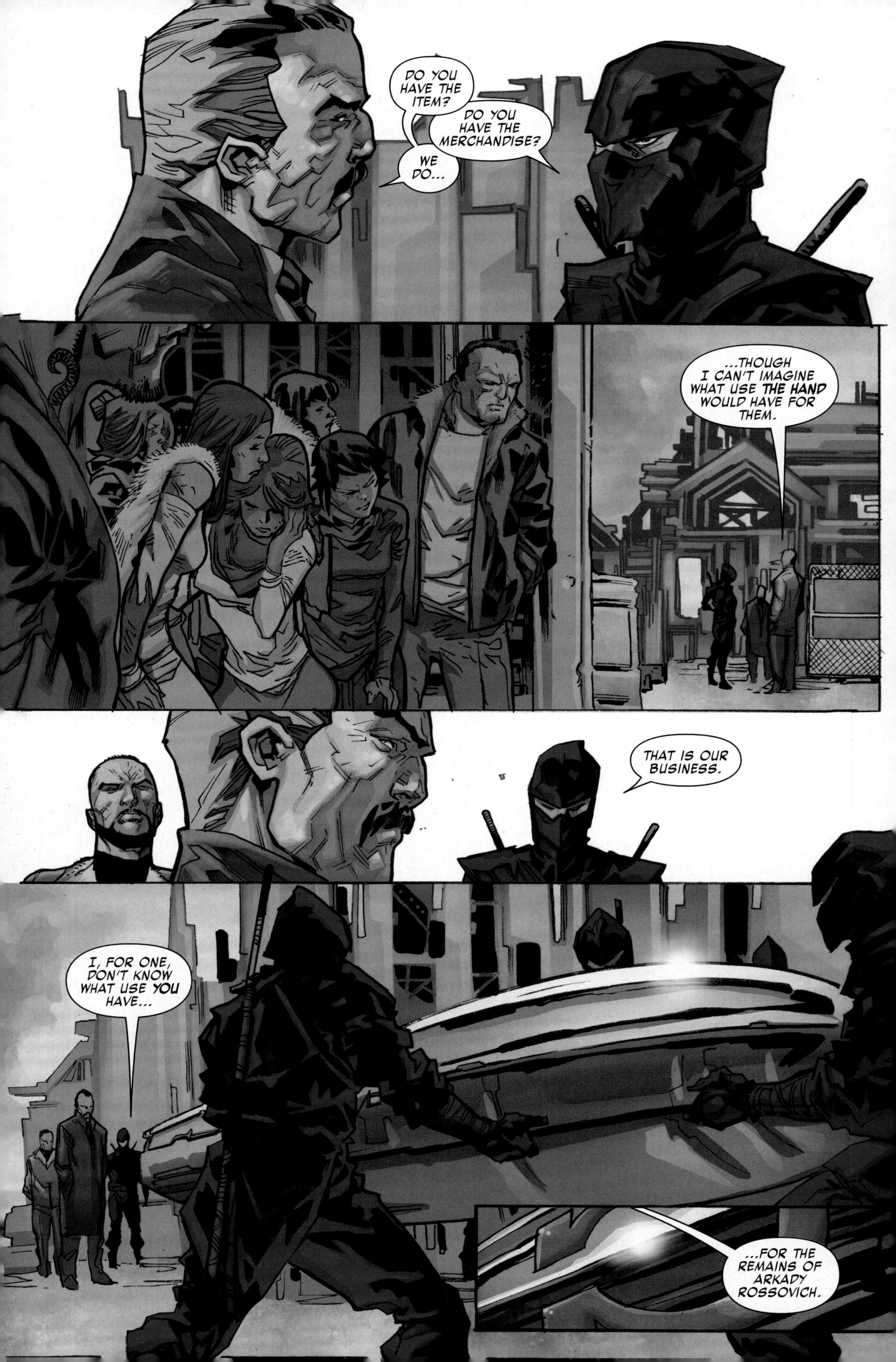
DO YOU HAVE THE ITEM?
DO YOU HAVE THE MERCHANDISE?
WE DO...
...THOUGH I CAN'T IMAGINE WHAT USE **THE HAND** WOULD HAVE FOR THEM.
THAT IS OUR BUSINESS.
I, FOR ONE, DON'T KNOW WHAT USE **YOU** HAVE...
...FOR THE REMAINS OF ARKADY ROSSOVICH.

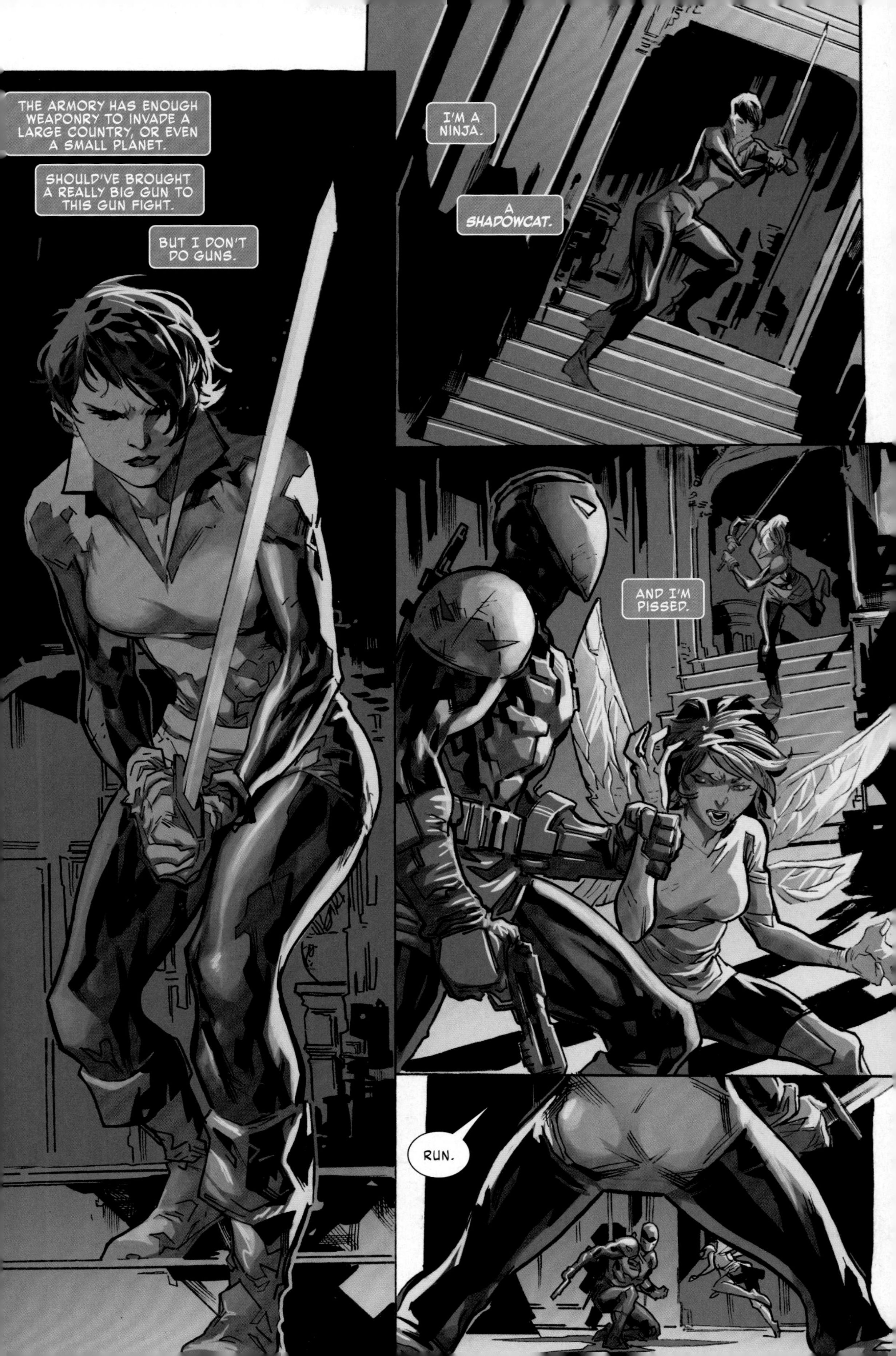
THE ARMORY HAS ENOUGH WEAPONRY TO INVADE A LARGE COUNTRY, OR EVEN A SMALL PLANET.
SHOULD'VE BROUGHT A REALLY BIG GUN TO THIS GUN FIGHT.
BUT I DON'T DO GUNS.
I'M A NINJA.
A *SHADOWCAT.*
AND I'M PISSED.
RUN.

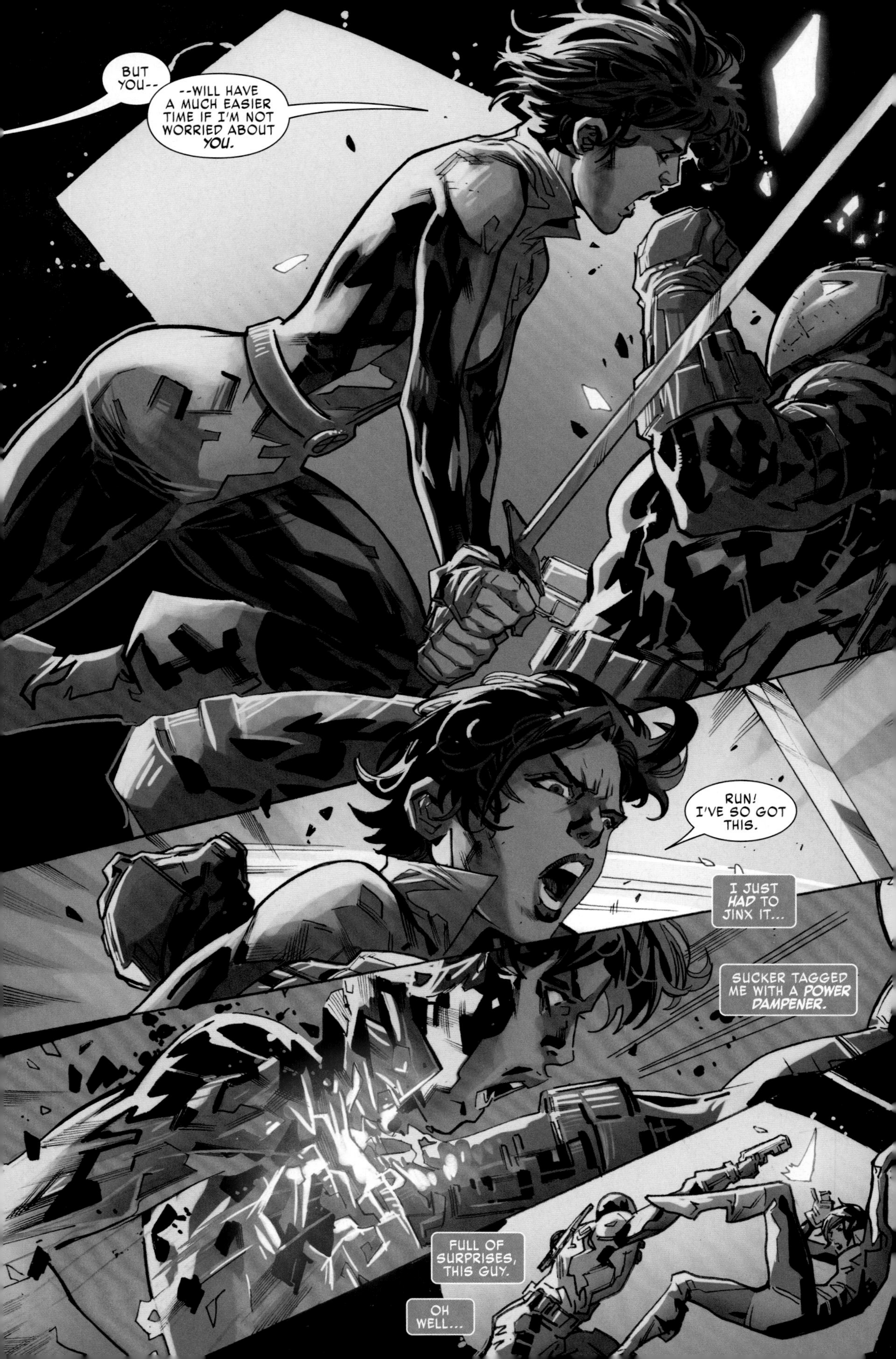
BUT YOU--
--WILL HAVE A MUCH EASIER TIME IF I'M NOT WORRIED ABOUT YOU.
RUN! I'VE SO GOT THIS.
I JUST HAD TO JINX IT...
SUCKER TAGGED ME WITH A POWER DAMPENER.
FULL OF SURPRISES, THIS GUY.
OH WELL...

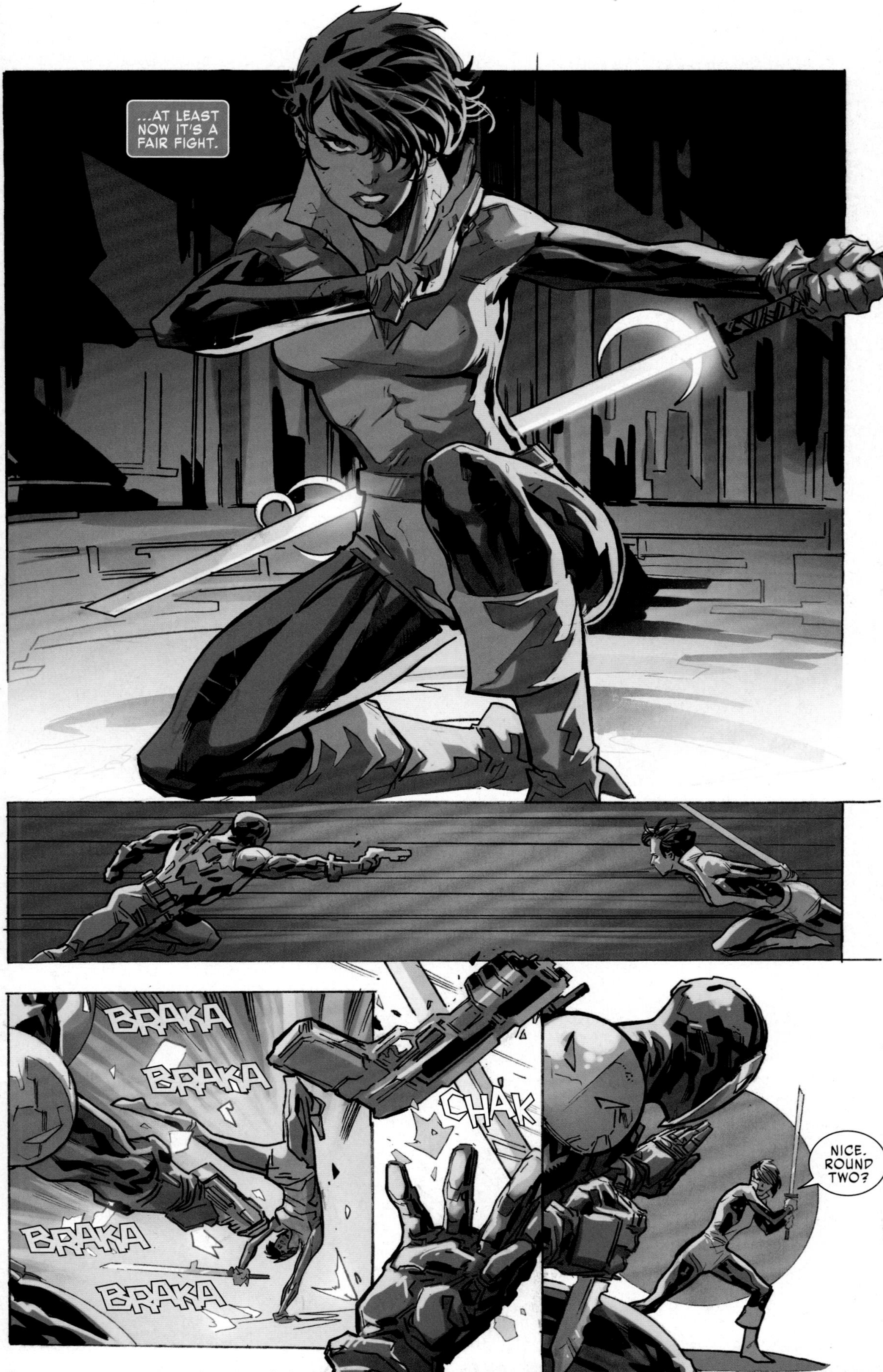
...AT LEAST NOW IT'S A FAIR FIGHT.
BRAKA
BRAKA
BRAKA
BRAKA
CHAK
NICE. ROUND TWO?

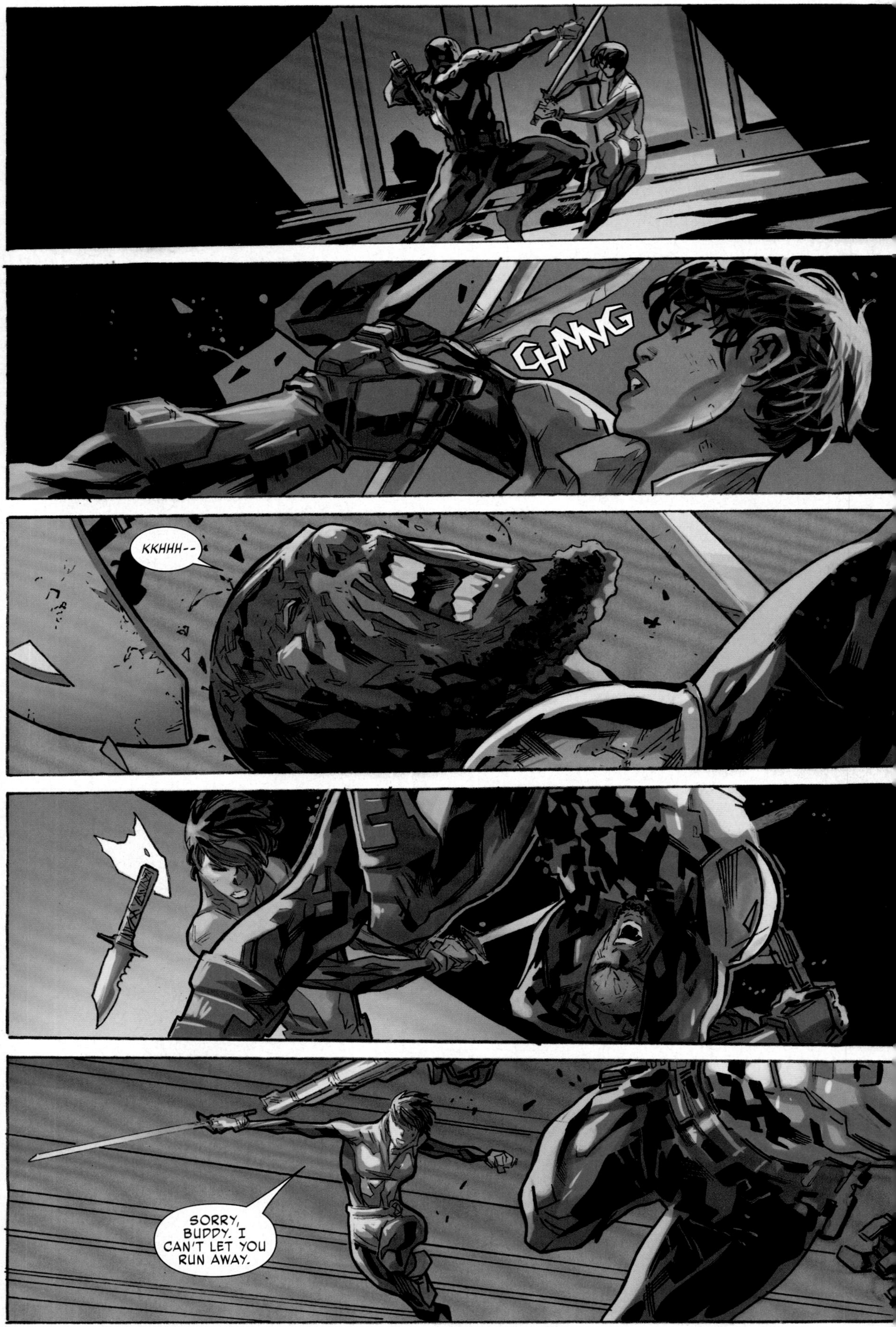
CHNNG
KKHHH--
SORRY, BUDDY. I CAN'T LET YOU RUN AWAY.

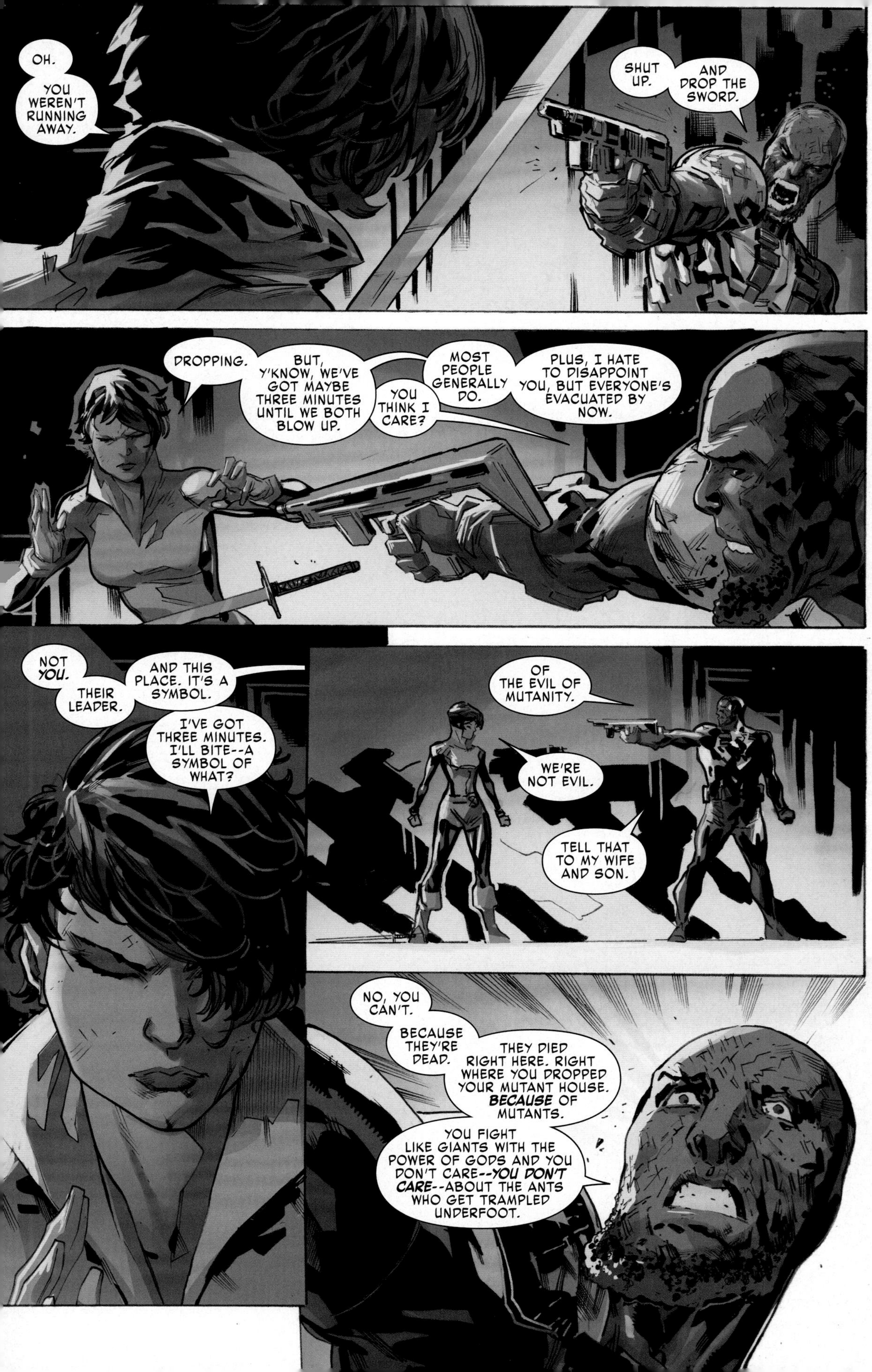
OH.
YOU WEREN'T RUNNING AWAY.
SHUT UP.
AND DROP THE SWORD.
DROPPING.
BUT, Y'KNOW, WE'VE GOT MAYBE THREE MINUTES UNTIL WE BOTH BLOW UP.
YOU THINK I CARE?
MOST PEOPLE GENERALLY DO.
PLUS, I HATE TO DISAPPOINT YOU, BUT EVERYONE'S EVACUATED BY NOW.
NOT *YOU.*
THEIR LEADER.
AND THIS PLACE. IT'S A SYMBOL.
I'VE GOT THREE MINUTES. I'LL BITE--A SYMBOL OF WHAT?
OF THE EVIL OF MUTANITY.
WE'RE NOT EVIL.
TELL THAT TO MY WIFE AND SON.
NO, YOU CAN'T.
BECAUSE THEY'RE DEAD.
THEY DIED RIGHT HERE. RIGHT WHERE YOU DROPPED YOUR MUTANT HOUSE. ***BECAUSE*** OF MUTANTS.
YOU FIGHT LIKE GIANTS WITH THE POWER OF GODS AND YOU DON'T CARE--***YOU DON'T CARE***--ABOUT THE ANTS WHO GET TRAMPLED UNDERFOOT.

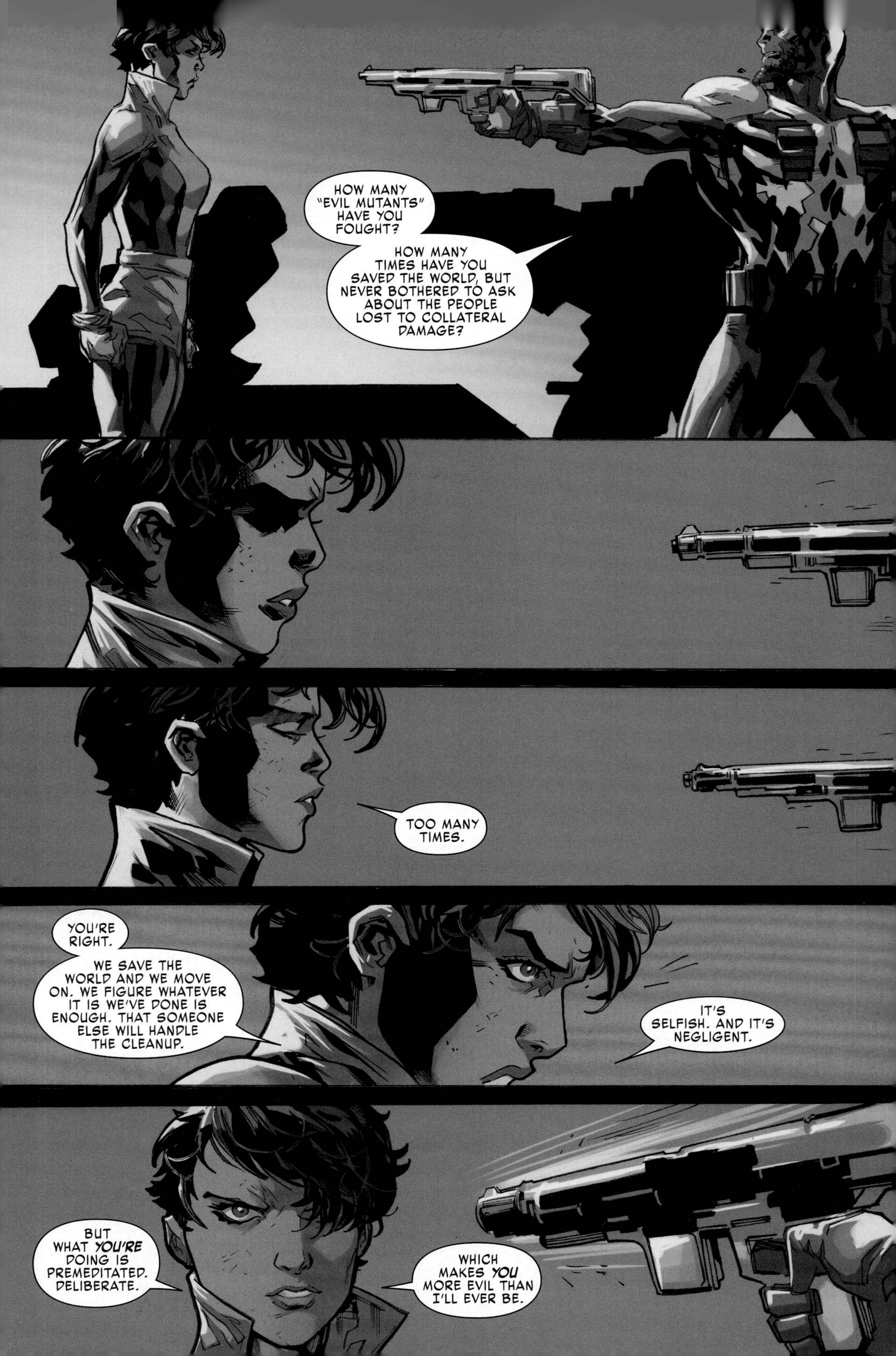
HOW MANY "EVIL MUTANTS" HAVE YOU FOUGHT?
HOW MANY TIMES HAVE YOU SAVED THE WORLD, BUT NEVER BOTHERED TO ASK ABOUT THE PEOPLE LOST TO COLLATERAL DAMAGE?
TOO MANY TIMES.
YOU'RE RIGHT.
WE SAVE THE WORLD AND WE MOVE ON. WE FIGURE WHATEVER IT IS WE'VE DONE IS ENOUGH. THAT SOMEONE ELSE WILL HANDLE THE CLEANUP.
IT'S SELFISH. AND IT'S NEGLIGENT.
BUT WHAT *YOU'RE* DOING IS PREMEDITATED. DELIBERATE.
WHICH MAKES *YOU* MORE EVIL THAN I'LL EVER BE.

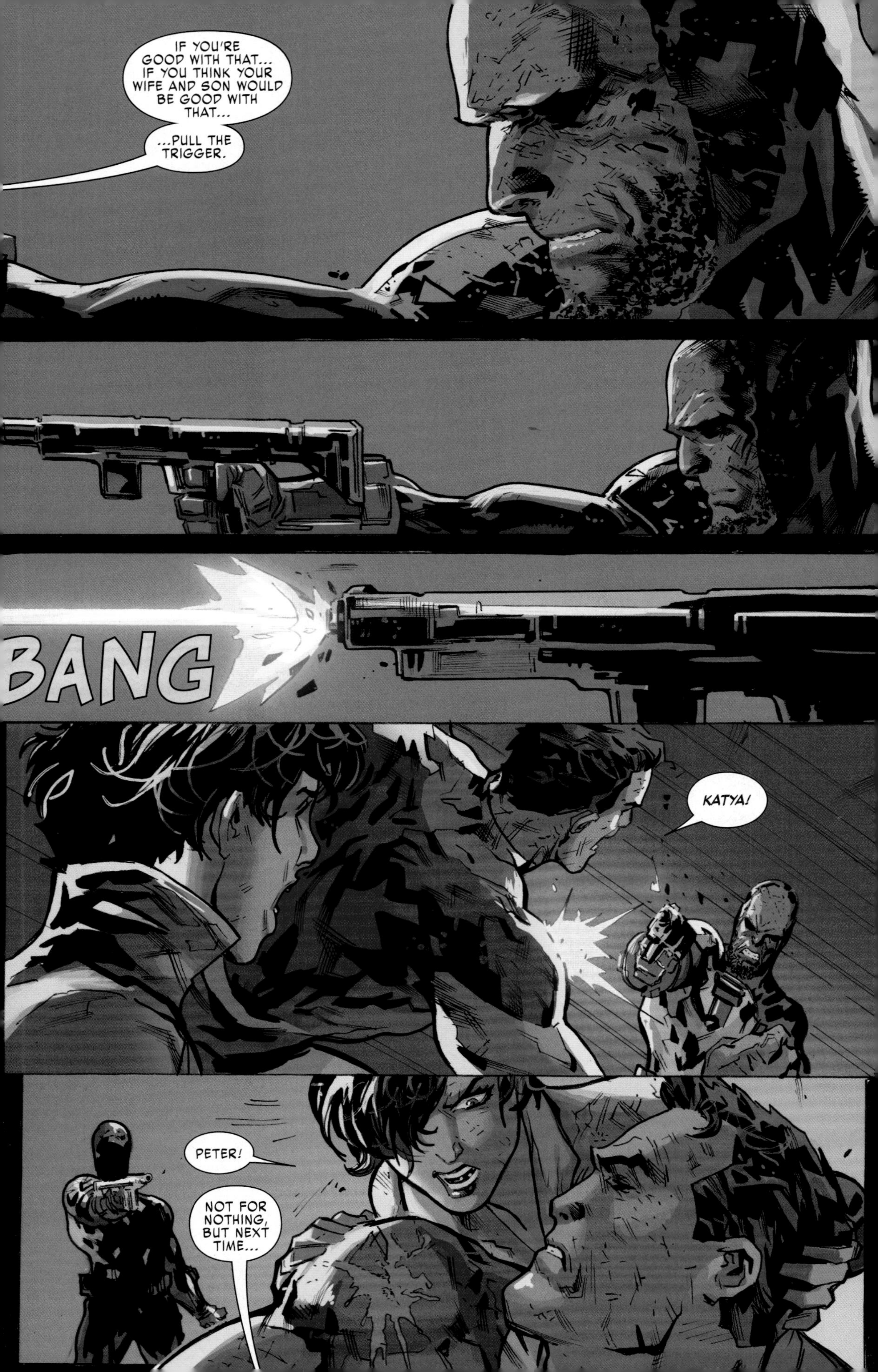
IF YOU'RE GOOD WITH THAT... IF YOU THINK YOUR WIFE AND SON WOULD BE GOOD WITH THAT...
...PULL THE TRIGGER.
BANG
KATYA!
PETER!
NOT FOR NOTHING, BUT NEXT TIME...

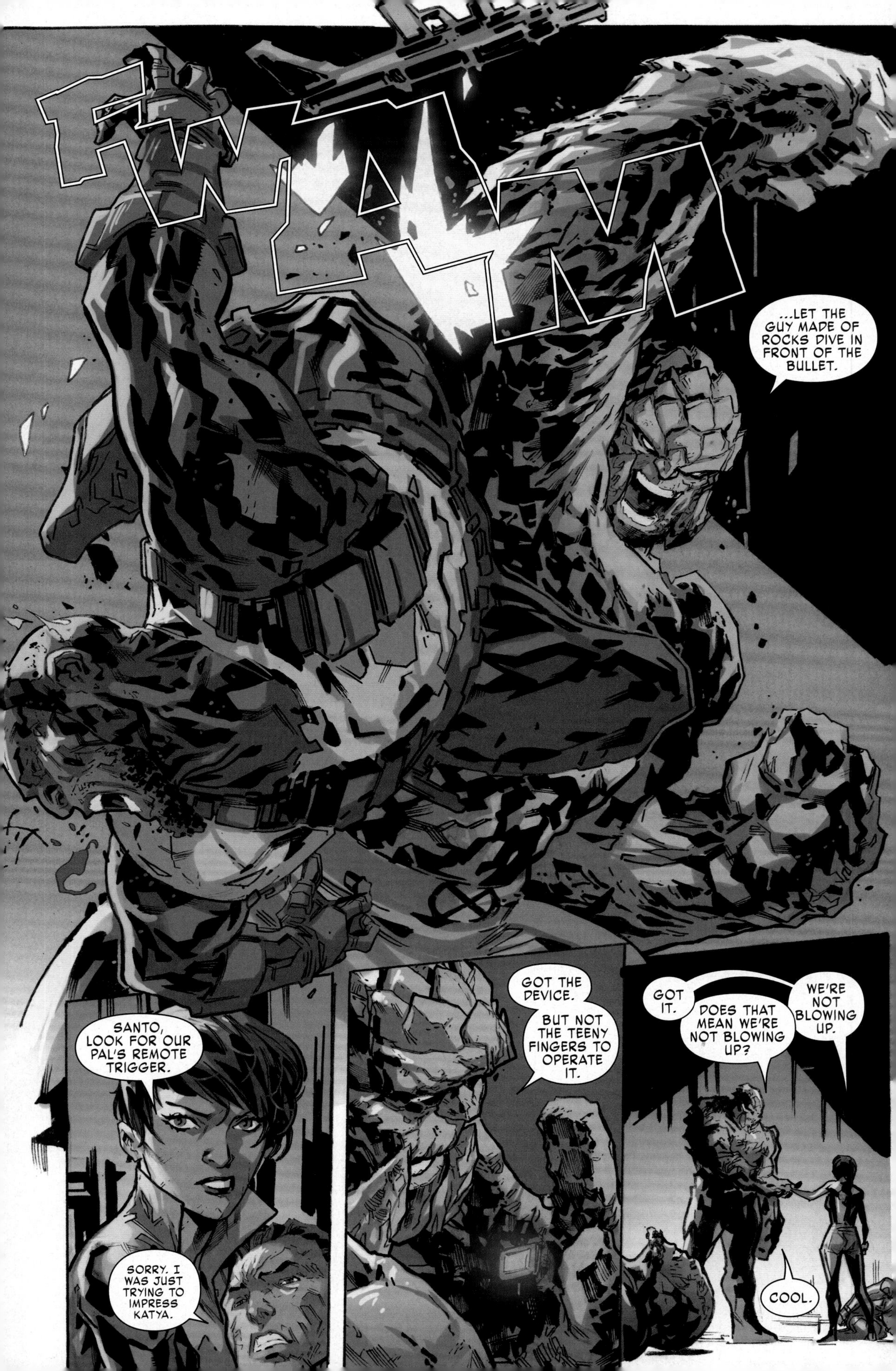
FWAM
...LET THE GUY MADE OF ROCKS DIVE IN FRONT OF THE BULLET.
SANTO, LOOK FOR OUR PAL'S REMOTE TRIGGER.
SORRY. I WAS JUST TRYING TO IMPRESS KATYA.
GOT THE DEVICE.
BUT NOT THE TEENY FINGERS TO OPERATE IT.
GOT IT.
DOES THAT MEAN WE'RE NOT BLOWING UP?
WE'RE NOT BLOWING UP.
COOL.

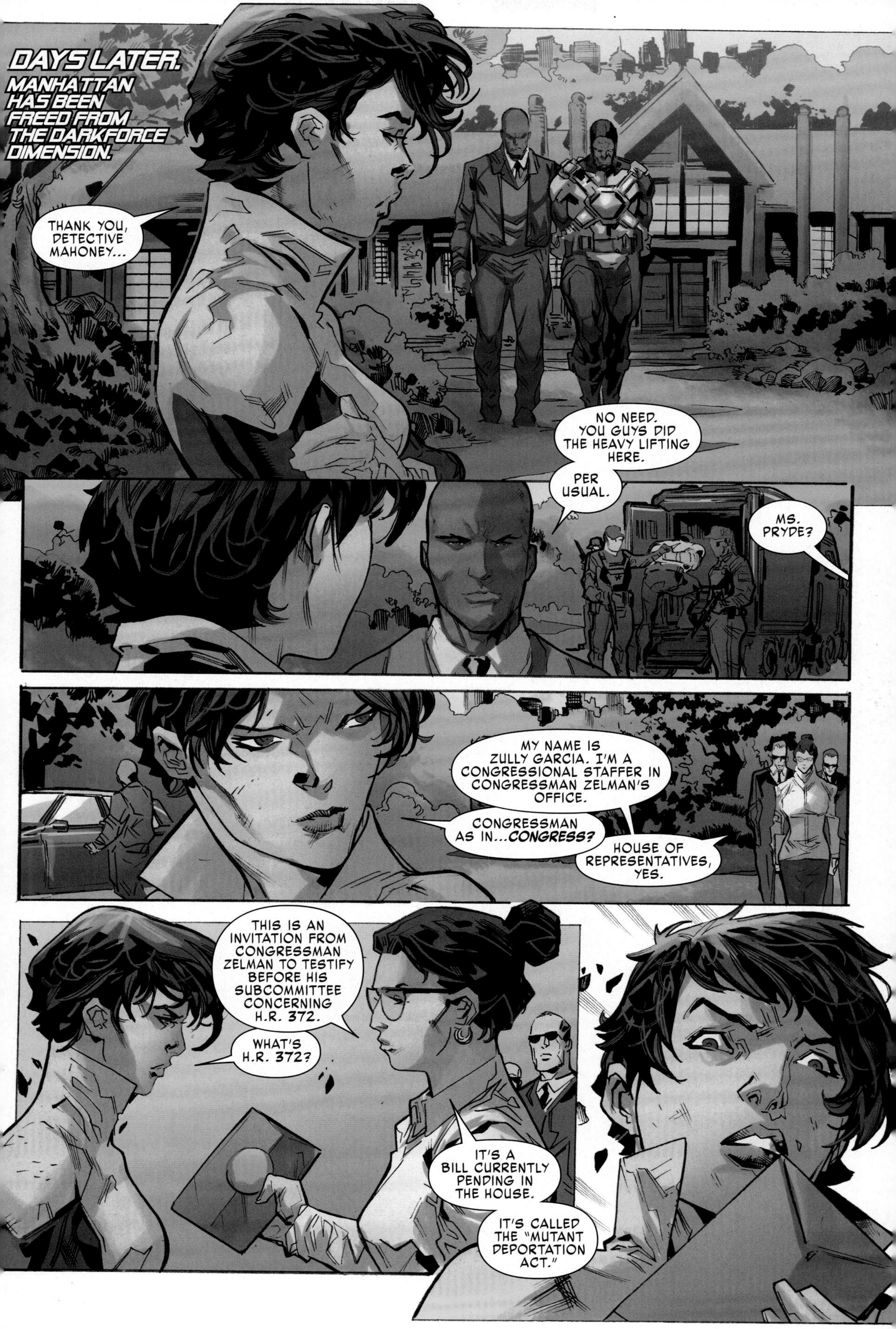
DAYS LATER. MANHATTAN HAS BEEN FREED FROM THE DARKFORCE DIMENSION.
THANK YOU, DETECTIVE MAHONEY...
NO NEED. YOU GUYS DID THE HEAVY LIFTING HERE.
PER USUAL.
MS. PRYDE?
MY NAME IS ZULLY GARCIA. I'M A CONGRESSIONAL STAFFER IN CONGRESSMAN ZELMAN'S OFFICE.
CONGRESSMAN AS IN...CONGRESS?
HOUSE OF REPRESENTATIVES, YES.
THIS IS AN INVITATION FROM CONGRESSMAN ZELMAN TO TESTIFY BEFORE HIS SUBCOMMITTEE CONCERNING H.R. 372.
WHAT'S H.R. 372?
IT'S A BILL CURRENTLY PENDING IN THE HOUSE.
IT'S CALLED THE "MUTANT DEPORTATION ACT."

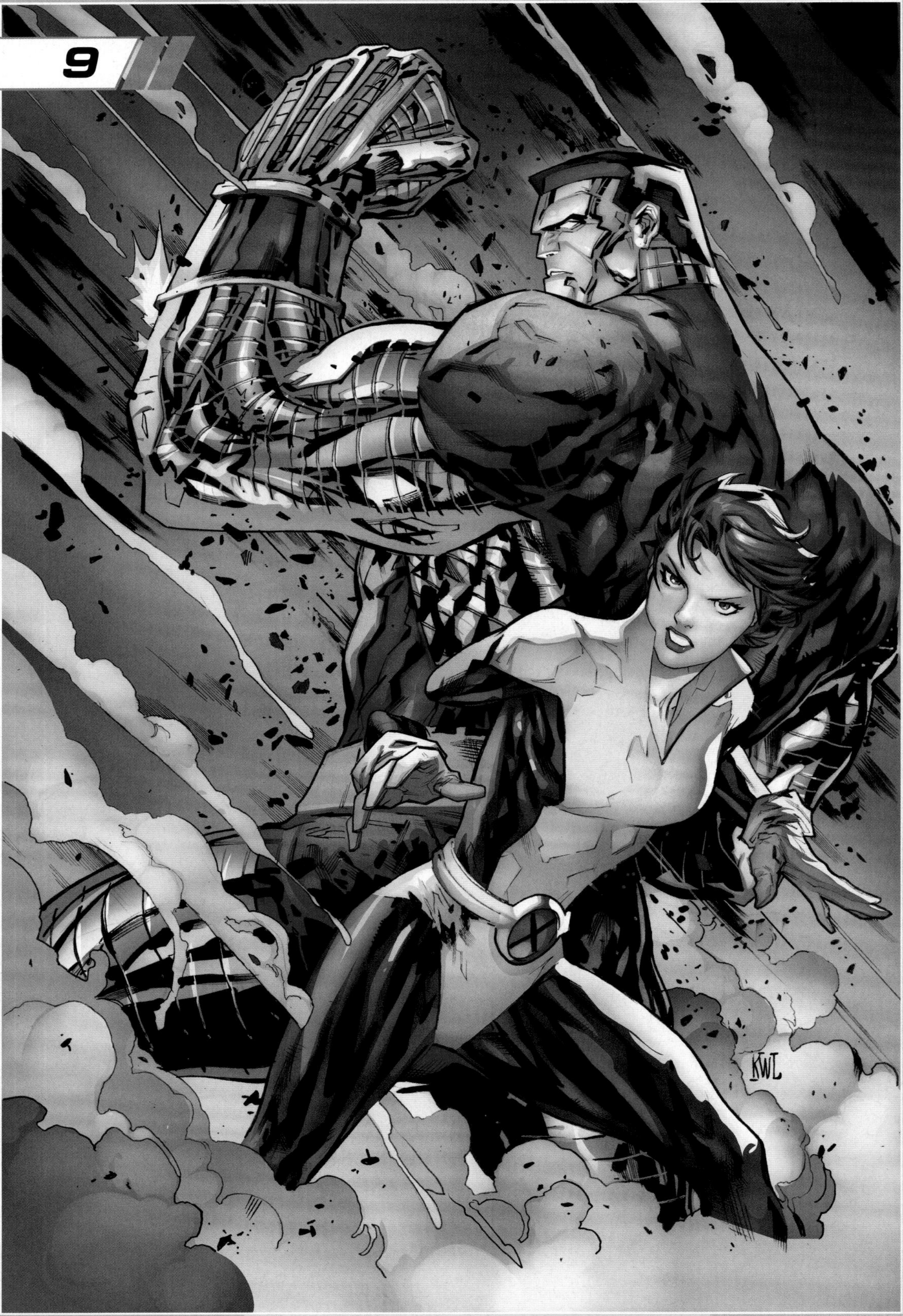

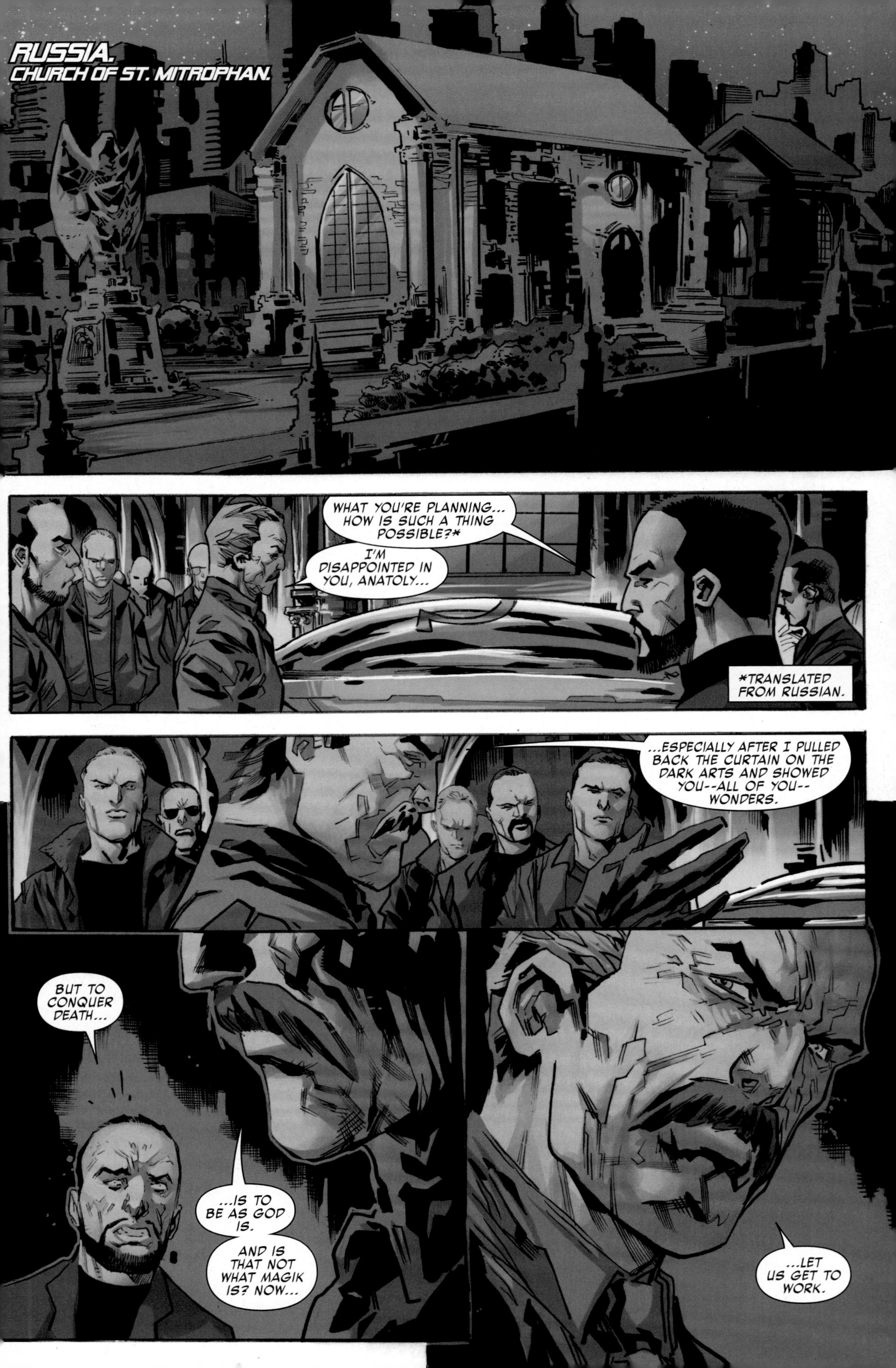
RUSSIA.
CHURCH OF ST. MITROPHAN.
WHAT YOU'RE PLANNING... HOW IS SUCH A THING POSSIBLE?*
I'M DISAPPOINTED IN YOU, ANATOLY...
*TRANSLATED FROM RUSSIAN.
...ESPECIALLY AFTER I PULLED BACK THE CURTAIN ON THE DARK ARTS AND SHOWED YOU--ALL OF YOU--WONDERS.
BUT TO CONQUER DEATH...
...IS TO BE AS GOD IS.
AND IS THAT NOT WHAT MAGIK IS? NOW...
...LET US GET TO WORK.

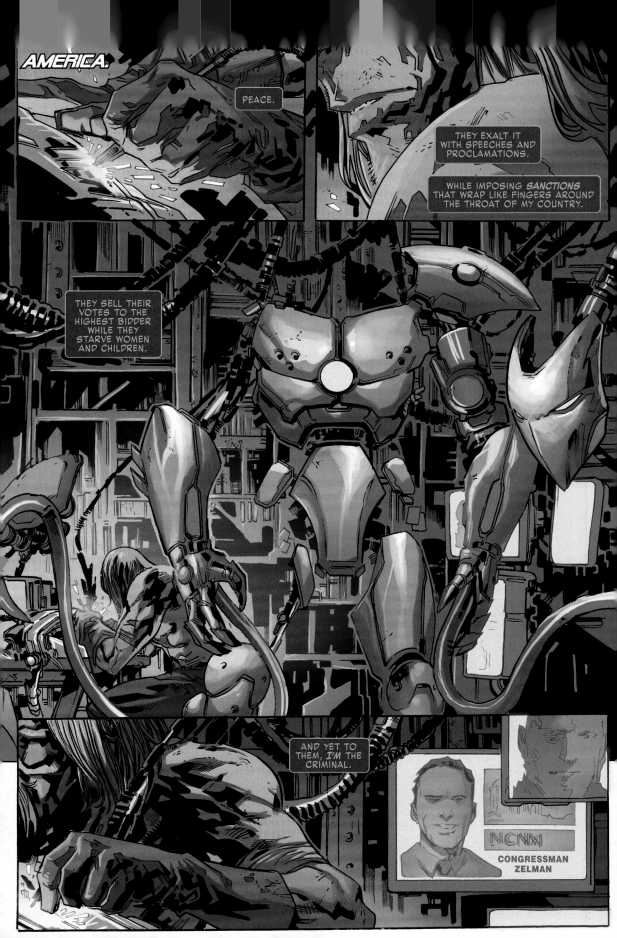

AMERICA.

PEACE.

THEY EXALT IT WITH SPEECHES AND PROCLAMATIONS.

WHILE IMPOSING *SANCTIONS* THAT WRAP LIKE FINGERS AROUND THE THROAT OF MY COUNTRY.

THEY SELL THEIR VOTES TO THE HIGHEST BIDDER WHILE THEY STARVE WOMEN AND CHILDREN.

AND YET TO THEM, *I'M* THE CRIMINAL.

CONGRESSMAN ZELMAN

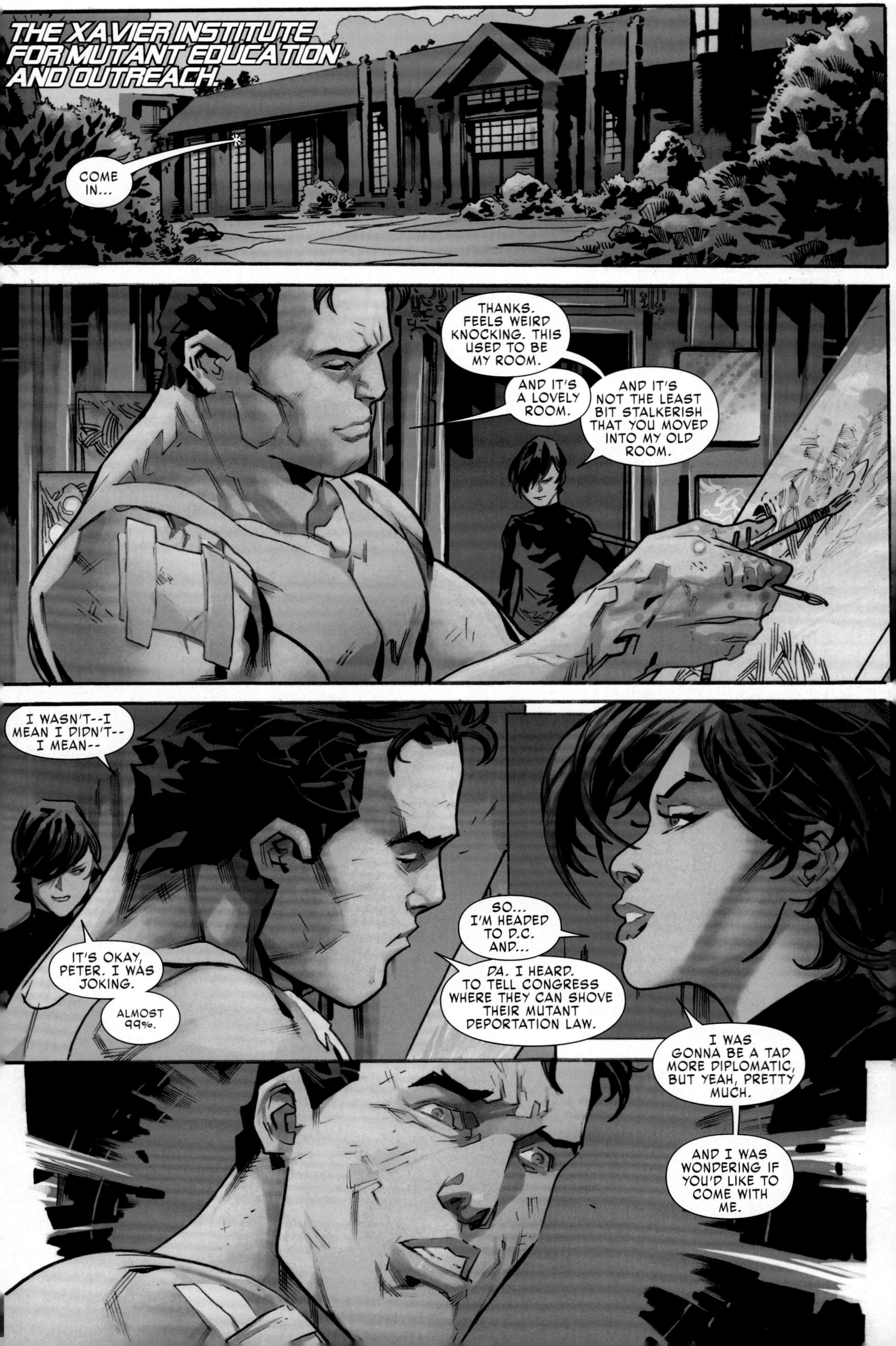
THE XAVIER INSTITUTE FOR MUTANT EDUCATION AND OUTREACH.
COME IN...
THANKS. FEELS WEIRD KNOCKING. THIS USED TO BE MY ROOM.
AND IT'S A LOVELY ROOM.
AND IT'S NOT THE LEAST BIT STALKERISH THAT YOU MOVED INTO MY OLD ROOM.
I WASN'T--I MEAN I DIDN'T--I MEAN--
IT'S OKAY, PETER. I WAS JOKING.
ALMOST 99%.
SO... I'M HEADED TO D.C. AND...
DA. I HEARD. TO TELL CONGRESS WHERE THEY CAN SHOVE THEIR MUTANT DEPORTATION LAW.
I WAS GONNA BE A TAD MORE DIPLOMATIC, BUT YEAH, PRETTY MUCH.
AND I WAS WONDERING IF YOU'D LIKE TO COME WITH ME.

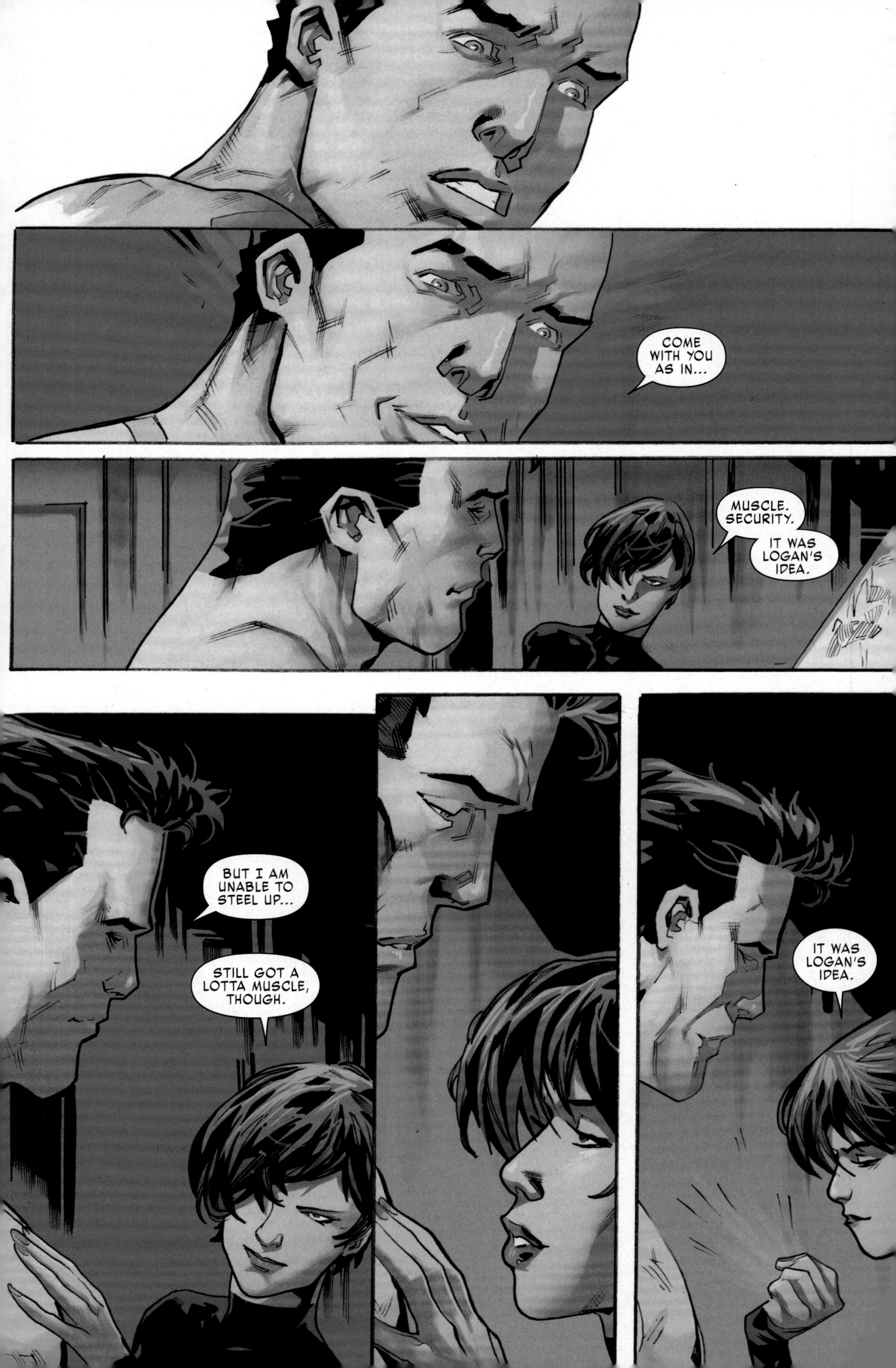
COME WITH YOU AS IN...
MUSCLE. SECURITY.
IT WAS LOGAN'S IDEA.
BUT I AM UNABLE TO STEEL UP...
STILL GOT A LOTTA MUSCLE, THOUGH.
IT WAS LOGAN'S IDEA.

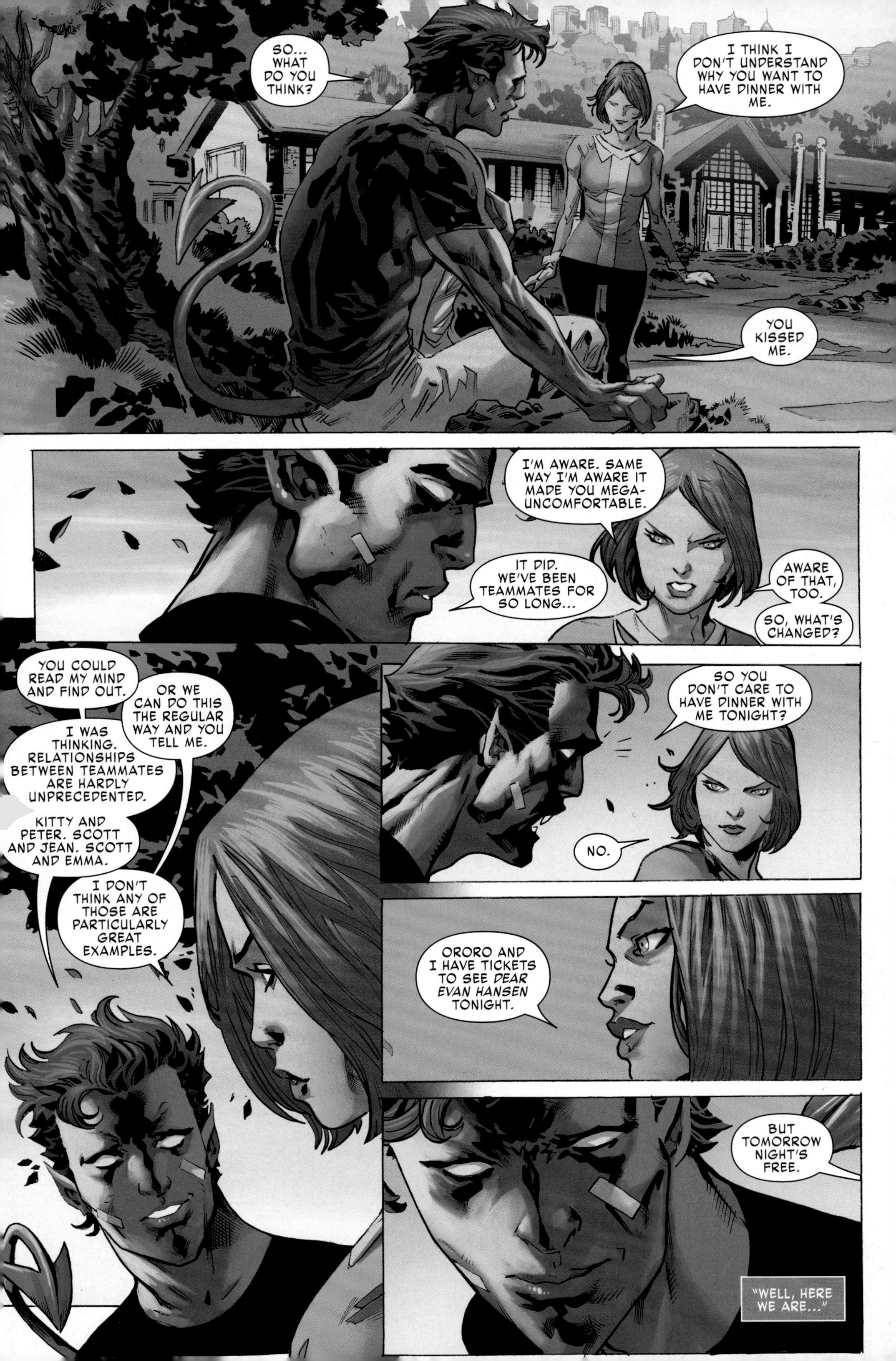
SO... WHAT DO YOU THINK?
I THINK I DON'T UNDERSTAND WHY YOU WANT TO HAVE DINNER WITH ME.
YOU KISSED ME.
I'M AWARE. SAME WAY I'M AWARE IT MADE YOU MEGA-UNCOMFORTABLE.
IT DID. WE'VE BEEN TEAMMATES FOR SO LONG...
AWARE OF THAT, TOO.
SO, WHAT'S CHANGED?
YOU COULD READ MY MIND AND FIND OUT.
OR WE CAN DO THIS THE REGULAR WAY AND YOU TELL ME.
I WAS THINKING. RELATIONSHIPS BETWEEN TEAMMATES ARE HARDLY UNPRECEDENTED.
KITTY AND PETER. SCOTT AND JEAN. SCOTT AND EMMA.
I DON'T THINK ANY OF THOSE ARE PARTICULARLY GREAT EXAMPLES.
SO YOU DON'T CARE TO HAVE DINNER WITH ME TONIGHT?
NO.
ORORO AND I HAVE TICKETS TO SEE *DEAR EVAN HANSEN* TONIGHT.
BUT TOMORROW NIGHT'S FREE.
"WELL, HERE WE ARE..."

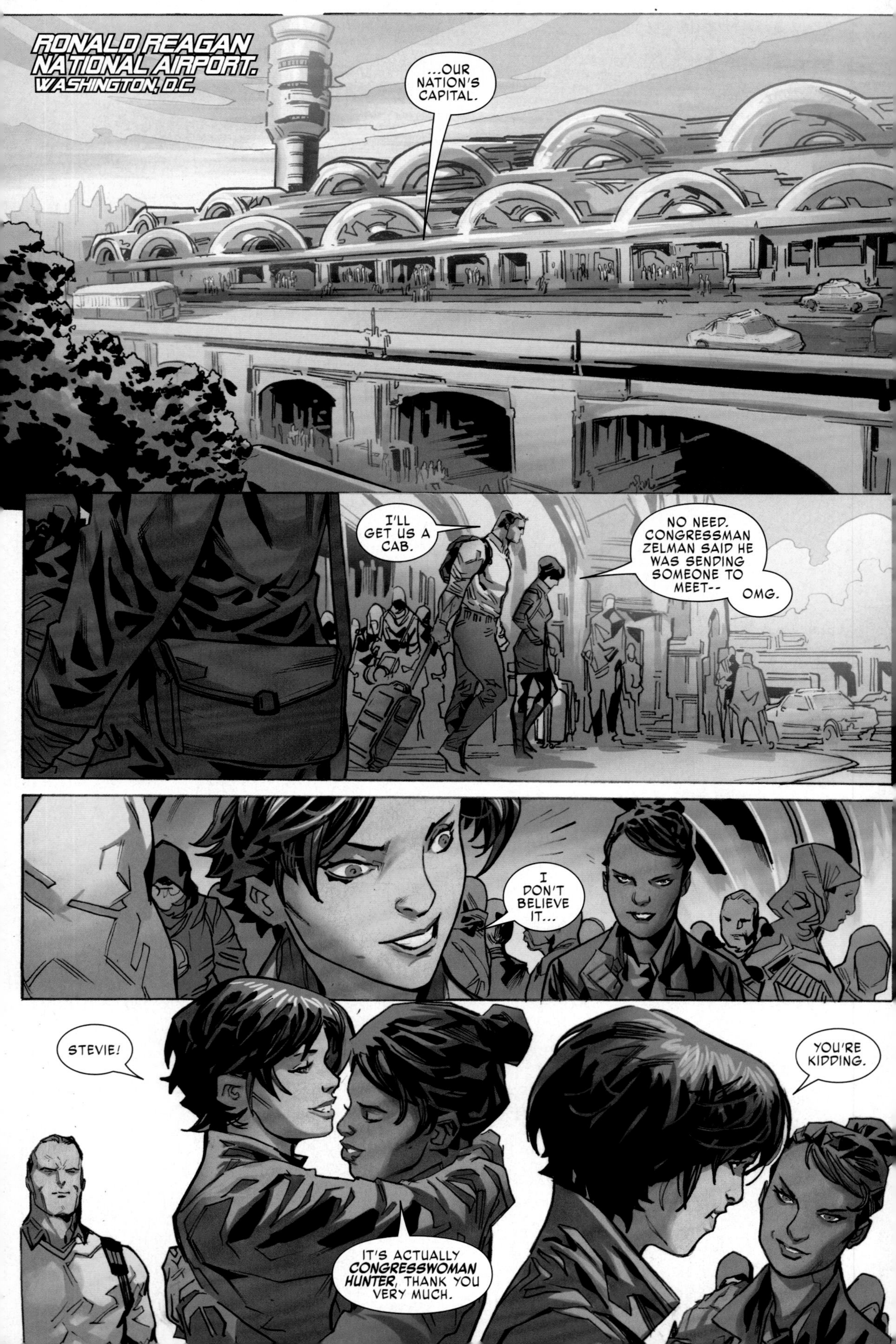
RONALD REAGAN NATIONAL AIRPORT. WASHINGTON, D.C.
...OUR NATION'S CAPITAL.
I'LL GET US A CAB.
NO NEED. CONGRESSMAN ZELMAN SAID HE WAS SENDING SOMEONE TO MEET--
OMG.
I DON'T BELIEVE IT...
STEVIE!
YOU'RE KIDDING.
IT'S ACTUALLY ***CONGRESSWOMAN HUNTER***, THANK YOU VERY MUCH.

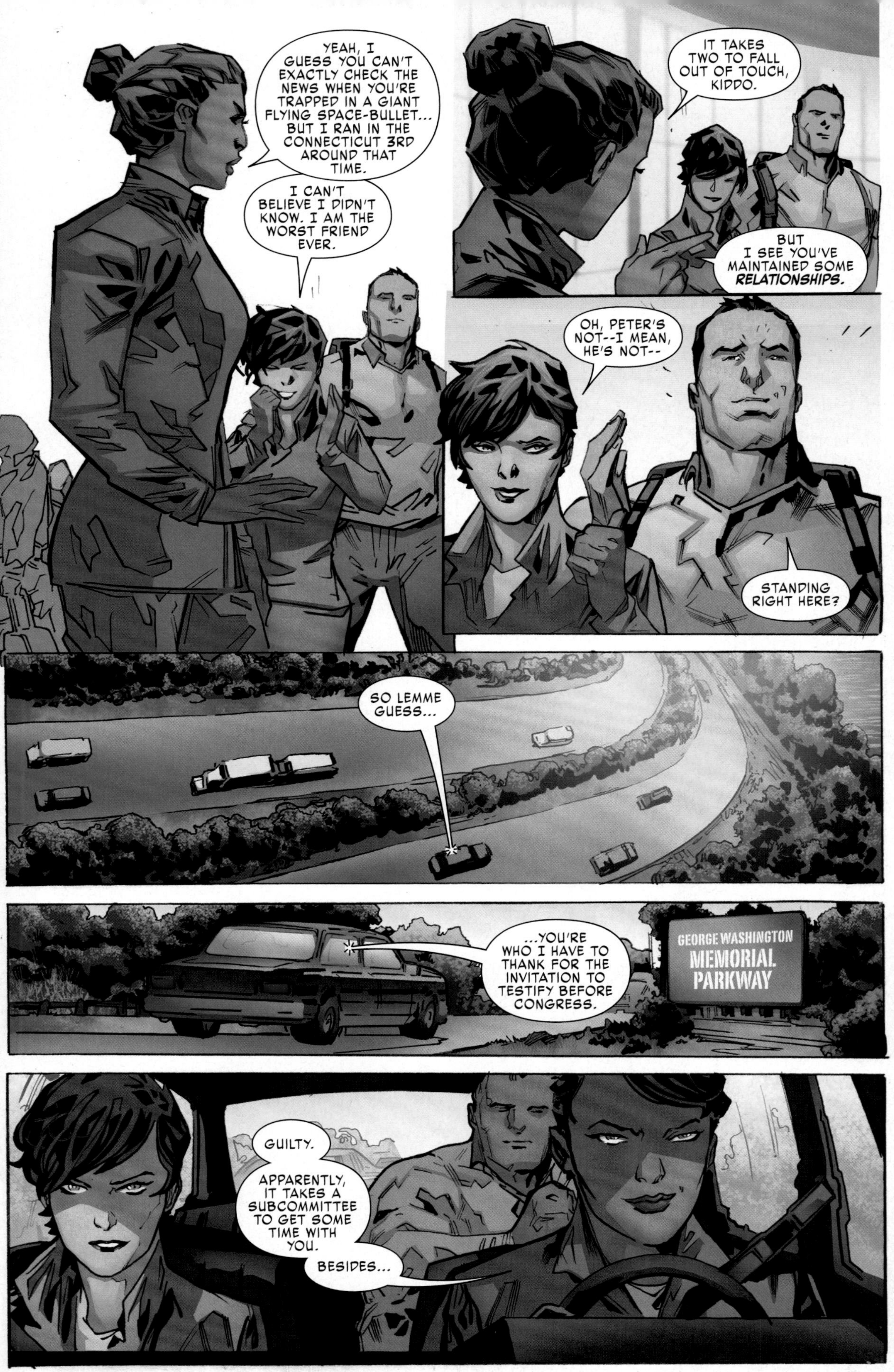
YEAH, I GUESS YOU CAN'T EXACTLY CHECK THE NEWS WHEN YOU'RE TRAPPED IN A GIANT FLYING SPACE-BULLET... BUT I RAN IN THE CONNECTICUT 3RD AROUND THAT TIME.
I CAN'T BELIEVE I DIDN'T KNOW. I AM THE WORST FRIEND EVER.
IT TAKES TWO TO FALL OUT OF TOUCH, KIDDO.
BUT I SEE YOU'VE MAINTAINED SOME ***RELATIONSHIPS.***
OH, PETER'S NOT--I MEAN, HE'S NOT--
STANDING RIGHT HERE?
SO LEMME GUESS...
...YOU'RE WHO I HAVE TO THANK FOR THE INVITATION TO TESTIFY BEFORE CONGRESS.
GEORGE WASHINGTON MEMORIAL PARKWAY
GUILTY.
APPARENTLY, IT TAKES A SUBCOMMITTEE TO GET SOME TIME WITH YOU.
BESIDES...

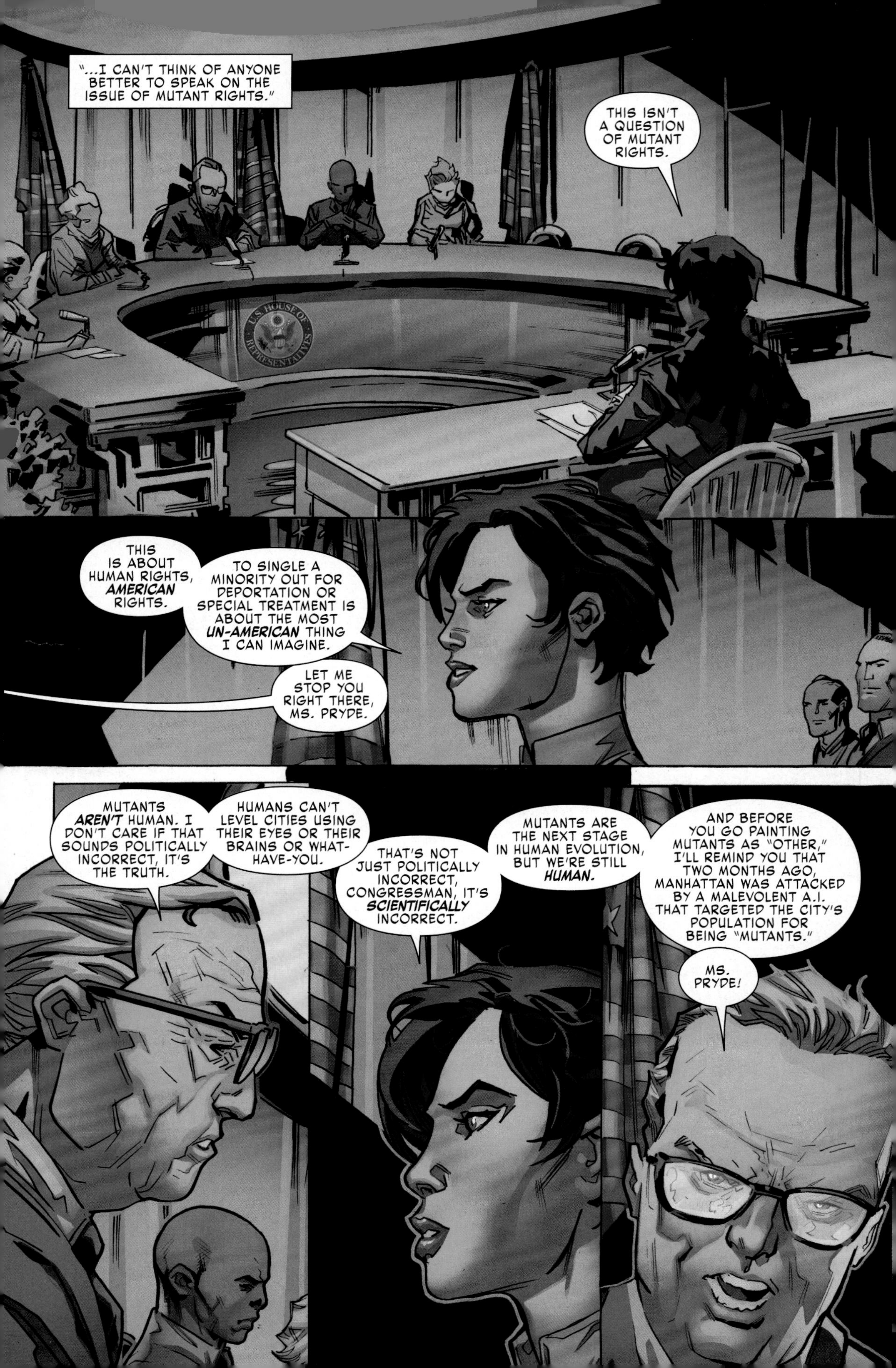
"...I CAN'T THINK OF ANYONE BETTER TO SPEAK ON THE ISSUE OF MUTANT RIGHTS."
THIS ISN'T A QUESTION OF MUTANT RIGHTS.
THIS IS ABOUT HUMAN RIGHTS, *AMERICAN* RIGHTS.
TO SINGLE A MINORITY OUT FOR DEPORTATION OR SPECIAL TREATMENT IS ABOUT THE MOST *UN-AMERICAN* THING I CAN IMAGINE.
LET ME STOP YOU RIGHT THERE, MS. PRYDE.
MUTANTS *AREN'T* HUMAN. I DON'T CARE IF THAT SOUNDS POLITICALLY INCORRECT, IT'S THE TRUTH.
HUMANS CAN'T LEVEL CITIES USING THEIR EYES OR THEIR BRAINS OR WHAT-HAVE-YOU.
THAT'S NOT JUST POLITICALLY INCORRECT, CONGRESSMAN, IT'S *SCIENTIFICALLY* INCORRECT.
MUTANTS ARE THE NEXT STAGE IN HUMAN EVOLUTION, BUT WE'RE STILL *HUMAN.*
AND BEFORE YOU GO PAINTING MUTANTS AS "OTHER," I'LL REMIND YOU THAT TWO MONTHS AGO, MANHATTAN WAS ATTACKED BY A MALEVOLENT A.I. THAT TARGETED THE CITY'S POPULATION FOR BEING "MUTANTS."
MS. PRYDE!

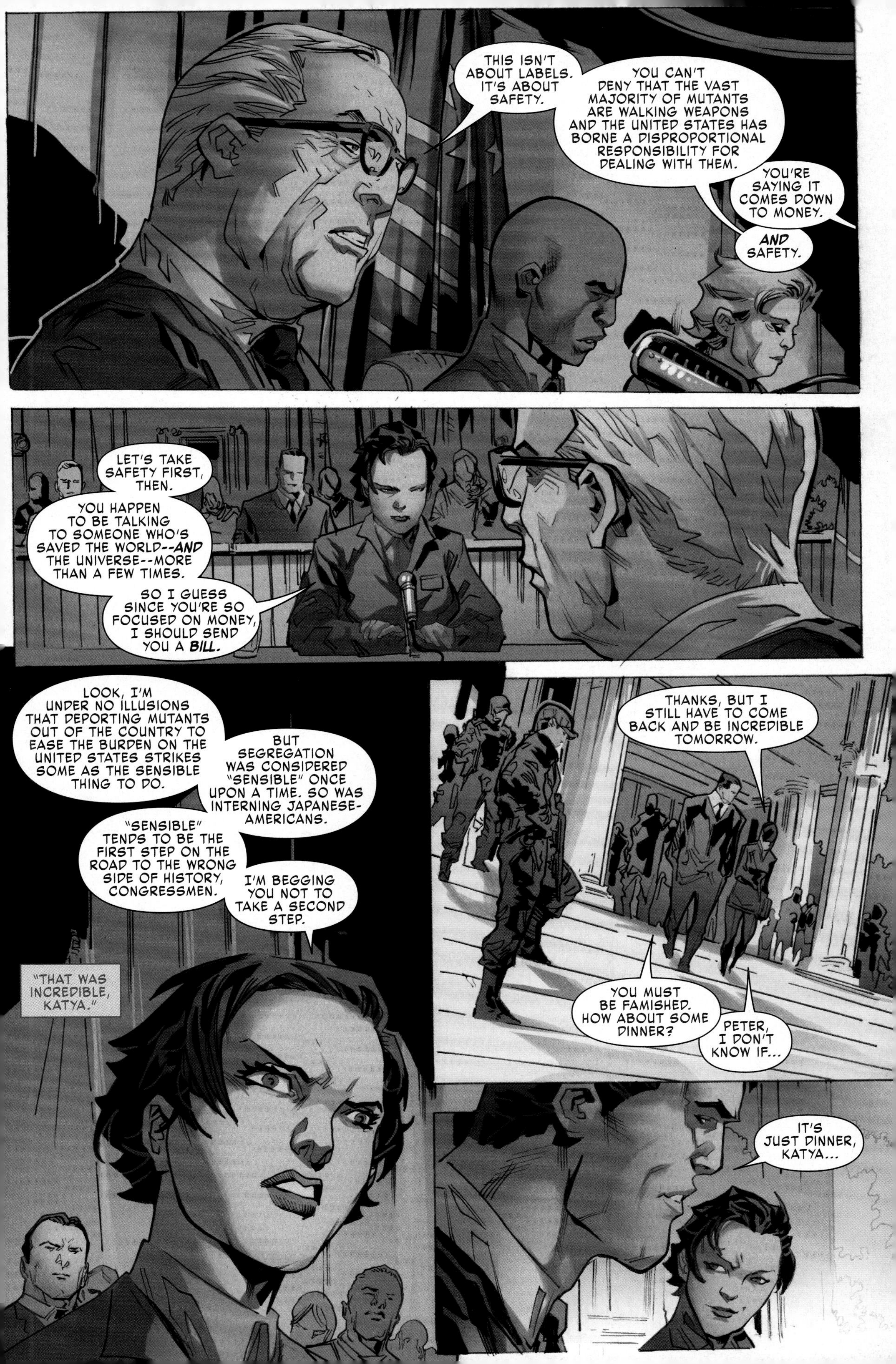
THIS ISN'T ABOUT LABELS. IT'S ABOUT SAFETY.
YOU CAN'T DENY THAT THE VAST MAJORITY OF MUTANTS ARE WALKING WEAPONS AND THE UNITED STATES HAS BORNE A DISPROPORTIONAL RESPONSIBILITY FOR DEALING WITH THEM.
YOU'RE SAYING IT COMES DOWN TO MONEY.
AND SAFETY.
LET'S TAKE SAFETY FIRST, THEN.
YOU HAPPEN TO BE TALKING TO SOMEONE WHO'S SAVED THE WORLD--AND THE UNIVERSE--MORE THAN A FEW TIMES.
SO I GUESS SINCE YOU'RE SO FOCUSED ON MONEY, I SHOULD SEND YOU A BILL.
LOOK, I'M UNDER NO ILLUSIONS THAT DEPORTING MUTANTS OUT OF THE COUNTRY TO EASE THE BURDEN ON THE UNITED STATES STRIKES SOME AS THE SENSIBLE THING TO DO.
BUT SEGREGATION WAS CONSIDERED "SENSIBLE" ONCE UPON A TIME. SO WAS INTERNING JAPANESE-AMERICANS.
"SENSIBLE" TENDS TO BE THE FIRST STEP ON THE ROAD TO THE WRONG SIDE OF HISTORY, CONGRESSMEN.
I'M BEGGING YOU NOT TO TAKE A SECOND STEP.
"THAT WAS INCREDIBLE, KATYA."
THANKS, BUT I STILL HAVE TO COME BACK AND BE INCREDIBLE TOMORROW.
YOU MUST BE FAMISHED. HOW ABOUT SOME DINNER?
PETER, I DON'T KNOW IF...
IT'S JUST DINNER, KATYA...

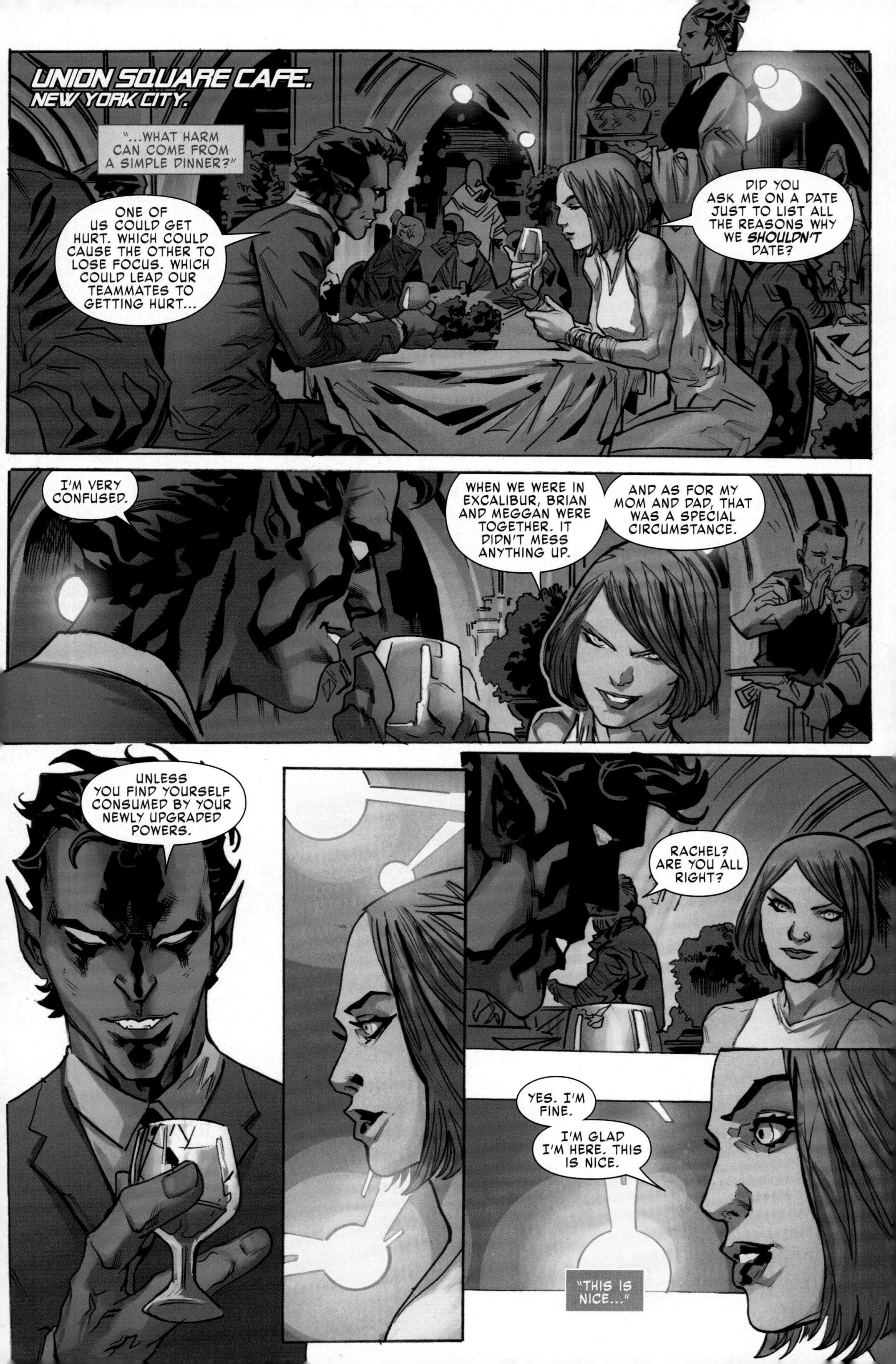
UNION SQUARE CAFE.
NEW YORK CITY.
"...WHAT HARM CAN COME FROM A SIMPLE DINNER?"
ONE OF US COULD GET HURT. WHICH COULD CAUSE THE OTHER TO LOSE FOCUS. WHICH COULD LEAD OUR TEAMMATES TO GETTING HURT...
DID YOU ASK ME ON A DATE JUST TO LIST ALL THE REASONS WHY WE SHOULDN'T DATE?
I'M VERY CONFUSED.
WHEN WE WERE IN EXCALIBUR, BRIAN AND MEGGAN WERE TOGETHER. IT DIDN'T MESS ANYTHING UP.
AND AS FOR MY MOM AND DAD, THAT WAS A SPECIAL CIRCUMSTANCE.
UNLESS YOU FIND YOURSELF CONSUMED BY YOUR NEWLY UPGRADED POWERS.
RACHEL? ARE YOU ALL RIGHT?
YES. I'M FINE.
I'M GLAD I'M HERE. THIS IS NICE.
"THIS IS NICE..."

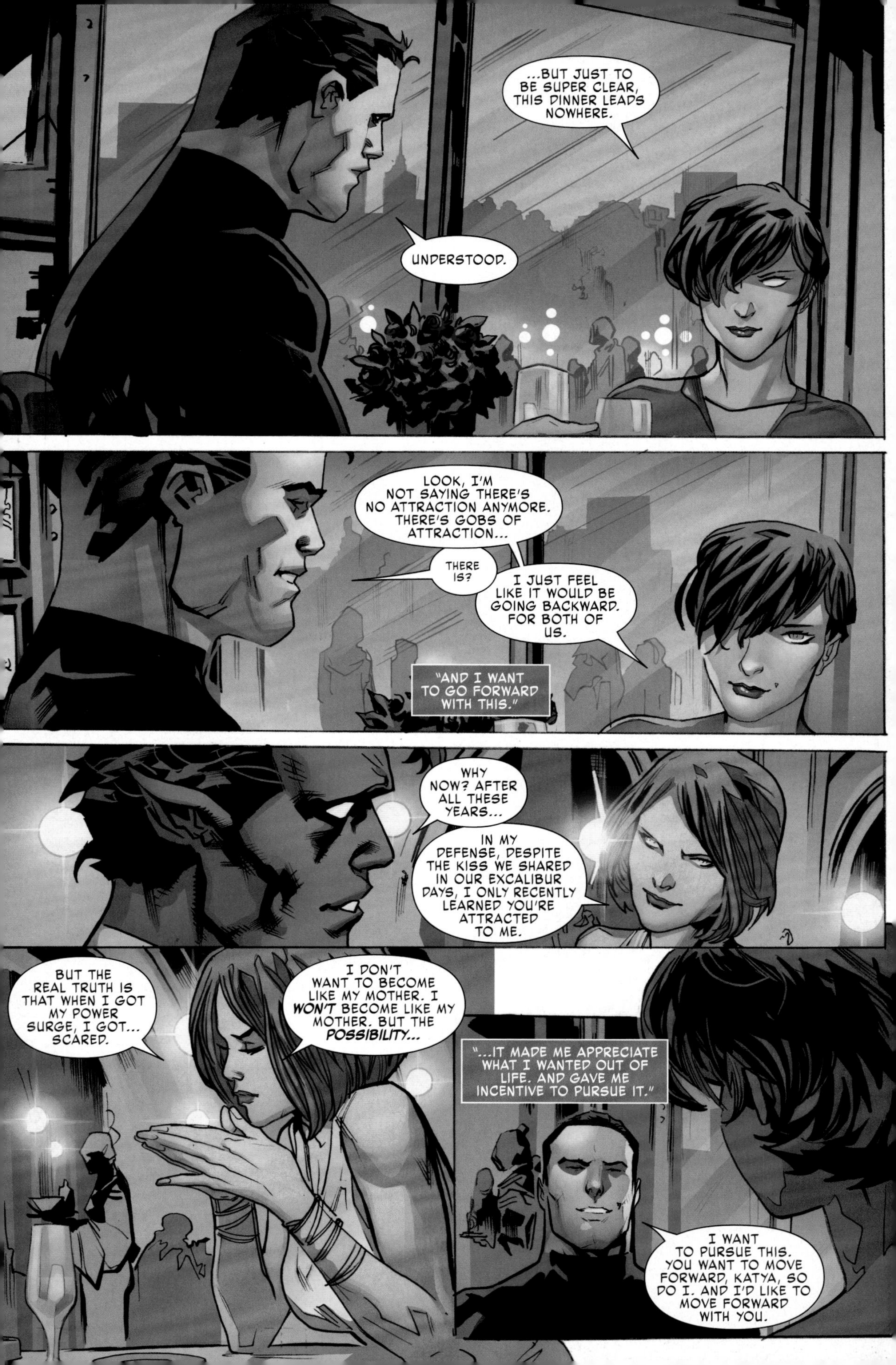
...BUT JUST TO BE SUPER CLEAR, THIS DINNER LEADS NOWHERE.
UNDERSTOOD.
LOOK, I'M NOT SAYING THERE'S NO ATTRACTION ANYMORE. THERE'S GOBS OF ATTRACTION...
THERE IS?
I JUST FEEL LIKE IT WOULD BE GOING BACKWARD. FOR BOTH OF US.
"AND I WANT TO GO FORWARD WITH THIS."
WHY NOW? AFTER ALL THESE YEARS...
IN MY DEFENSE, DESPITE THE KISS WE SHARED IN OUR EXCALIBUR DAYS, I ONLY RECENTLY LEARNED YOU'RE ATTRACTED TO ME.
BUT THE REAL TRUTH IS THAT WHEN I GOT MY POWER SURGE, I GOT... SCARED.
I DON'T WANT TO BECOME LIKE MY MOTHER. I *WON'T* BECOME LIKE MY MOTHER. BUT THE ***POSSIBILITY...***
"...IT MADE ME APPRECIATE WHAT I WANTED OUT OF LIFE. AND GAVE ME INCENTIVE TO PURSUE IT."
I WANT TO PURSUE THIS. YOU WANT TO MOVE FORWARD, KATYA, SO DO I. AND I'D LIKE TO MOVE FORWARD WITH YOU.

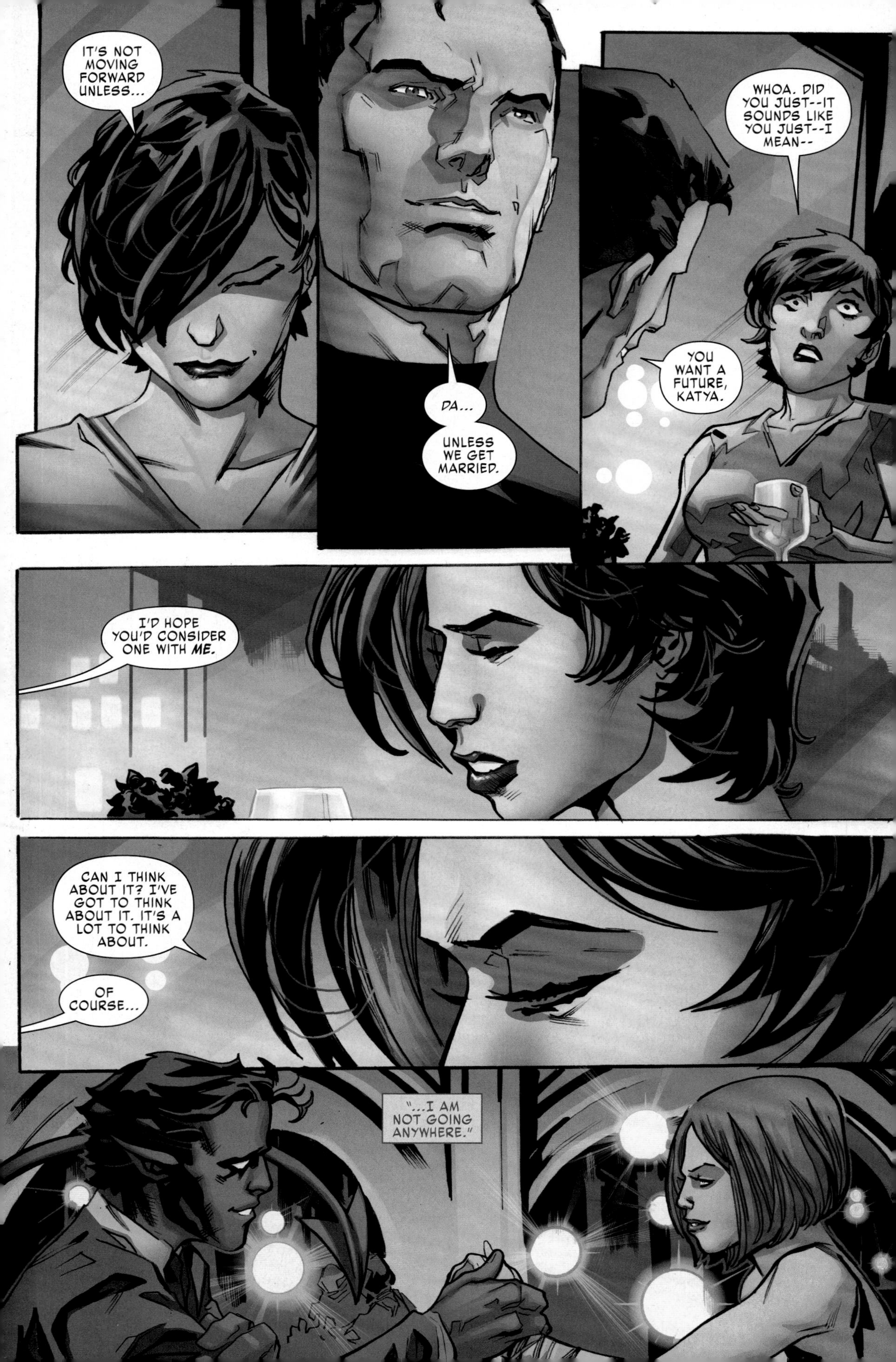
IT'S NOT MOVING FORWARD UNLESS...
DA...
UNLESS WE GET MARRIED.
WHOA. DID YOU JUST--IT SOUNDS LIKE YOU JUST--I MEAN--
YOU WANT A FUTURE, KATYA.
I'D HOPE YOU'D CONSIDER ONE WITH ME.
CAN I THINK ABOUT IT? I'VE GOT TO THINK ABOUT IT. IT'S A LOT TO THINK ABOUT.
OF COURSE...
"...I AM NOT GOING ANYWHERE."

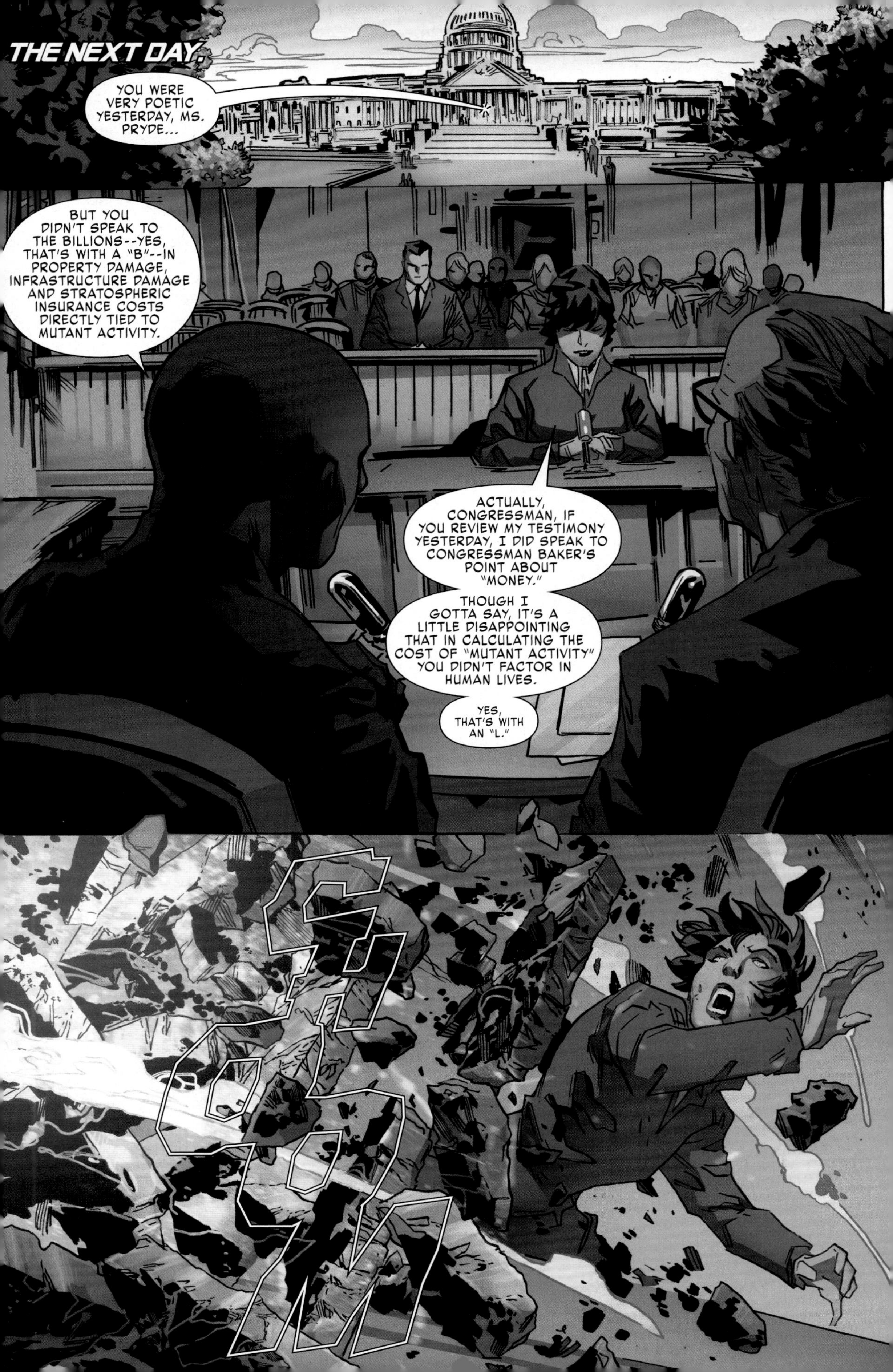
THE NEXT DAY.
YOU WERE VERY POETIC YESTERDAY, MS. PRYDE...
BUT YOU DIDN'T SPEAK TO THE BILLIONS--YES, THAT'S WITH A "B"--IN PROPERTY DAMAGE, INFRASTRUCTURE DAMAGE AND STRATOSPHERIC INSURANCE COSTS DIRECTLY TIED TO MUTANT ACTIVITY.
ACTUALLY, CONGRESSMAN, IF YOU REVIEW MY TESTIMONY YESTERDAY, I DID SPEAK TO CONGRESSMAN BAKER'S POINT ABOUT "MONEY."
THOUGH I GOTTA SAY, IT'S A LITTLE DISAPPOINTING THAT IN CALCULATING THE COST OF "MUTANT ACTIVITY" YOU DIDN'T FACTOR IN HUMAN LIVES.
YES, THAT'S WITH AN "L."
SHOOM

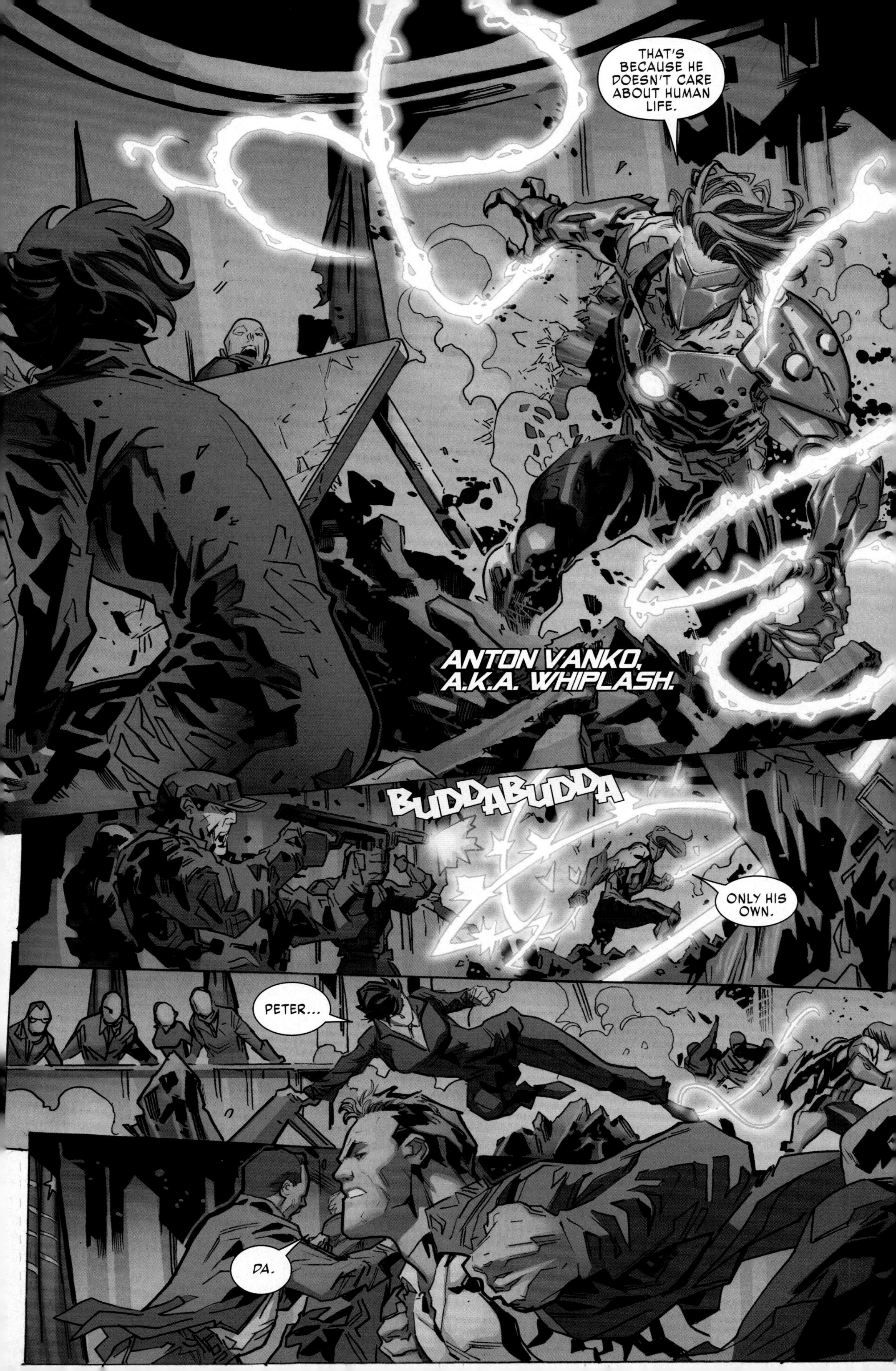
THAT'S BECAUSE HE DOESN'T CARE ABOUT HUMAN LIFE.
ANTON VANKO, A.K.A. WHIPLASH.
BUDDABUDDA
ONLY HIS OWN.
PETER...
DA.

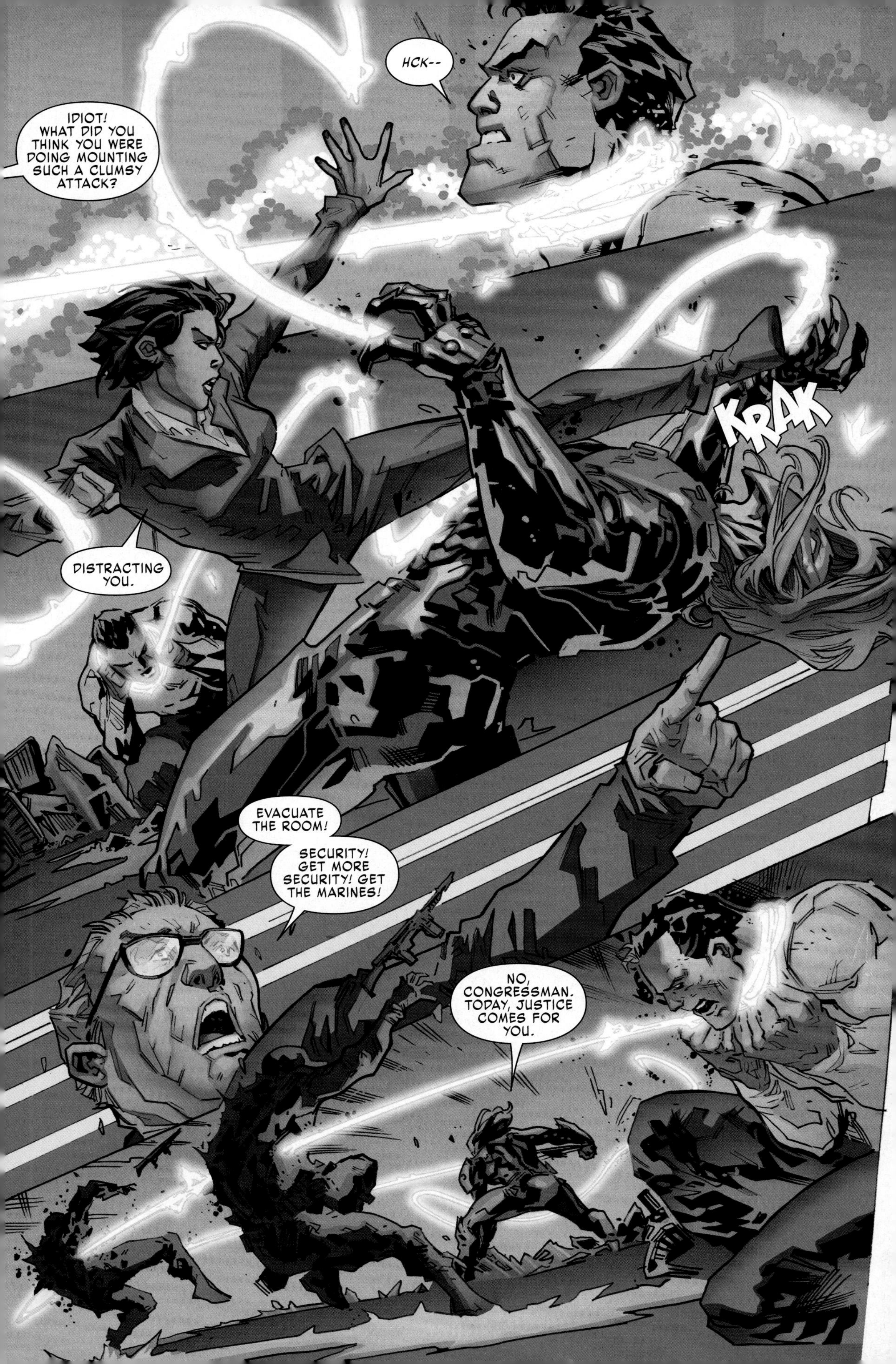
HCK--
IDIOT! WHAT DID YOU THINK YOU WERE DOING MOUNTING SUCH A CLUMSY ATTACK?
KRAK
DISTRACTING YOU.
EVACUATE THE ROOM!
SECURITY! GET MORE SECURITY! GET THE MARINES!
NO, CONGRESSMAN. TODAY, JUSTICE COMES FOR YOU.

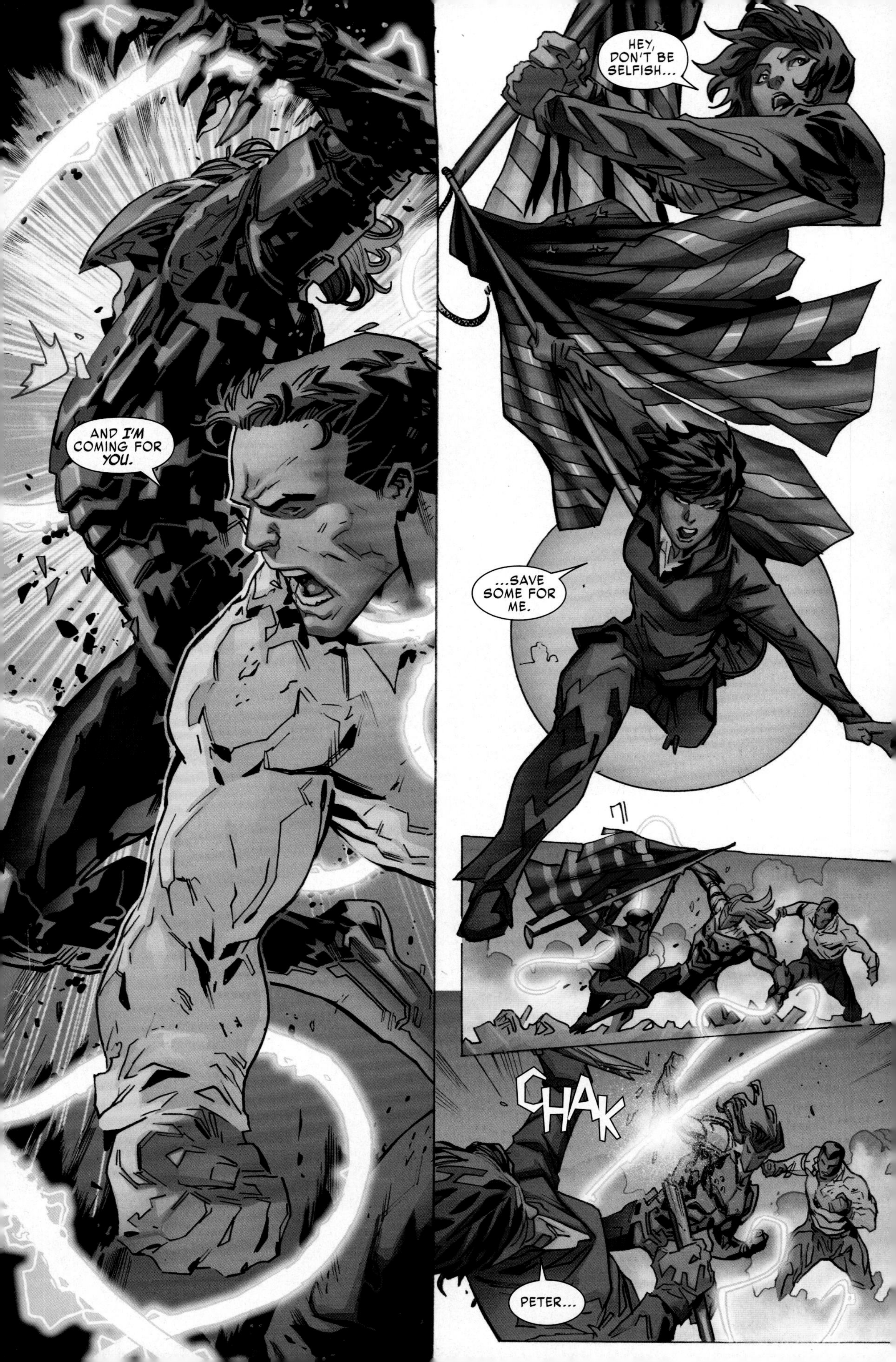
AND I'M COMING FOR YOU.
HEY, DON'T BE SELFISH...
...SAVE SOME FOR ME.
CHAK
PETER...

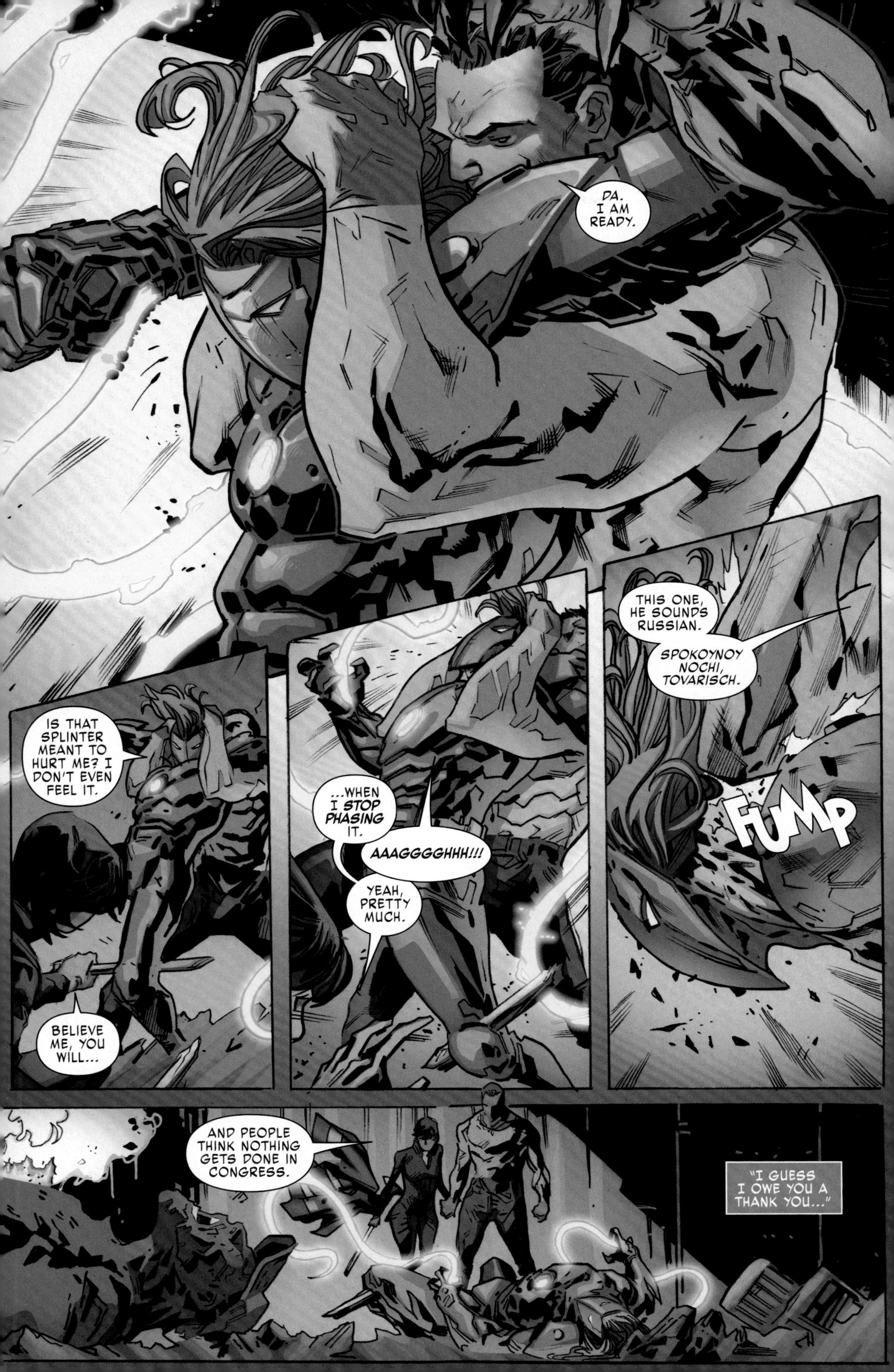
DA. I AM READY.
IS THAT SPLINTER MEANT TO HURT ME? I DON'T EVEN FEEL IT.
BELIEVE ME, YOU WILL...
...WHEN I STOP PHASING IT.
AAAGGGGHHH!!!
YEAH, PRETTY MUCH.
THIS ONE, HE SOUNDS RUSSIAN.
SPOKOYNOY NOCHI, TOVARISCH.
FUMP
AND PEOPLE THINK NOTHING GETS DONE IN CONGRESS.
"I GUESS I OWE YOU A THANK YOU..."

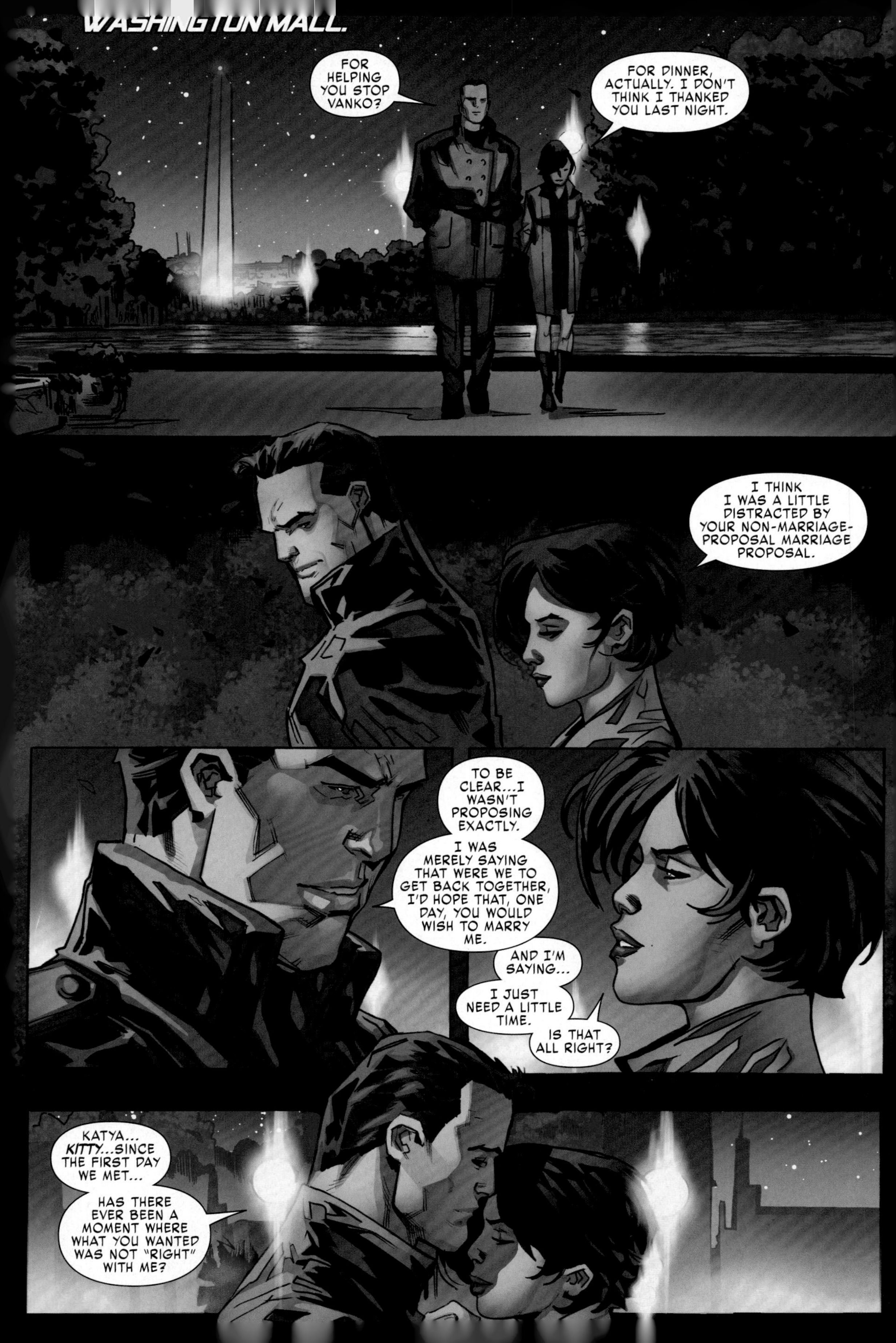
WASHINGTON MALL.
FOR DINNER, ACTUALLY. I DON'T THINK I THANKED YOU LAST NIGHT.
FOR HELPING YOU STOP VANKO?
I THINK I WAS A LITTLE DISTRACTED BY YOUR NON-MARRIAGE-PROPOSAL MARRIAGE PROPOSAL.
TO BE CLEAR...I WASN'T PROPOSING EXACTLY.
I WAS MERELY SAYING THAT WERE WE TO GET BACK TOGETHER, I'D HOPE THAT, ONE DAY, YOU WOULD WISH TO MARRY ME.
AND I'M SAYING...
I JUST NEED A LITTLE TIME.
IS THAT ALL RIGHT?
KATYA... KITTY...SINCE THE FIRST DAY WE MET...
HAS THERE EVER BEEN A MOMENT WHERE WHAT YOU WANTED WAS NOT "RIGHT" WITH ME?

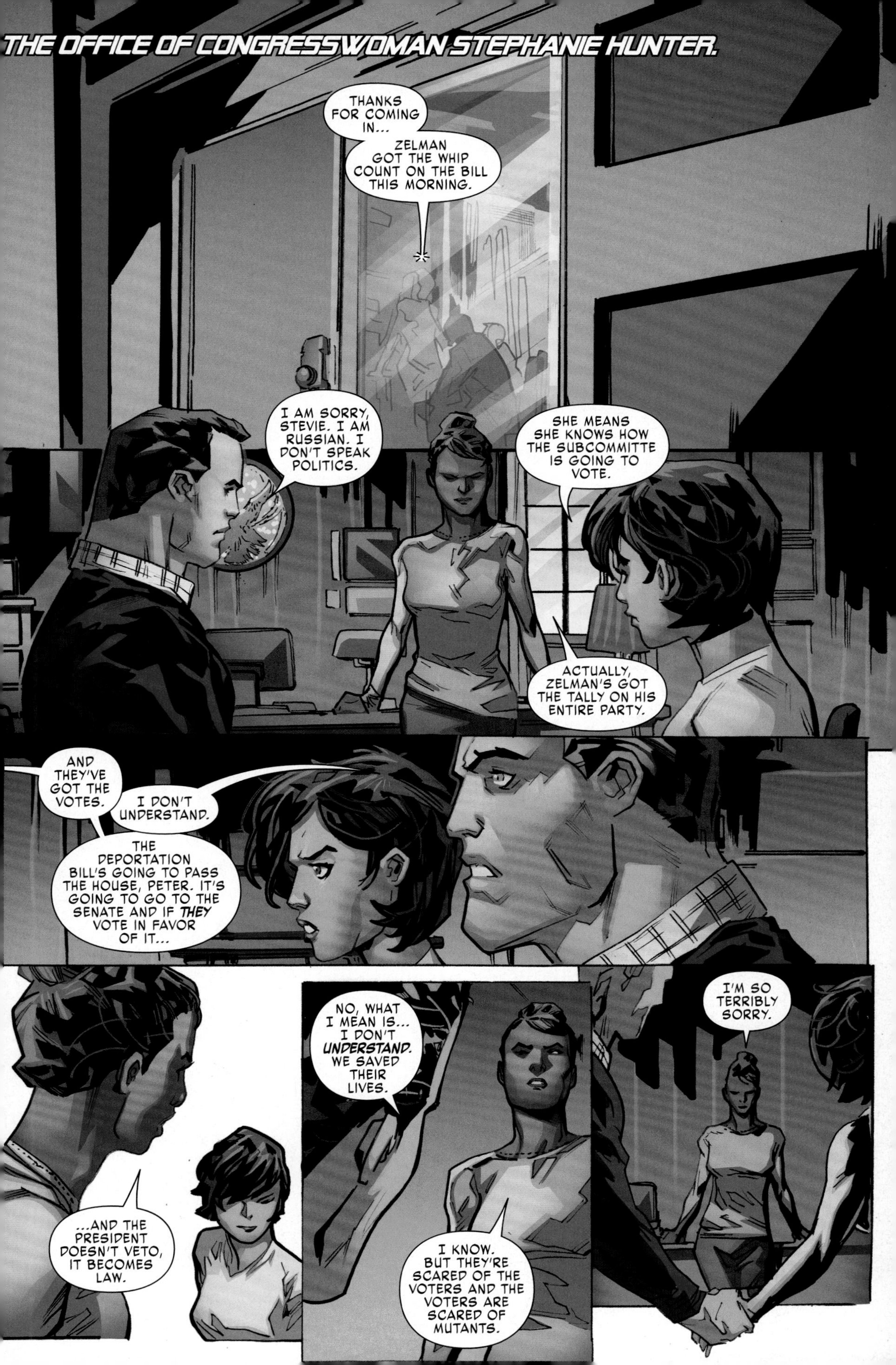
THE OFFICE OF CONGRESSWOMAN STEPHANIE HUNTER.
THANKS FOR COMING IN...
ZELMAN GOT THE WHIP COUNT ON THE BILL THIS MORNING.
I AM SORRY, STEVIE. I AM RUSSIAN. I DON'T SPEAK POLITICS.
SHE MEANS SHE KNOWS HOW THE SUBCOMMITTE IS GOING TO VOTE.
ACTUALLY, ZELMAN'S GOT THE TALLY ON HIS ENTIRE PARTY.
AND THEY'VE GOT THE VOTES.
I DON'T UNDERSTAND.
THE DEPORTATION BILL'S GOING TO PASS THE HOUSE, PETER. IT'S GOING TO GO TO THE SENATE AND IF *THEY* VOTE IN FAVOR OF IT...
...AND THE PRESIDENT DOESN'T VETO, IT BECOMES LAW.
NO, WHAT I MEAN IS... I DON'T ***UNDERSTAND.*** WE SAVED THEIR LIVES.
I KNOW. BUT THEY'RE SCARED OF THE VOTERS AND THE VOTERS ARE SCARED OF MUTANTS.
I'M SO TERRIBLY SORRY.

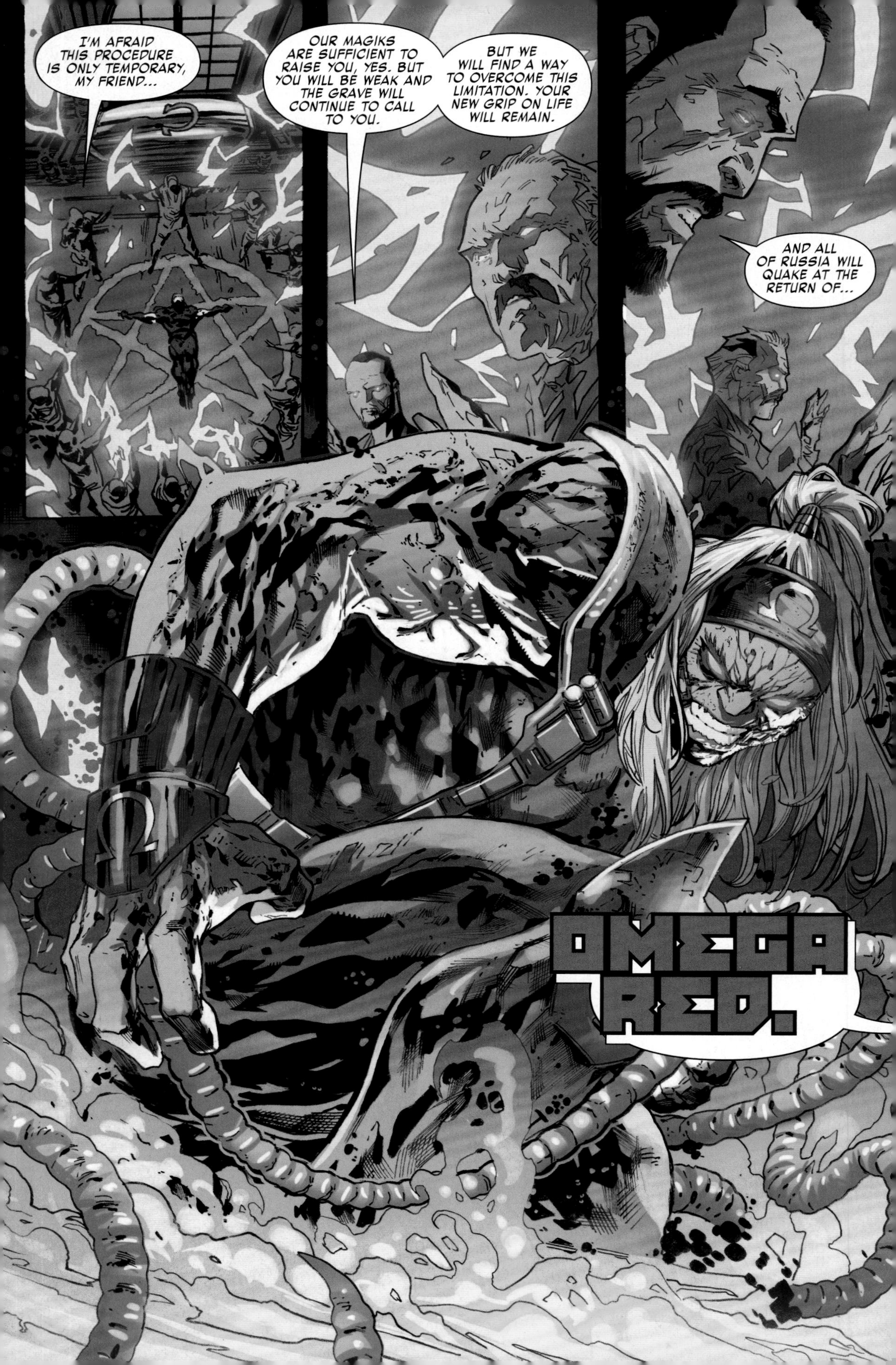
I'M AFRAID THIS PROCEDURE IS ONLY TEMPORARY, MY FRIEND...
OUR MAGIKS ARE SUFFICIENT TO RAISE YOU, YES. BUT YOU WILL BE WEAK AND THE GRAVE WILL CONTINUE TO CALL TO YOU.
BUT WE WILL FIND A WAY TO OVERCOME THIS LIMITATION. YOUR NEW GRIP ON LIFE WILL REMAIN.
AND ALL OF RUSSIA WILL QUAKE AT THE RETURN OF...
OMEGA RED.

10

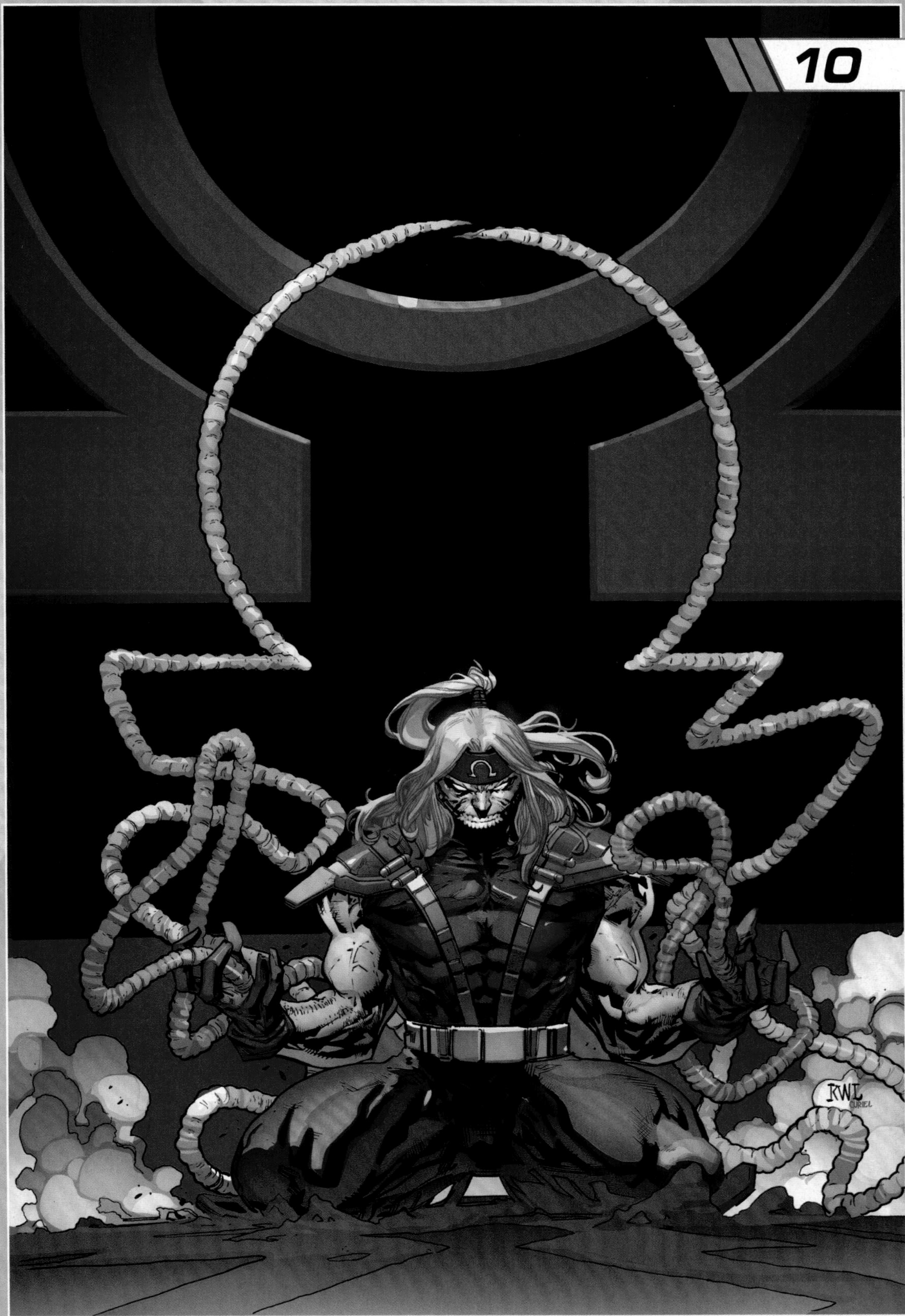

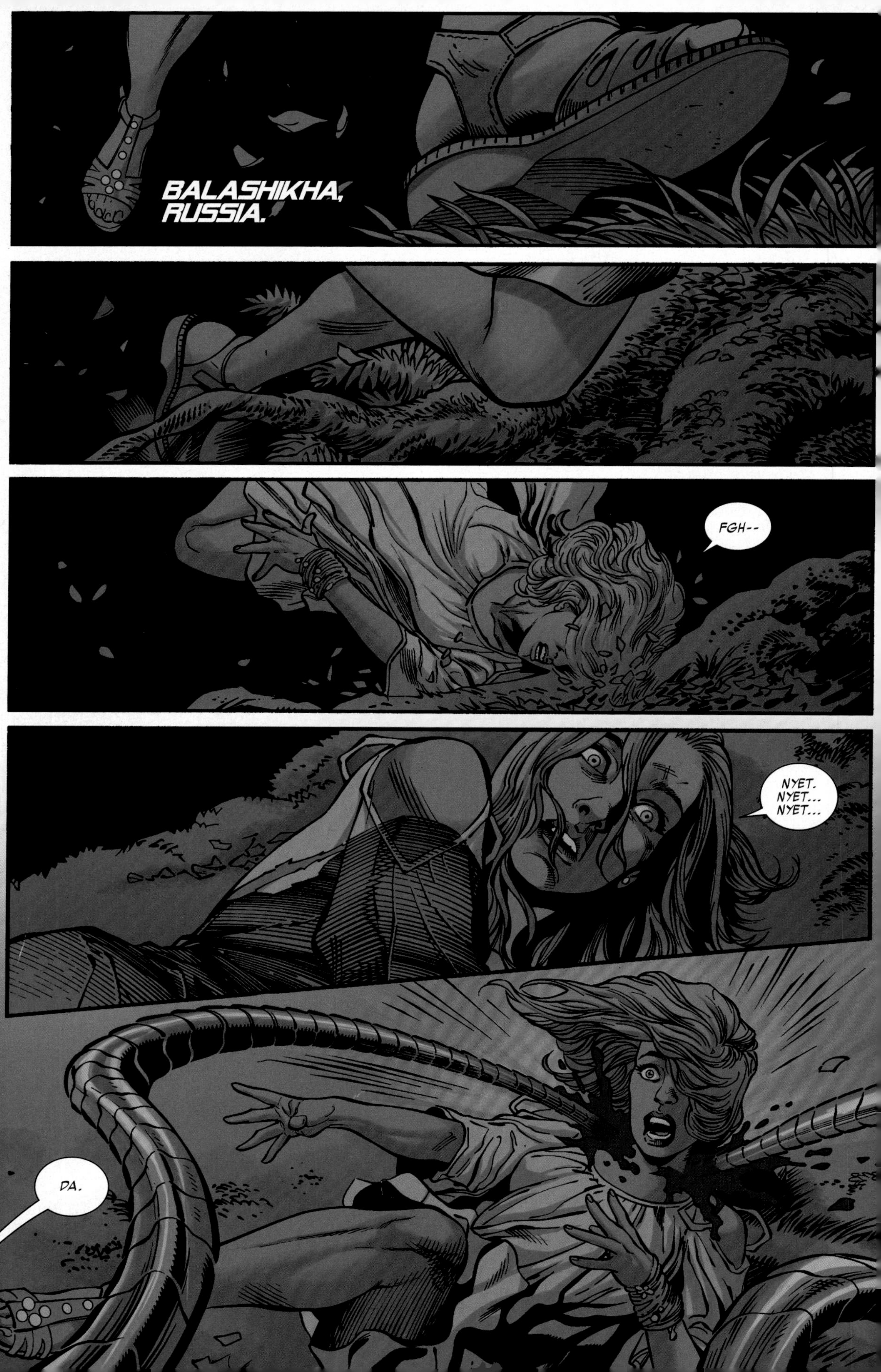
BALASHIKHA, RUSSIA.
FGH--
NYET. NYET... NYET...
DA.

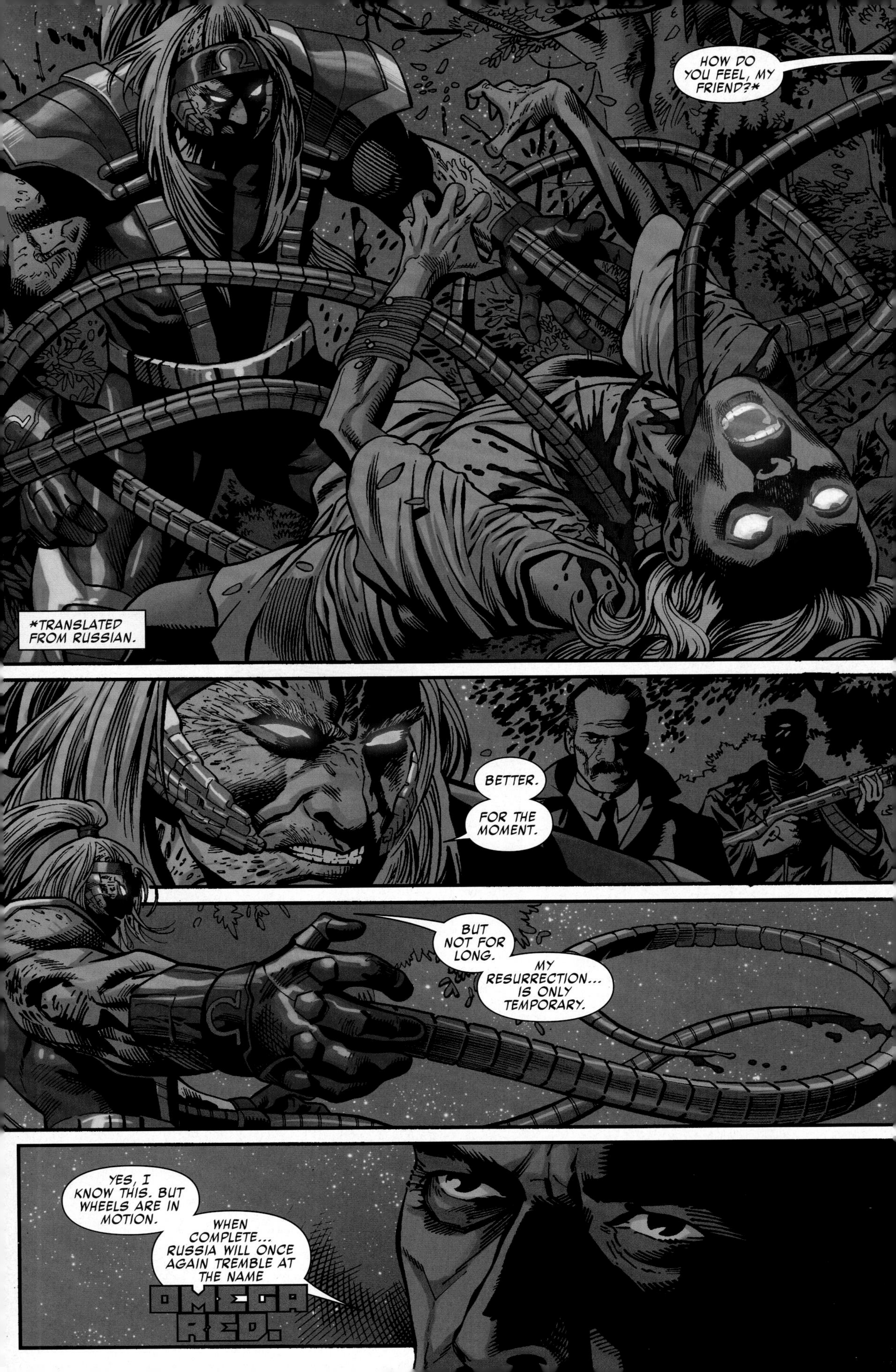
HOW DO YOU FEEL, MY FRIEND?*
*TRANSLATED FROM RUSSIAN.
BETTER.
FOR THE MOMENT.
BUT NOT FOR LONG.
MY RESURRECTION... IS ONLY TEMPORARY.
YES, I KNOW THIS. BUT WHEELS ARE IN MOTION.
WHEN COMPLETE... RUSSIA WILL ONCE AGAIN TREMBLE AT THE NAME
OMEGA RED.

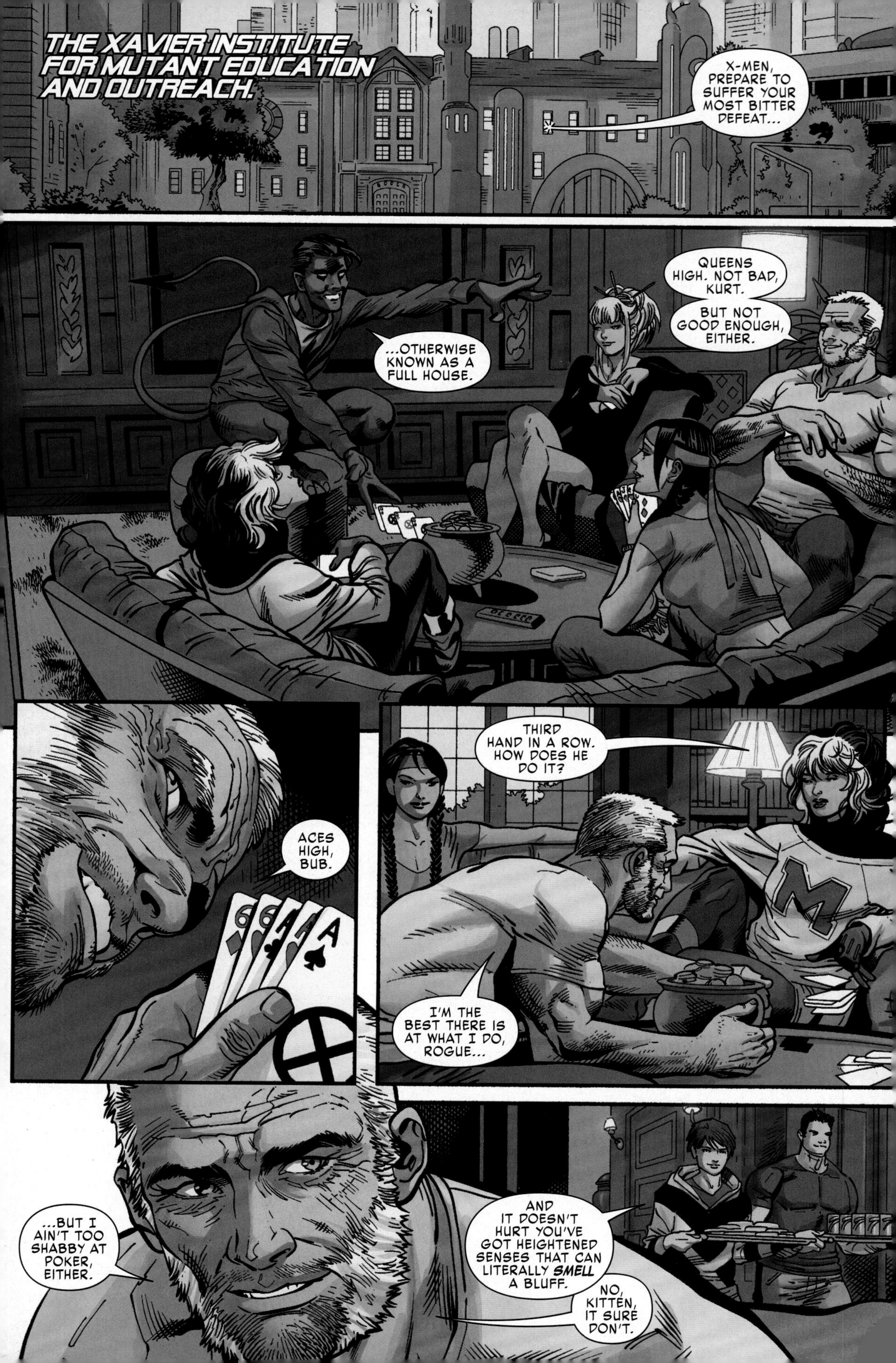
THE XAVIER INSTITUTE FOR MUTANT EDUCATION AND OUTREACH.
X-MEN, PREPARE TO SUFFER YOUR MOST BITTER DEFEAT...
...OTHERWISE KNOWN AS A FULL HOUSE.
QUEENS HIGH. NOT BAD, KURT.
BUT NOT GOOD ENOUGH, EITHER.
ACES HIGH, BUB.
THIRD HAND IN A ROW. HOW DOES HE DO IT?
I'M THE BEST THERE IS AT WHAT I DO, ROGUE...
...BUT I AIN'T TOO SHABBY AT POKER, EITHER.
AND IT DOESN'T HURT YOU'VE GOT HEIGHTENED SENSES THAT CAN LITERALLY SMELL A BLUFF.
NO, KITTEN, IT SURE DON'T.

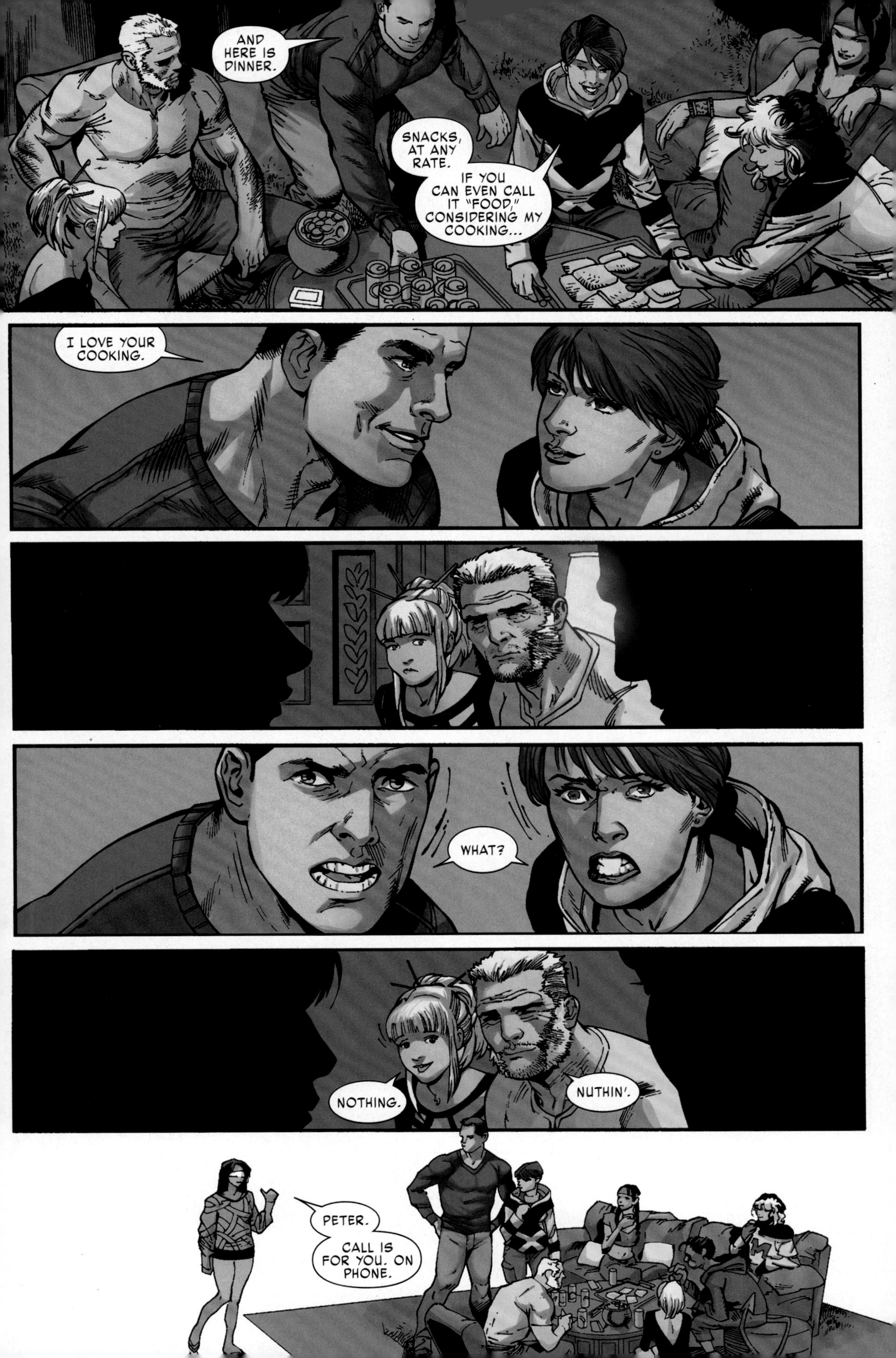
AND HERE IS DINNER.
SNACKS, AT ANY RATE.
IF YOU CAN EVEN CALL IT "FOOD," CONSIDERING MY COOKING...
I LOVE YOUR COOKING.
WHAT?
NOTHING.
NUTHIN'.
PETER.
CALL IS FOR YOU. ON PHONE.

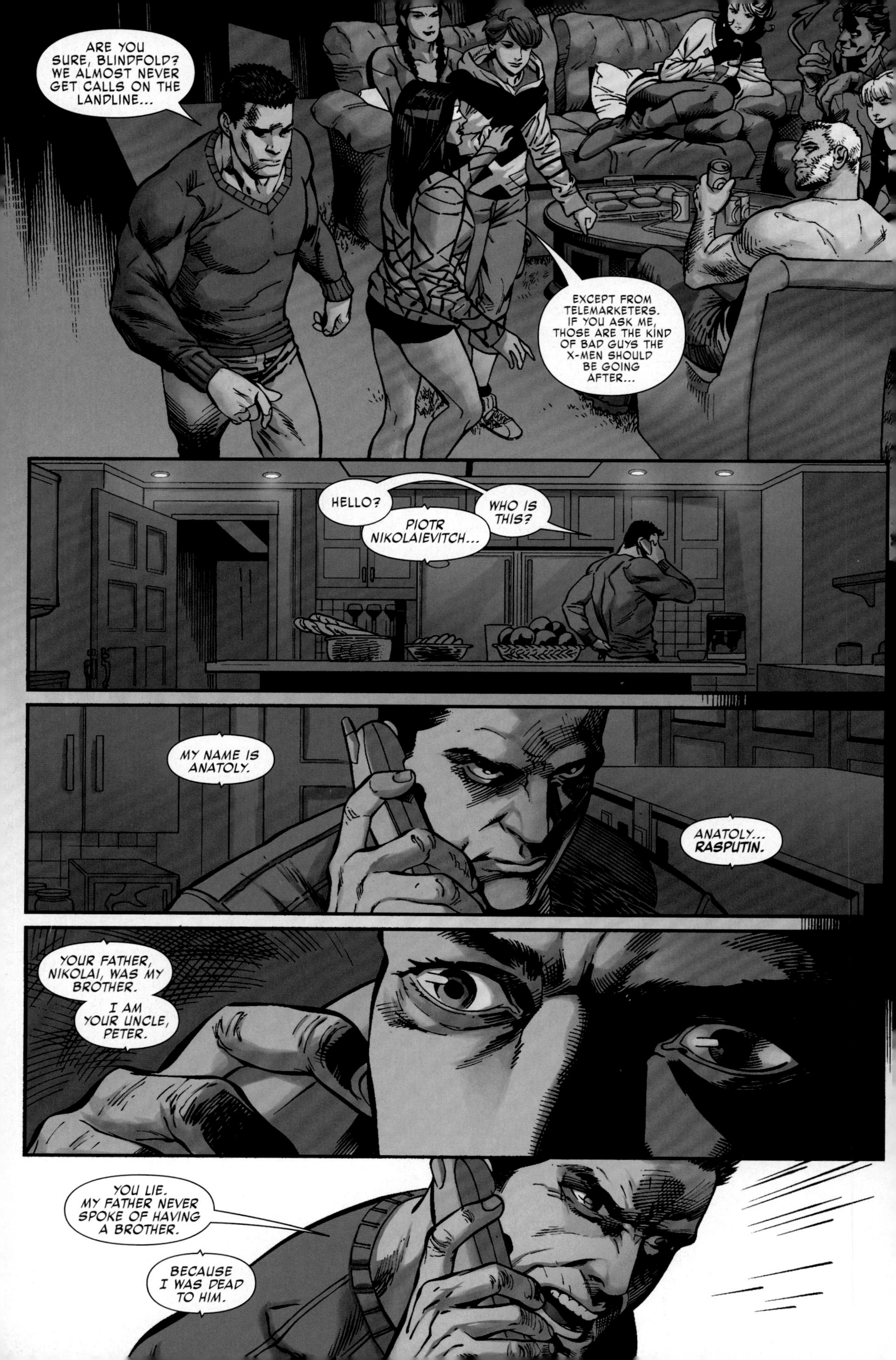
ARE YOU SURE, BLINDFOLD? WE ALMOST NEVER GET CALLS ON THE LANDLINE...
EXCEPT FROM TELEMARKETERS. IF YOU ASK ME, THOSE ARE THE KIND OF BAD GUYS THE X-MEN SHOULD BE GOING AFTER...
HELLO?
WHO IS THIS?
PIOTR NIKOLAIEVITCH...
MY NAME IS ANATOLY.
ANATOLY... RASPUTIN.
YOUR FATHER, NIKOLAI, WAS MY BROTHER.
I AM YOUR UNCLE, PETER.
YOU LIE. MY FATHER NEVER SPOKE OF HAVING A BROTHER.
BECAUSE I WAS DEAD TO HIM.

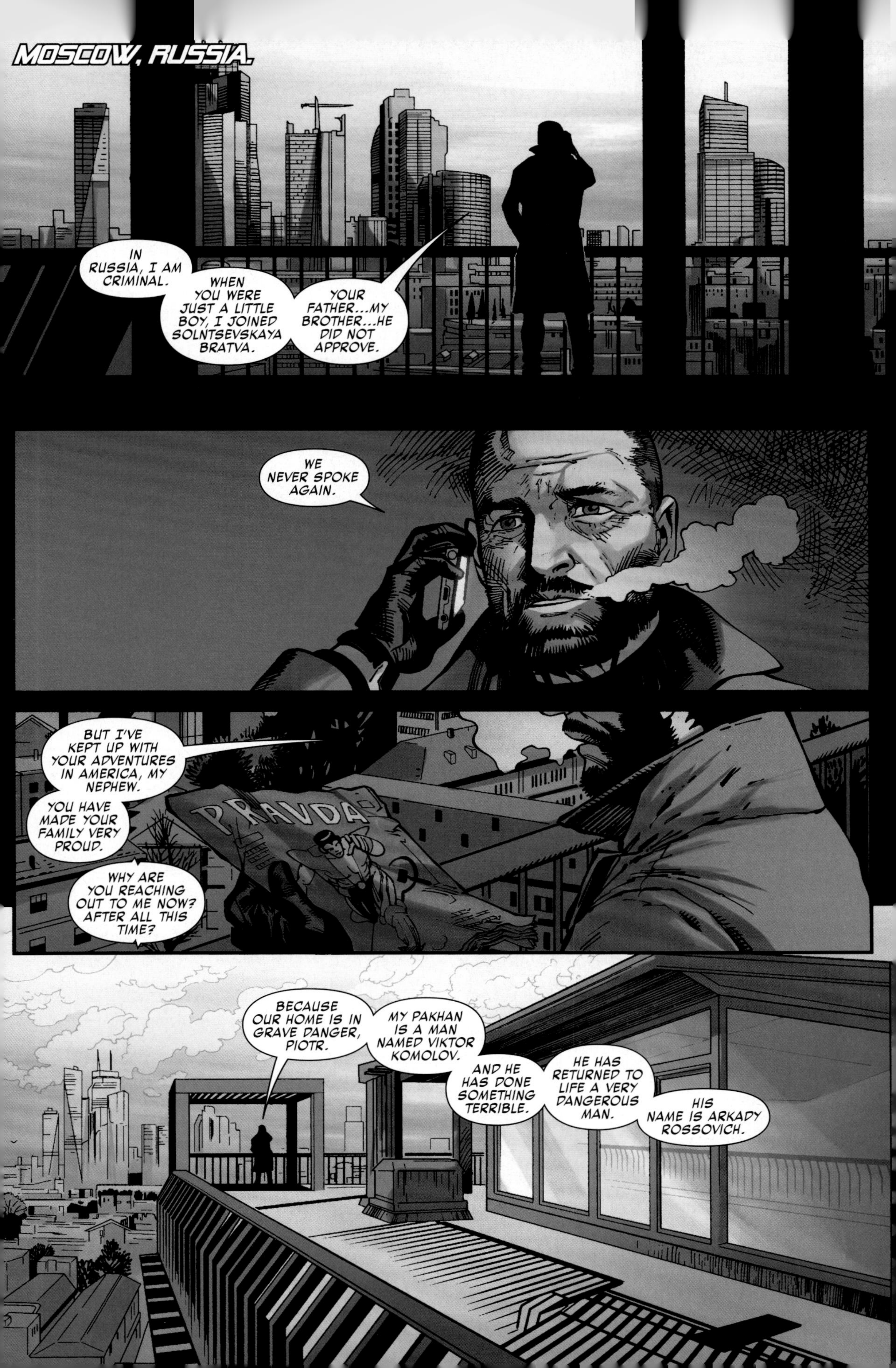
MOSCOW, RUSSIA.
IN RUSSIA, I AM CRIMINAL.
WHEN YOU WERE JUST A LITTLE BOY, I JOINED SOLNTSEVSKAYA BRATVA.
YOUR FATHER...MY BROTHER...HE DID NOT APPROVE.
WE NEVER SPOKE AGAIN.
BUT I'VE KEPT UP WITH YOUR ADVENTURES IN AMERICA, MY NEPHEW.
YOU HAVE MADE YOUR FAMILY VERY PROUD.
PRAVDA
WHY ARE YOU REACHING OUT TO ME NOW? AFTER ALL THIS TIME?
BECAUSE OUR HOME IS IN GRAVE DANGER, PIOTR.
MY PAKHAN IS A MAN NAMED VIKTOR KOMOLOV.
AND HE HAS DONE SOMETHING TERRIBLE.
HE HAS RETURNED TO LIFE A VERY DANGEROUS MAN.
HIS NAME IS ARKADY ROSSOVICH.

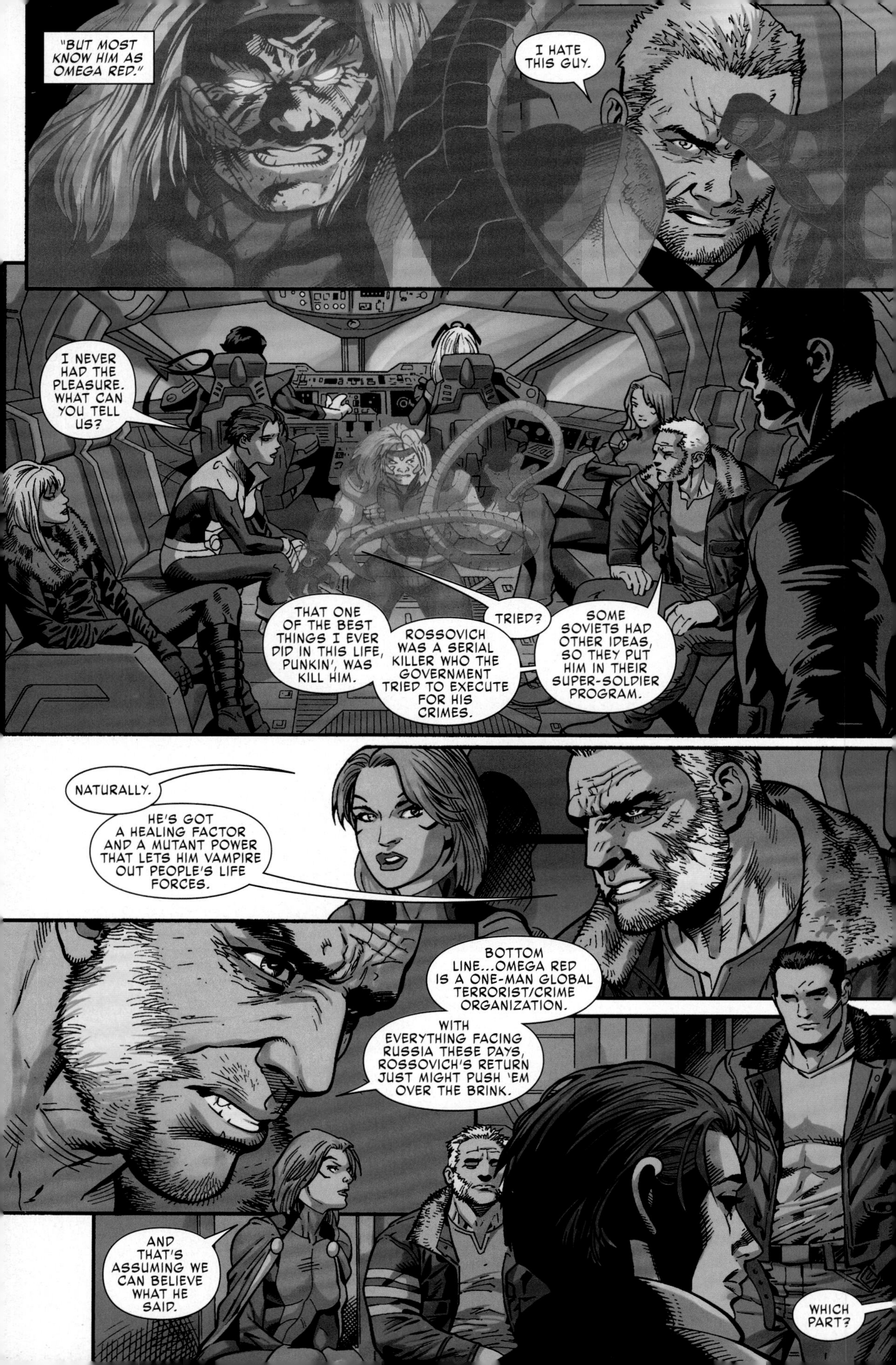
"BUT MOST KNOW HIM AS OMEGA RED."
I HATE THIS GUY.
I NEVER HAD THE PLEASURE. WHAT CAN YOU TELL US?
THAT ONE OF THE BEST THINGS I EVER DID IN THIS LIFE, PUNKIN', WAS KILL HIM.
ROSSOVICH WAS A SERIAL KILLER WHO THE GOVERNMENT TRIED TO EXECUTE FOR HIS CRIMES.
TRIED?
SOME SOVIETS HAD OTHER IDEAS, SO THEY PUT HIM IN THEIR SUPER-SOLDIER PROGRAM.
NATURALLY.
HE'S GOT A HEALING FACTOR AND A MUTANT POWER THAT LETS HIM VAMPIRE OUT PEOPLE'S LIFE FORCES.
BOTTOM LINE...OMEGA RED IS A ONE-MAN GLOBAL TERRORIST/CRIME ORGANIZATION.
WITH EVERYTHING FACING RUSSIA THESE DAYS, ROSSOVICH'S RETURN JUST MIGHT PUSH 'EM OVER THE BRINK.
AND THAT'S ASSUMING WE CAN BELIEVE WHAT HE SAID.
WHICH PART?

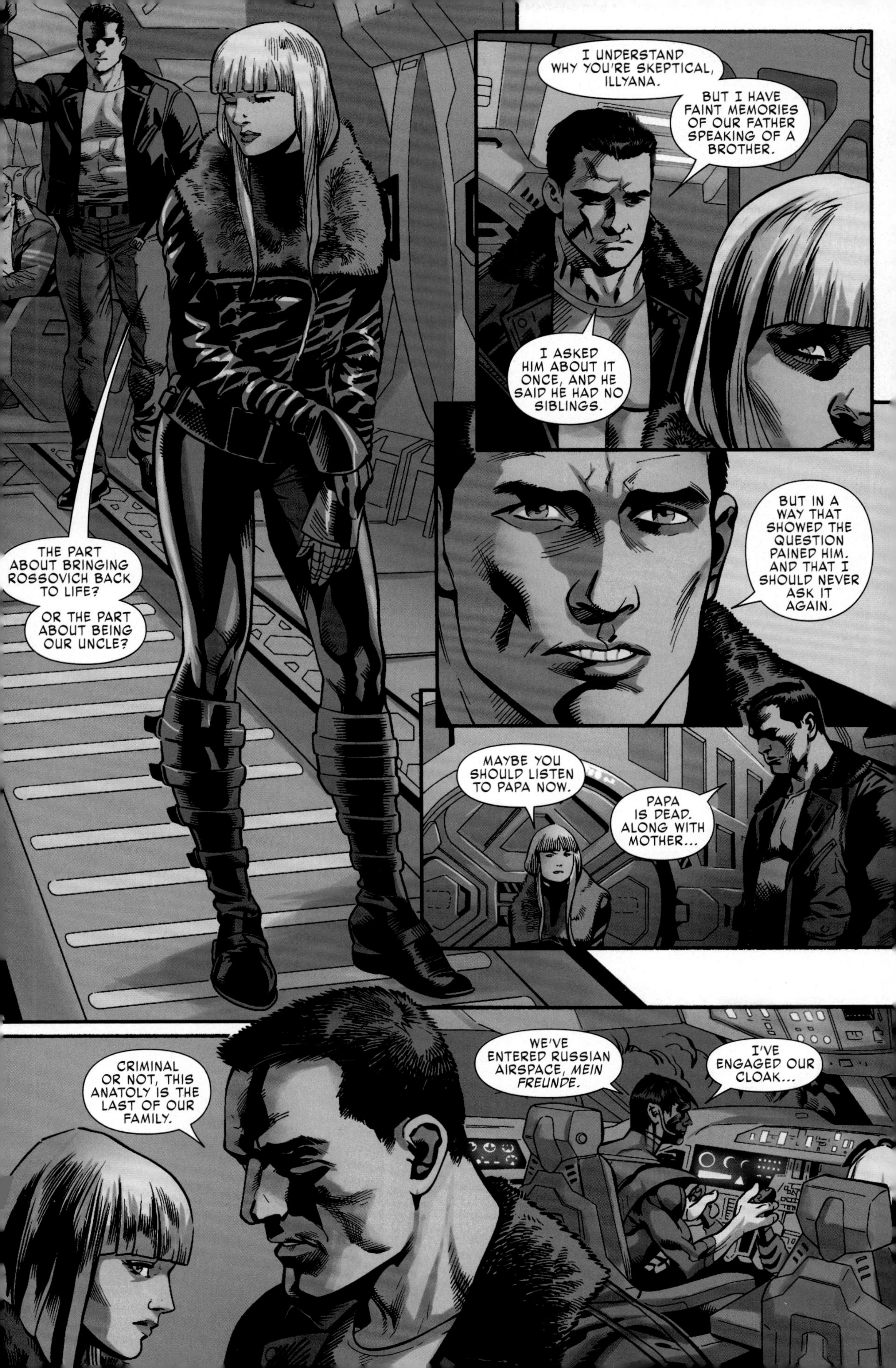
I UNDERSTAND WHY YOU'RE SKEPTICAL, ILLYANA.
BUT I HAVE FAINT MEMORIES OF OUR FATHER SPEAKING OF A BROTHER.
I ASKED HIM ABOUT IT ONCE, AND HE SAID HE HAD NO SIBLINGS.
BUT IN A WAY THAT SHOWED THE QUESTION PAINED HIM. AND THAT I SHOULD NEVER ASK IT AGAIN.
THE PART ABOUT BRINGING ROSSOVICH BACK TO LIFE?
OR THE PART ABOUT BEING OUR UNCLE?
MAYBE YOU SHOULD LISTEN TO PAPA NOW.
PAPA IS DEAD. ALONG WITH MOTHER...
CRIMINAL OR NOT, THIS ANATOLY IS THE LAST OF OUR FAMILY.
WE'VE ENTERED RUSSIAN AIRSPACE, *MEIN FREUNDE*.
I'VE ENGAGED OUR CLOAK...

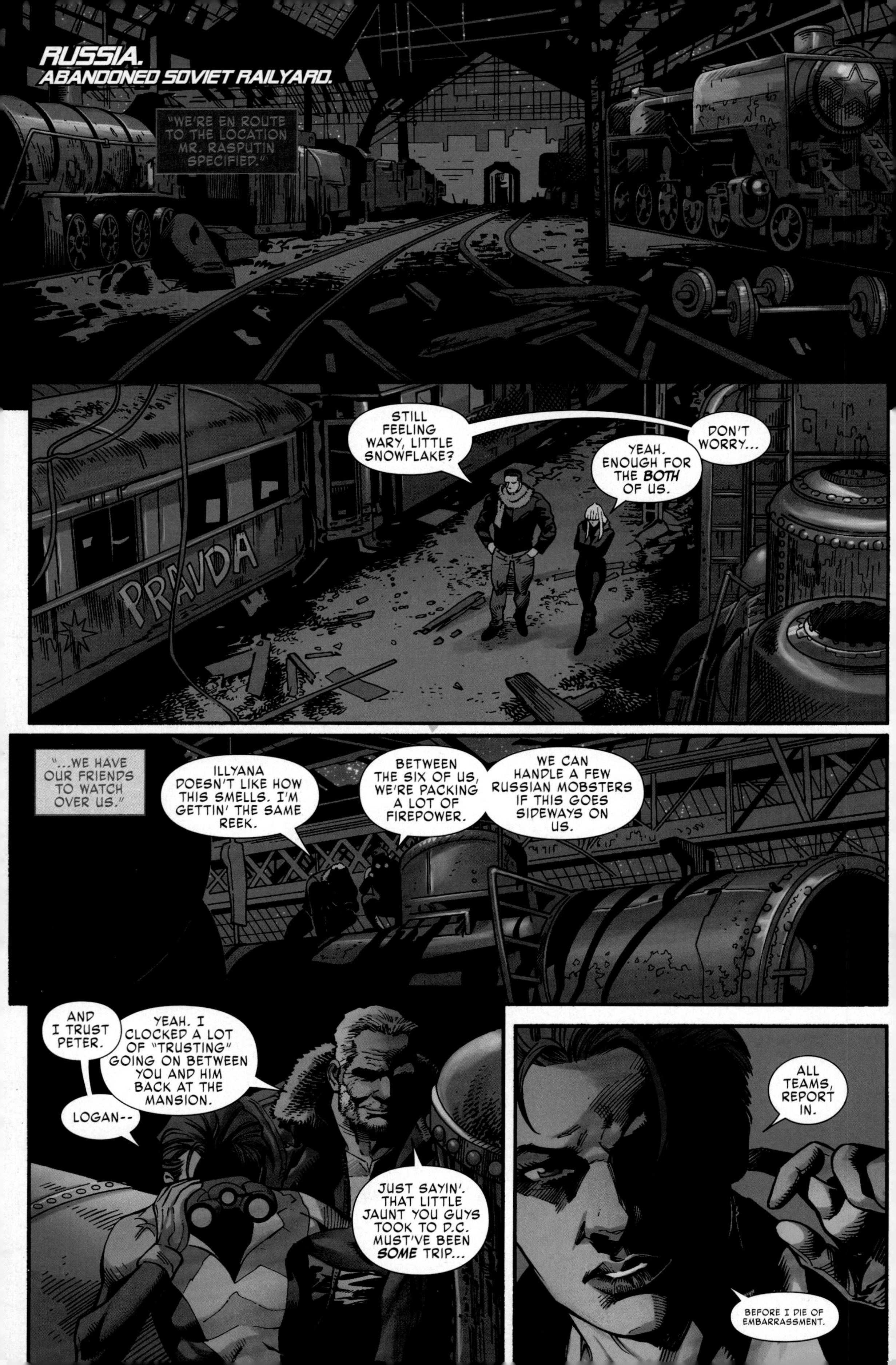
RUSSIA.
ABANDONED SOVIET RAILYARD.
"WE'RE EN ROUTE TO THE LOCATION MR. RASPUTIN SPECIFIED."
STILL FEELING WARY, LITTLE SNOWFLAKE?
YEAH. ENOUGH FOR THE BOTH OF US.
DON'T WORRY...
PRAVDA
"...WE HAVE OUR FRIENDS TO WATCH OVER US."
ILLYANA DOESN'T LIKE HOW THIS SMELLS. I'M GETTIN' THE SAME REEK.
BETWEEN THE SIX OF US, WE'RE PACKING A LOT OF FIREPOWER.
WE CAN HANDLE A FEW RUSSIAN MOBSTERS IF THIS GOES SIDEWAYS ON US.
AND I TRUST PETER.
YEAH. I CLOCKED A LOT OF "TRUSTING" GOING ON BETWEEN YOU AND HIM BACK AT THE MANSION.
LOGAN--
JUST SAYIN'. THAT LITTLE JAUNT YOU GUYS TOOK TO D.C. MUST'VE BEEN SOME TRIP...
ALL TEAMS, REPORT IN.
BEFORE I DIE OF EMBARRASSMENT.

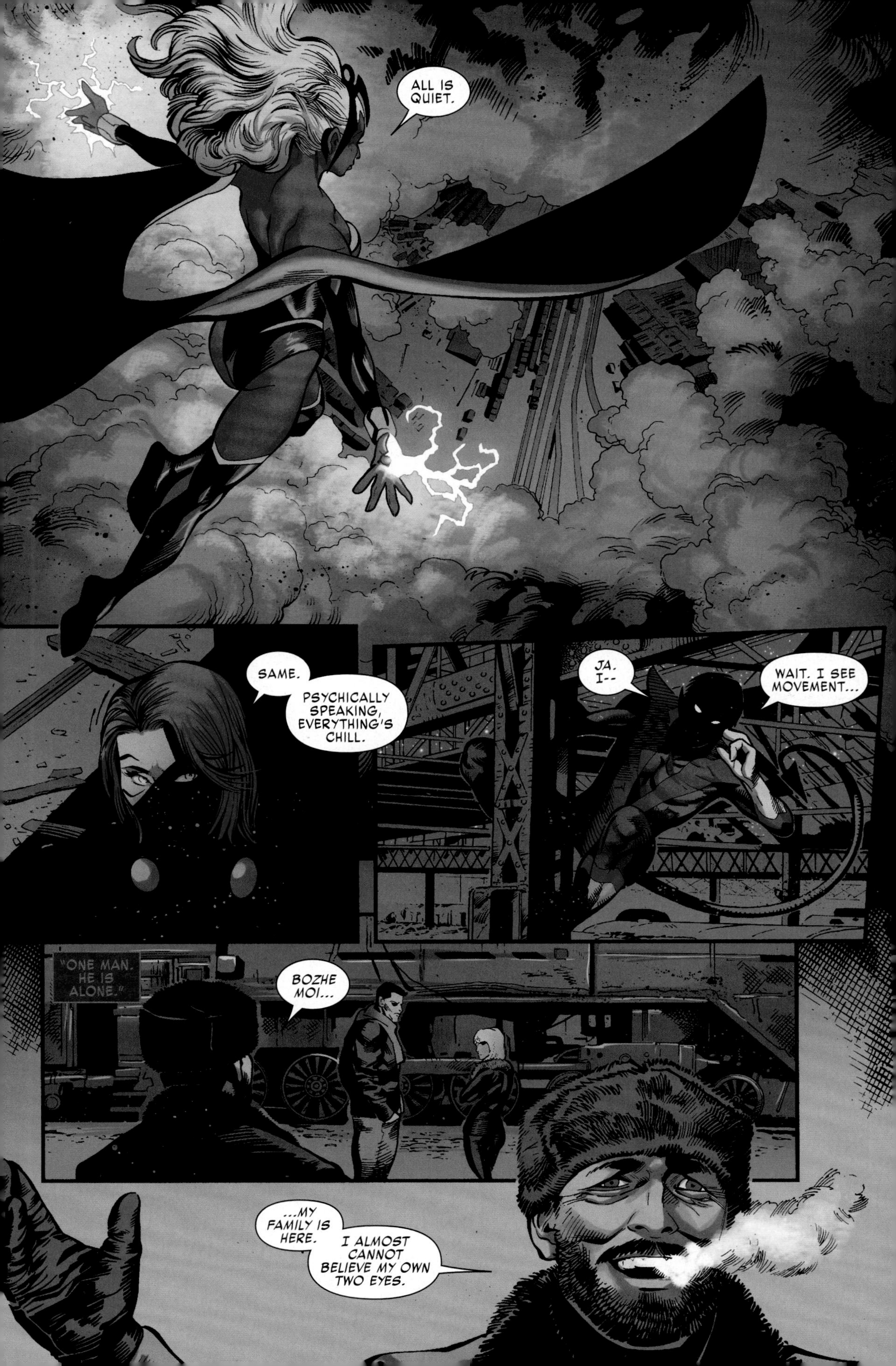
ALL IS QUIET.
SAME.
PSYCHICALLY SPEAKING, EVERYTHING'S CHILL.
JA. I--
WAIT. I SEE MOVEMENT...
"ONE MAN. HE IS ALONE."
BOZHE MOI...
...MY FAMILY IS HERE.
I ALMOST CANNOT BELIEVE MY OWN TWO EYES.

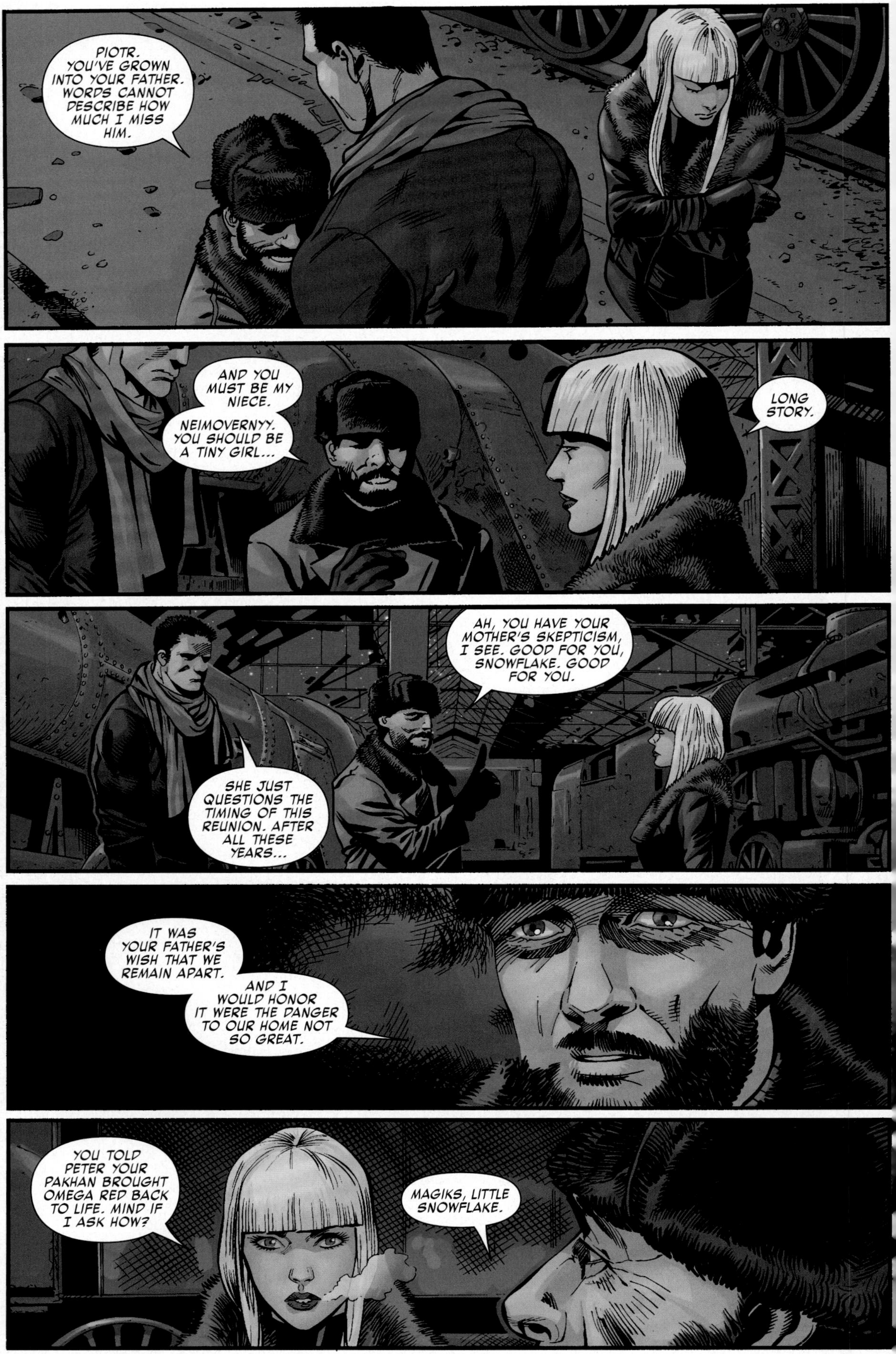
PIOTR. YOU'VE GROWN INTO YOUR FATHER. WORDS CANNOT DESCRIBE HOW MUCH I MISS HIM.
AND YOU MUST BE MY NIECE.
NEIMOVERNYY. YOU SHOULD BE A TINY GIRL...
LONG STORY.
AH, YOU HAVE YOUR MOTHER'S SKEPTICISM, I SEE. GOOD FOR YOU, SNOWFLAKE. GOOD FOR YOU.
SHE JUST QUESTIONS THE TIMING OF THIS REUNION. AFTER ALL THESE YEARS...
IT WAS YOUR FATHER'S WISH THAT WE REMAIN APART.
AND I WOULD HONOR IT WERE THE DANGER TO OUR HOME NOT SO GREAT.
YOU TOLD PETER YOUR PAKHAN BROUGHT OMEGA RED BACK TO LIFE. MIND IF I ASK HOW?
MAGIKS, LITTLE SNOWFLAKE.

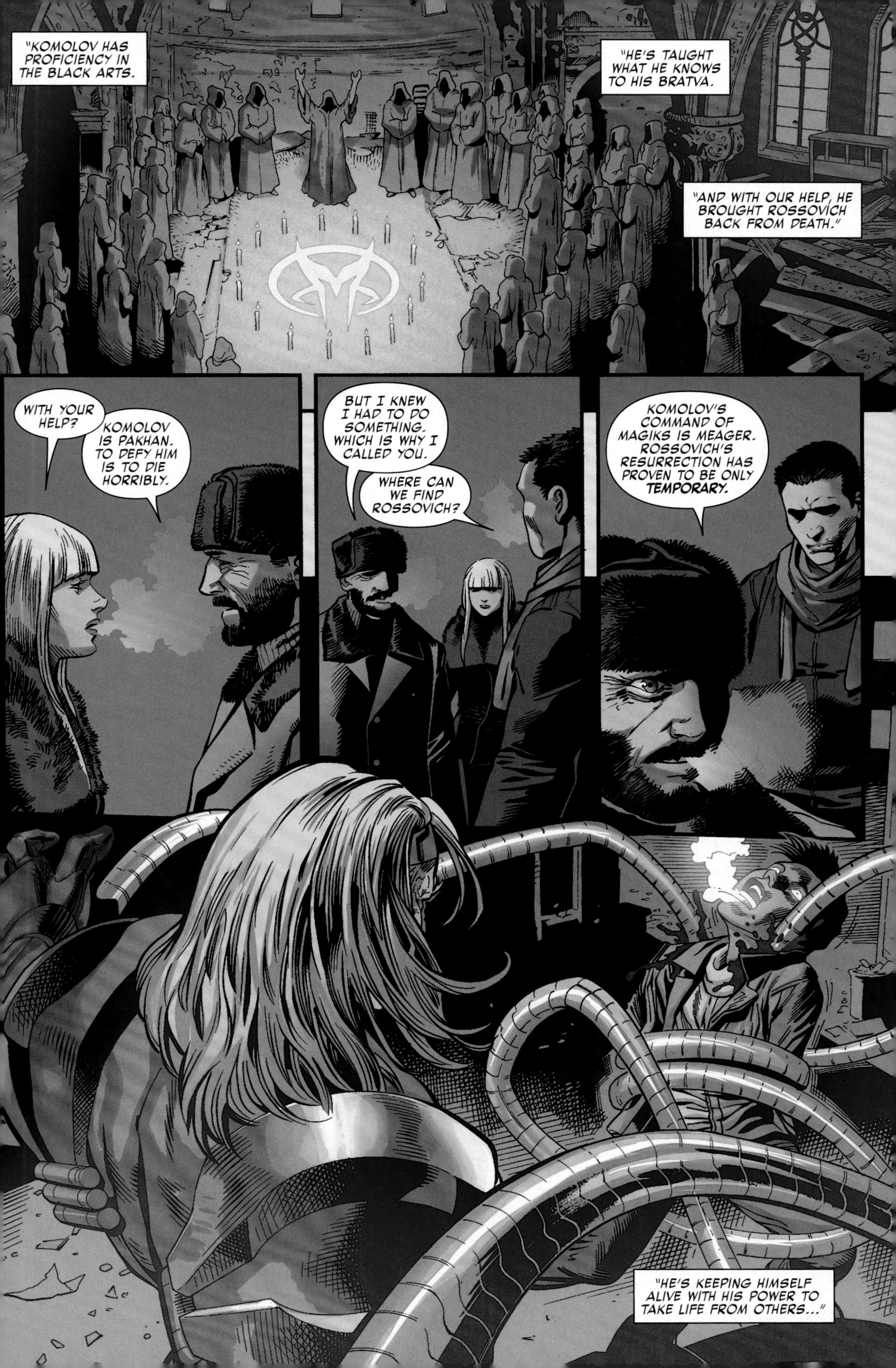
"KOMOLOV HAS PROFICIENCY IN THE BLACK ARTS.
"HE'S TAUGHT WHAT HE KNOWS TO HIS BRATVA.
"AND WITH OUR HELP, HE BROUGHT ROSSOVICH BACK FROM DEATH."
WITH YOUR HELP?
KOMOLOV IS PAKHAN. TO DEFY HIM IS TO DIE HORRIBLY.
BUT I KNEW I HAD TO DO SOMETHING. WHICH IS WHY I CALLED YOU.
WHERE CAN WE FIND ROSSOVICH?
KOMOLOV'S COMMAND OF MAGIKS IS MEAGER. ROSSOVICH'S RESURRECTION HAS PROVEN TO BE ONLY **TEMPORARY.**
"HE'S KEEPING HIMSELF ALIVE WITH HIS POWER TO TAKE LIFE FROM OTHERS..."

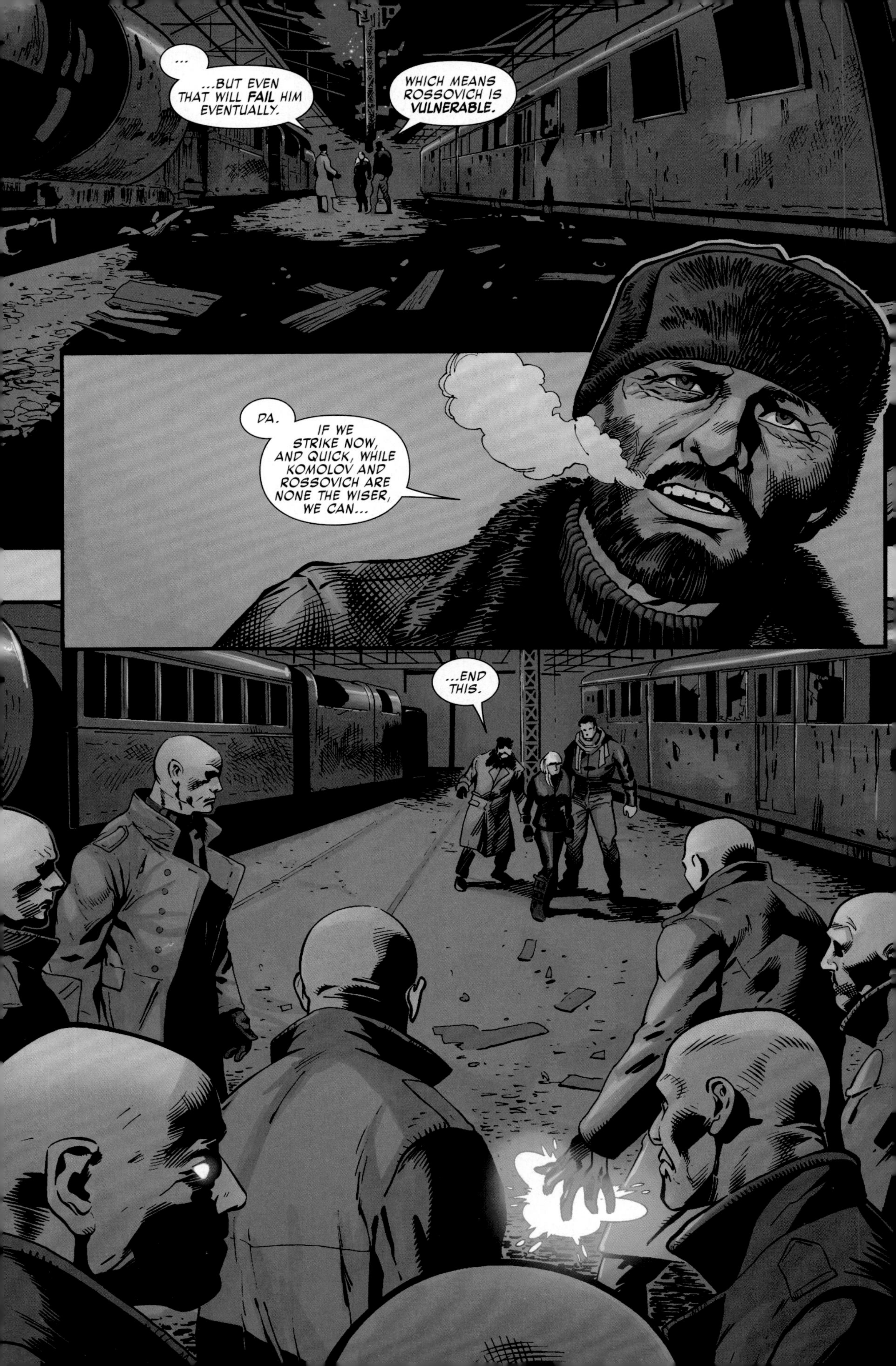
...
...BUT EVEN THAT WILL FAIL HIM EVENTUALLY.
WHICH MEANS ROSSOVICH IS VULNERABLE.
DA.
IF WE STRIKE NOW, AND QUICK, WHILE KOMOLOV AND ROSSOVICH ARE NONE THE WISER, WE CAN...
...END THIS.

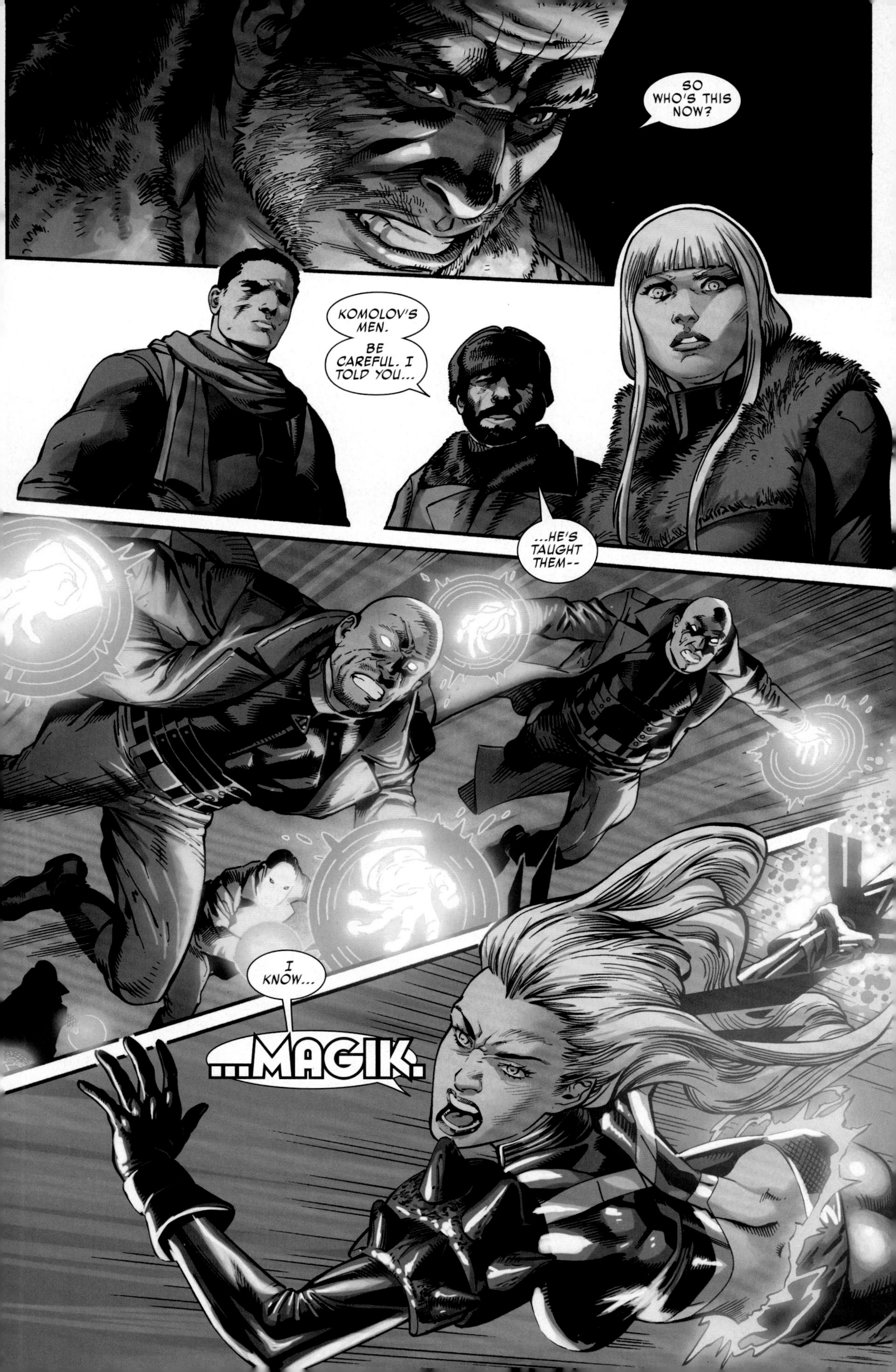
SO WHO'S THIS NOW?
KOMOLOV'S MEN.
BE CAREFUL. I TOLD YOU...
...HE'S TAUGHT THEM--
I KNOW...
...MAGIK.

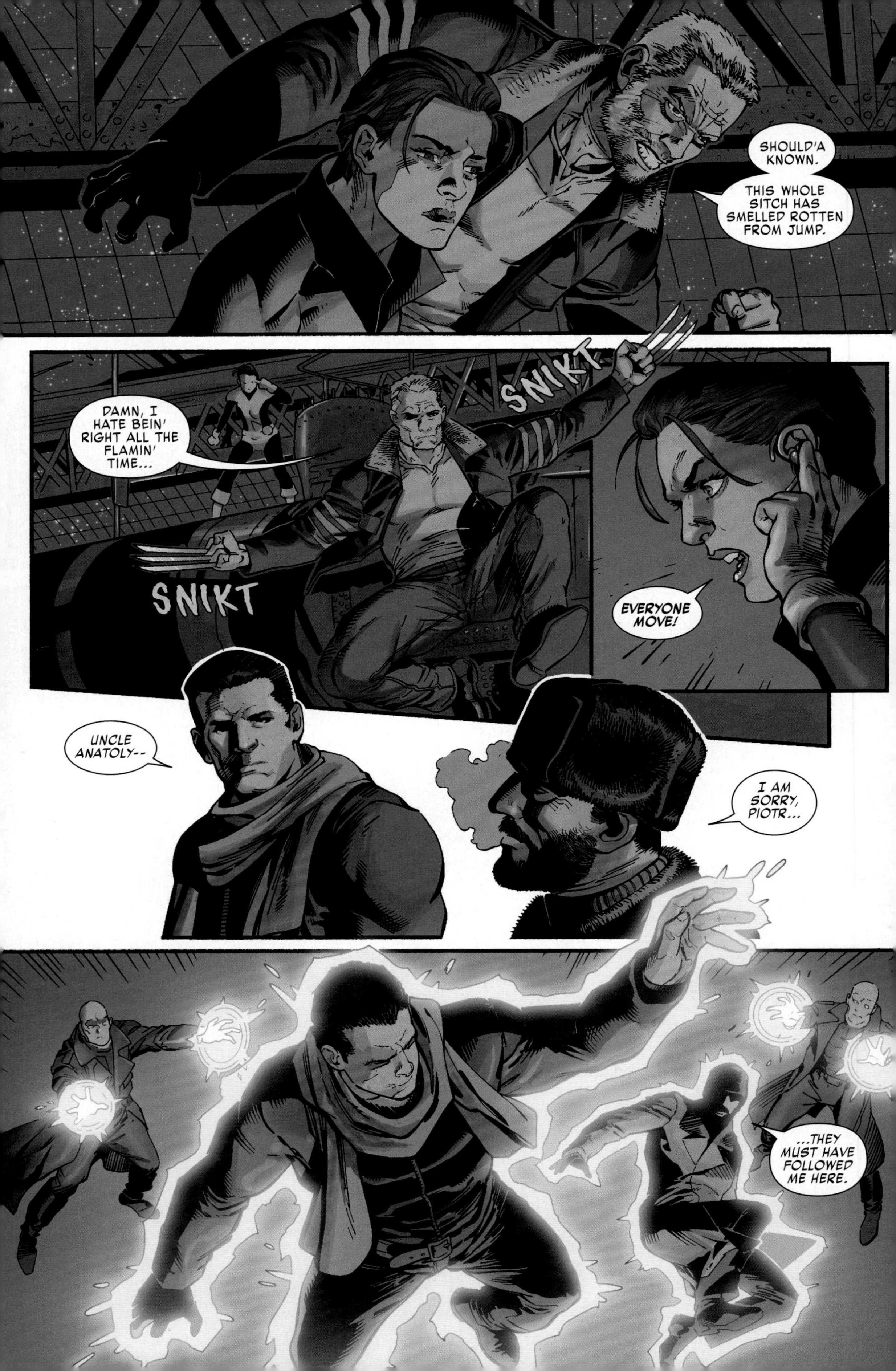
SHOULD'A KNOWN.
THIS WHOLE SITCH HAS SMELLED ROTTEN FROM JUMP.
DAMN, I HATE BEIN' RIGHT ALL THE FLAMIN' TIME...
SNIKT
SNIKT
EVERYONE MOVE!
UNCLE ANATOLY--
I AM SORRY, PIOTR...
...THEY MUST HAVE FOLLOWED ME HERE.

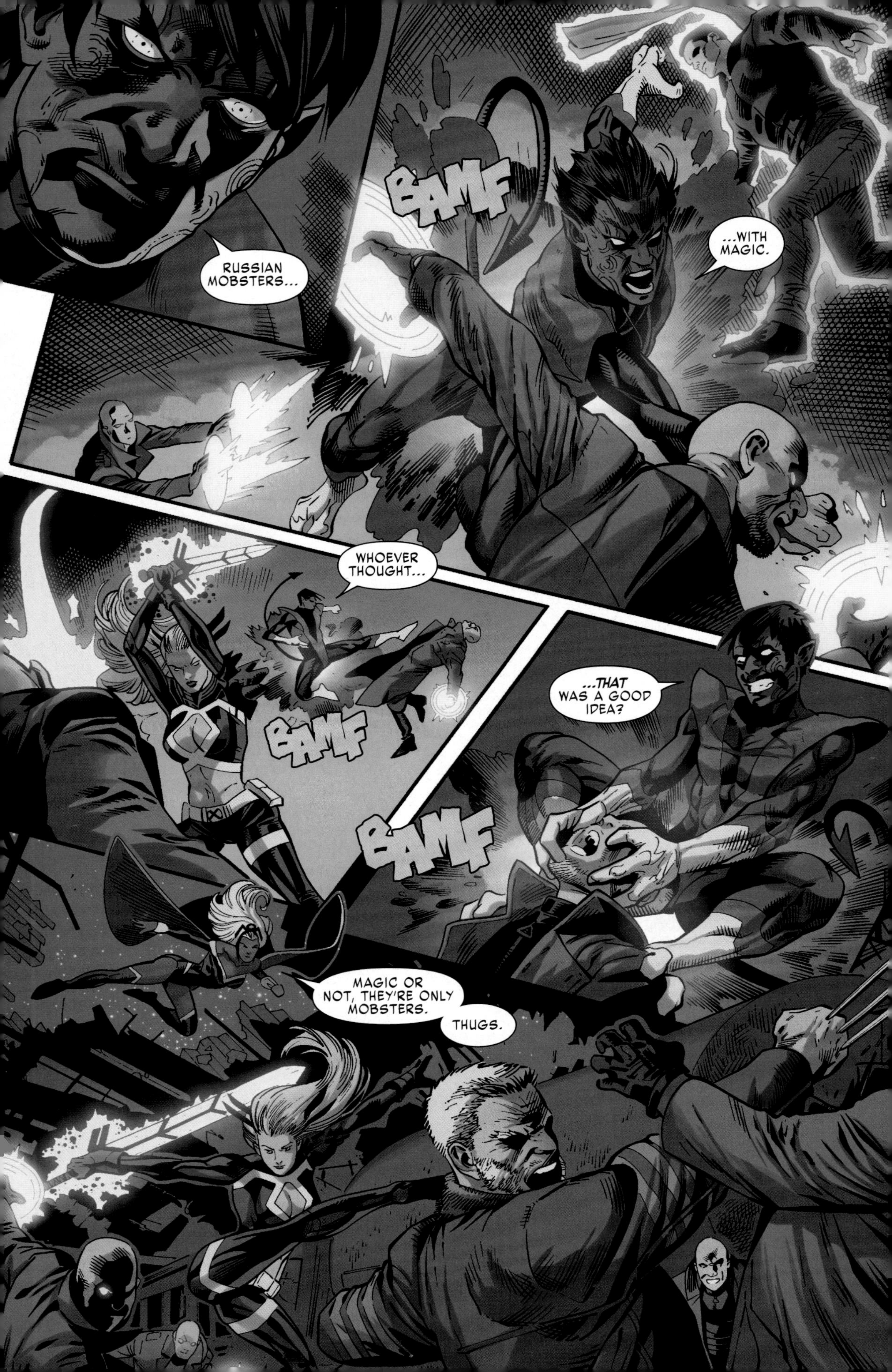
RUSSIAN MOBSTERS...
BAMF
...WITH MAGIC.
WHOEVER THOUGHT...
BAMF
...THAT WAS A GOOD IDEA?
BAMF
MAGIC OR NOT, THEY'RE ONLY MOBSTERS.
THUGS.

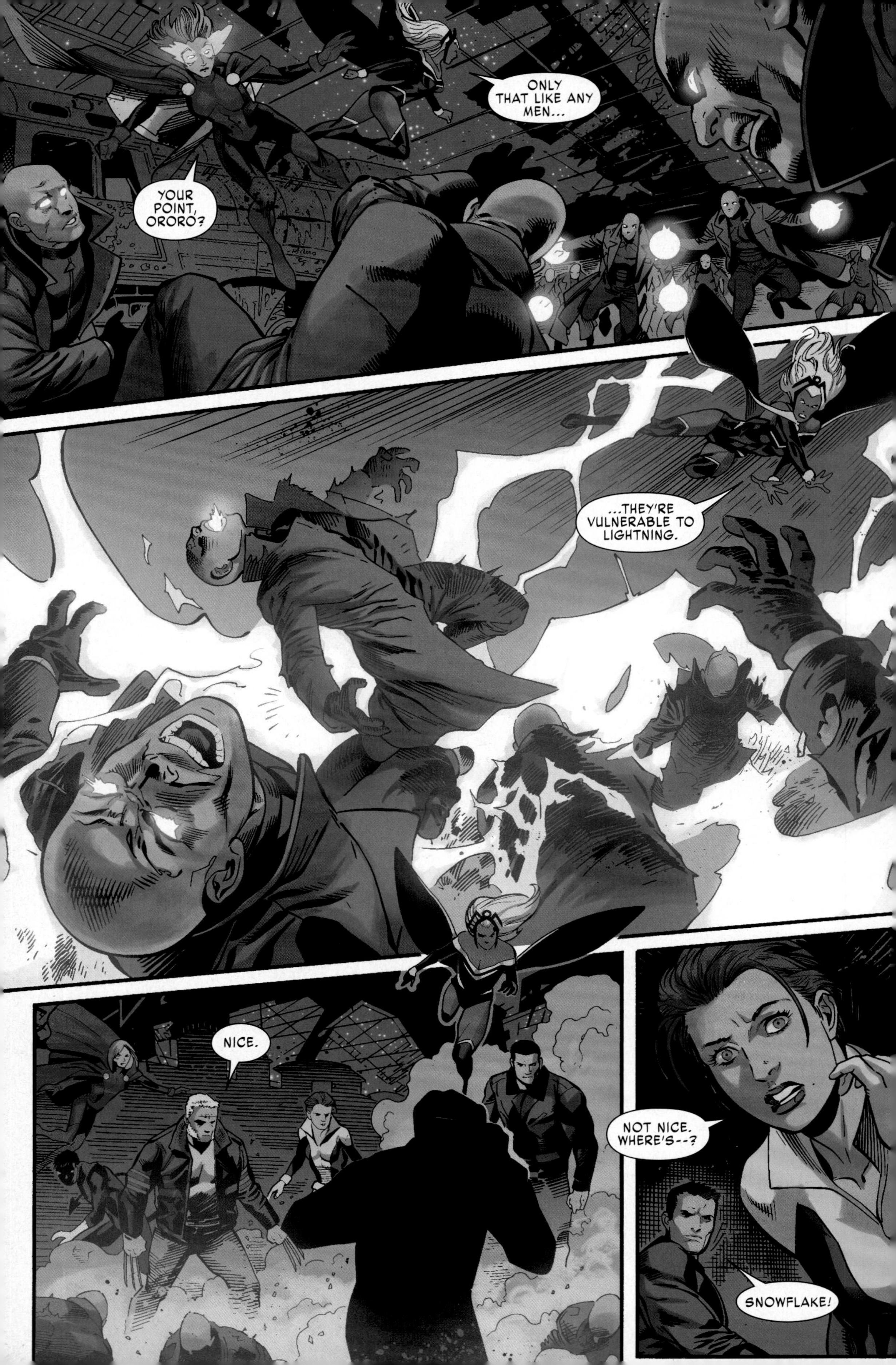
ONLY THAT LIKE ANY MEN...
YOUR POINT, ORORO?
...THEY'RE VULNERABLE TO LIGHTNING.
NICE.
NOT NICE. WHERE'S--?
SNOWFLAKE!

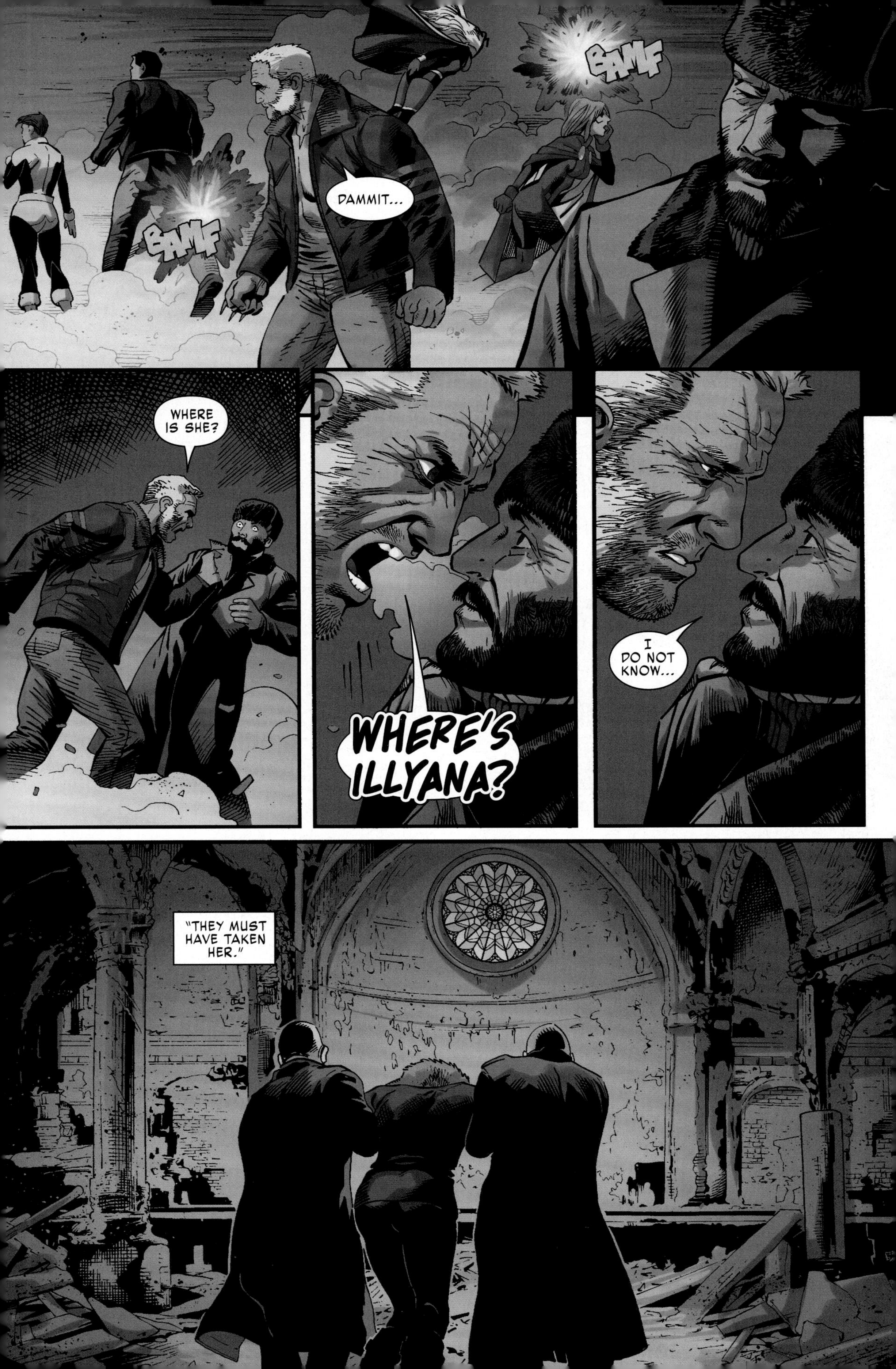
BAMF
DAMMIT...
BAMF
WHERE IS SHE?
WHERE'S ILLYANA?
I DO NOT KNOW...
"THEY MUST HAVE TAKEN HER."

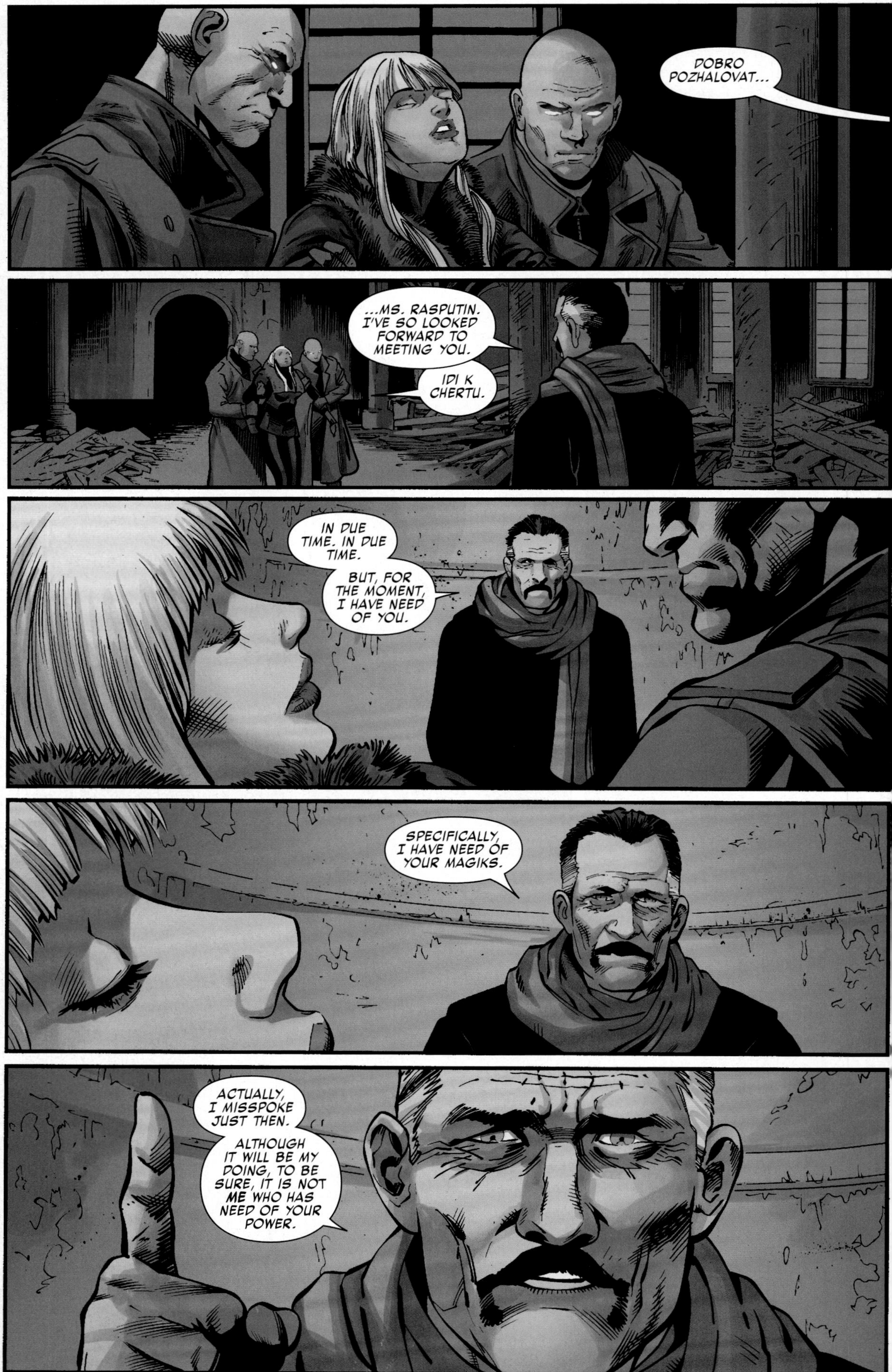
DOBRO POZHALOVAT...
...MS. RASPUTIN. I'VE SO LOOKED FORWARD TO MEETING YOU.
IDI K CHERTU.
IN DUE TIME. IN DUE TIME.
BUT, FOR THE MOMENT, I HAVE NEED OF YOU.
SPECIFICALLY, I HAVE NEED OF YOUR MAGIKS.
ACTUALLY, I MISSPOKE JUST THEN.
ALTHOUGH IT WILL BE MY DOING, TO BE SURE, IT IS NOT ME WHO HAS NEED OF YOUR POWER.

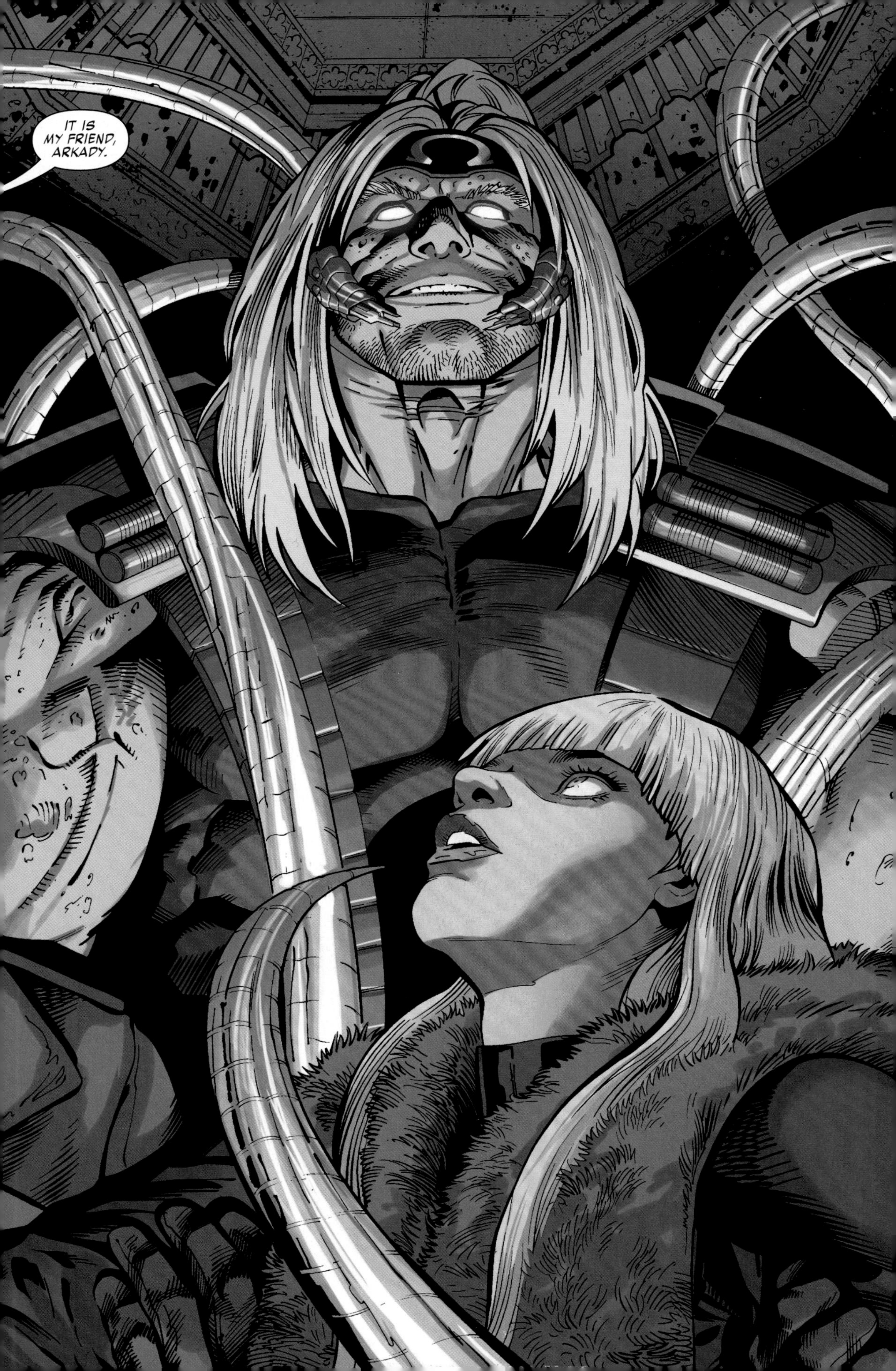
IT IS MY FRIEND, ARKADY.

11

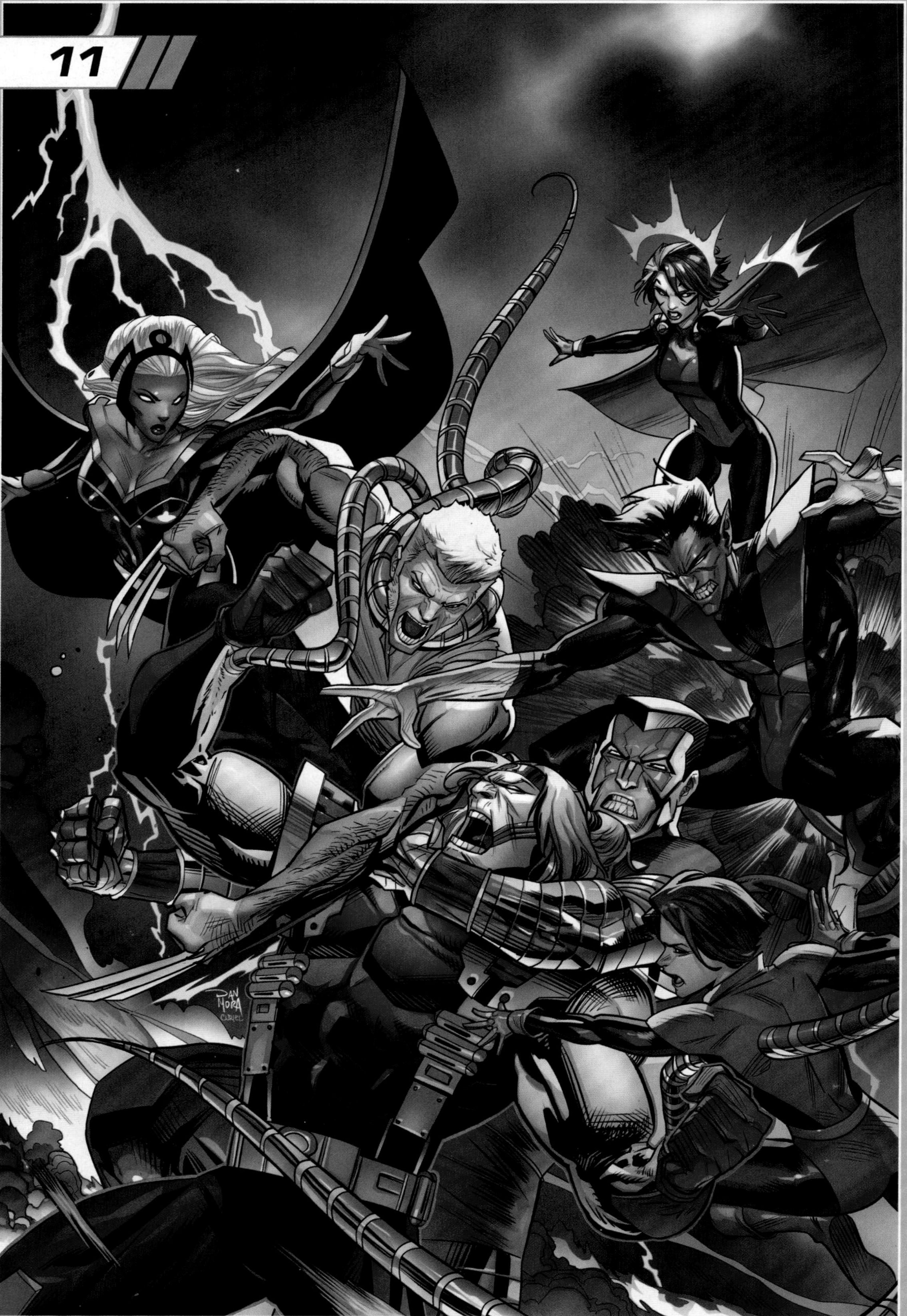

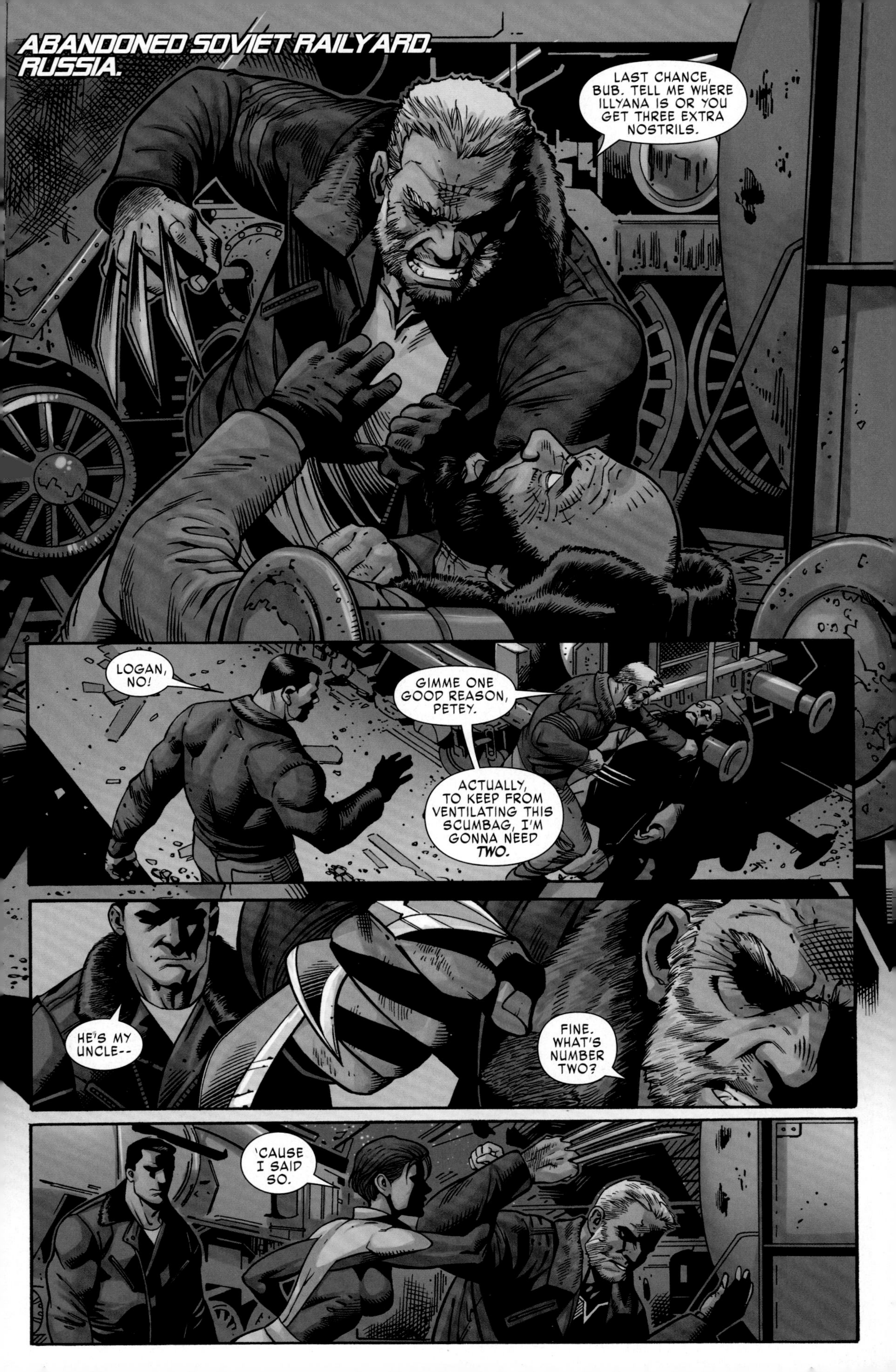
ABANDONED SOVIET RAILYARD. RUSSIA.
LAST CHANCE, BUB. TELL ME WHERE ILLYANA IS OR YOU GET THREE EXTRA NOSTRILS.
LOGAN, NO!
GIMME ONE GOOD REASON, PETEY.
ACTUALLY, TO KEEP FROM VENTILATING THIS SCUMBAG, I'M GONNA NEED TWO.
HE'S MY UNCLE--
FINE. WHAT'S NUMBER TWO?
'CAUSE I SAID SO.

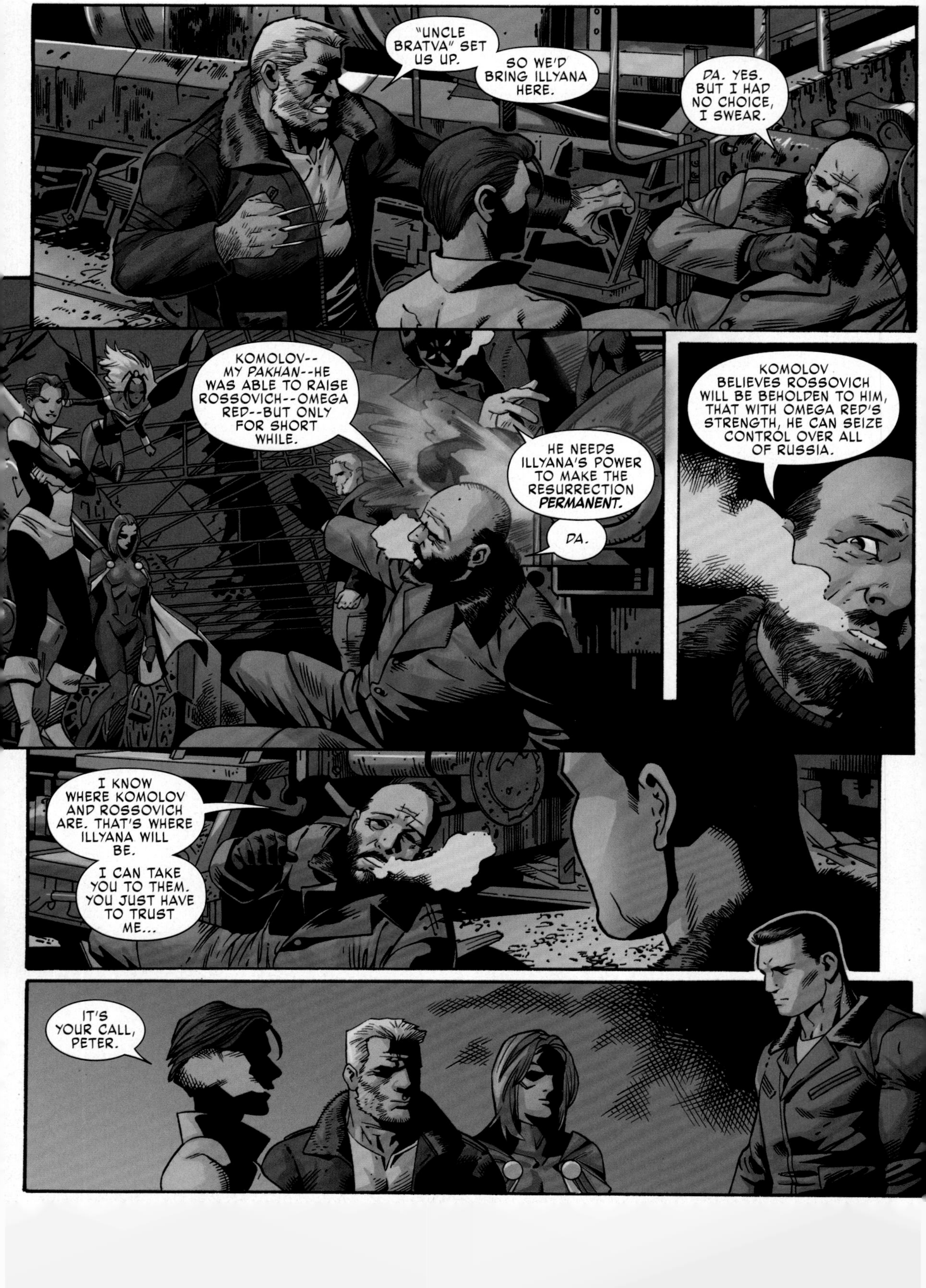
"UNCLE BRATVA" SET US UP.
SO WE'D BRING ILLYANA HERE.
DA. YES. BUT I HAD NO CHOICE, I SWEAR.
KOMOLOV-- MY PAKHAN--HE WAS ABLE TO RAISE ROSSOVICH--OMEGA RED--BUT ONLY FOR SHORT WHILE.
HE NEEDS ILLYANA'S POWER TO MAKE THE RESURRECTION PERMANENT.
DA.
KOMOLOV BELIEVES ROSSOVICH WILL BE BEHOLDEN TO HIM, THAT WITH OMEGA RED'S STRENGTH, HE CAN SEIZE CONTROL OVER ALL OF RUSSIA.
I KNOW WHERE KOMOLOV AND ROSSOVICH ARE. THAT'S WHERE ILLYANA WILL BE.
I CAN TAKE YOU TO THEM. YOU JUST HAVE TO TRUST ME...
IT'S YOUR CALL, PETER.

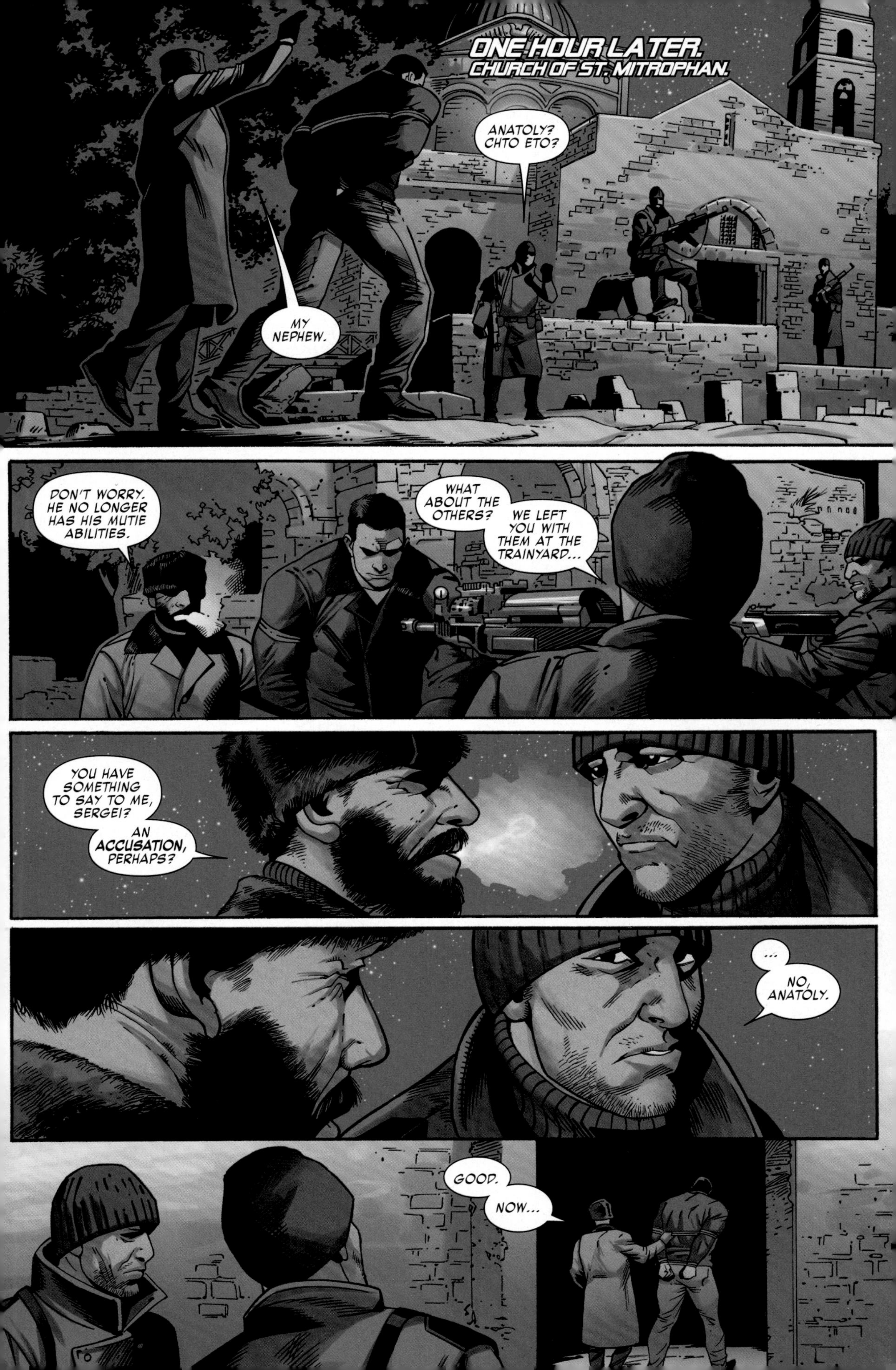
ONE HOUR LATER.
CHURCH OF ST. MITROPHAN.
ANATOLY? CHTO ETO?
MY NEPHEW.
DON'T WORRY. HE NO LONGER HAS HIS MUTIE ABILITIES.
WHAT ABOUT THE OTHERS?
WE LEFT YOU WITH THEM AT THE TRAINYARD...
YOU HAVE SOMETHING TO SAY TO ME, SERGEI?
AN ACCUSATION, PERHAPS?
...
NO, ANATOLY.
GOOD.
NOW...

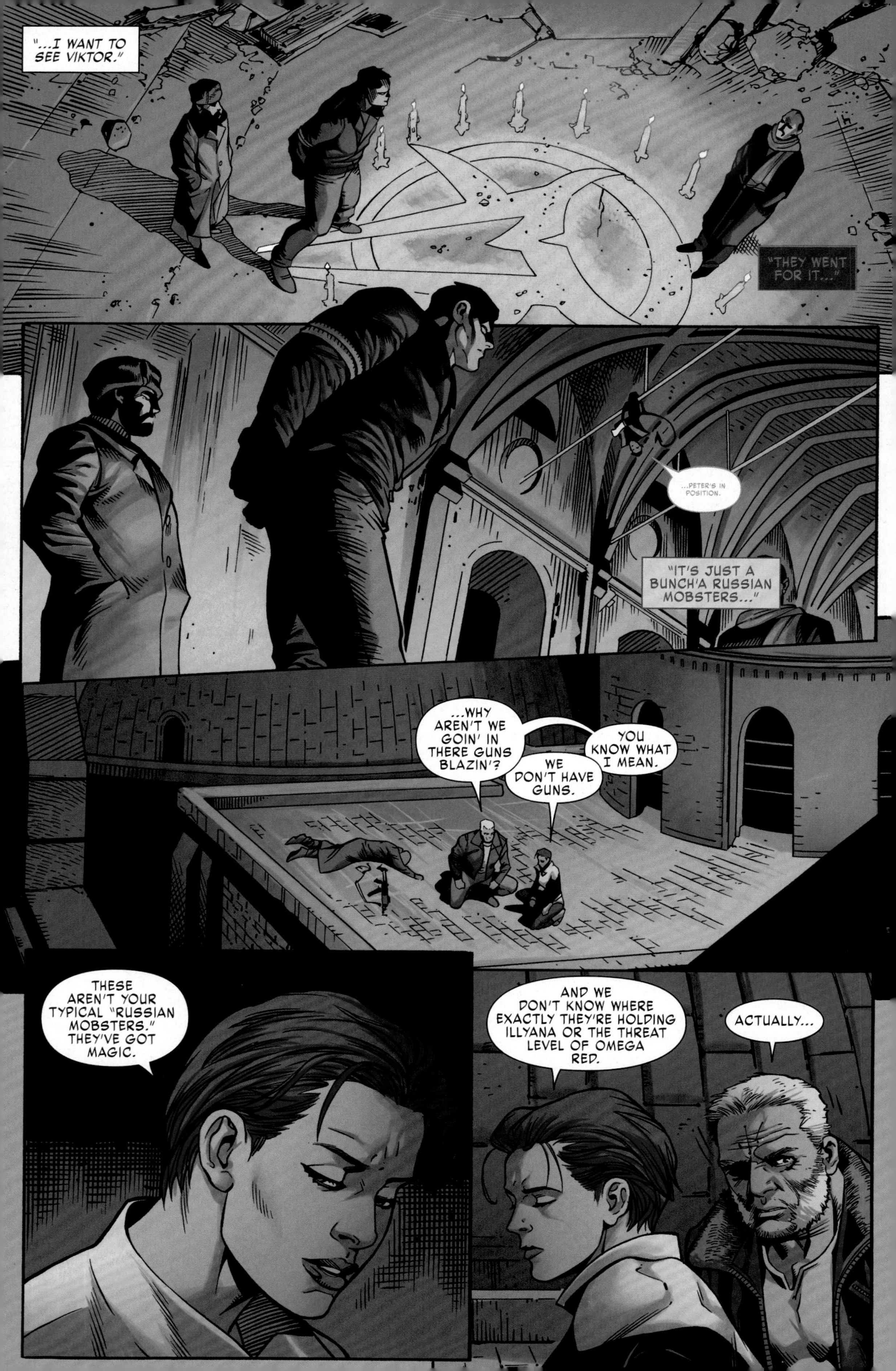
"...I WANT TO SEE VIKTOR."
"THEY WENT FOR IT..."
...PETER'S IN POSITION.
"IT'S JUST A BUNCH'A RUSSIAN MOBSTERS..."
...WHY AREN'T WE GOIN' IN THERE GUNS BLAZIN'?
WE DON'T HAVE GUNS.
YOU KNOW WHAT I MEAN.
THESE AREN'T YOUR TYPICAL "RUSSIAN MOBSTERS." THEY'VE GOT MAGIC.
AND WE DON'T KNOW WHERE EXACTLY THEY'RE HOLDING ILLYANA OR THE THREAT LEVEL OF OMEGA RED.
ACTUALLY...

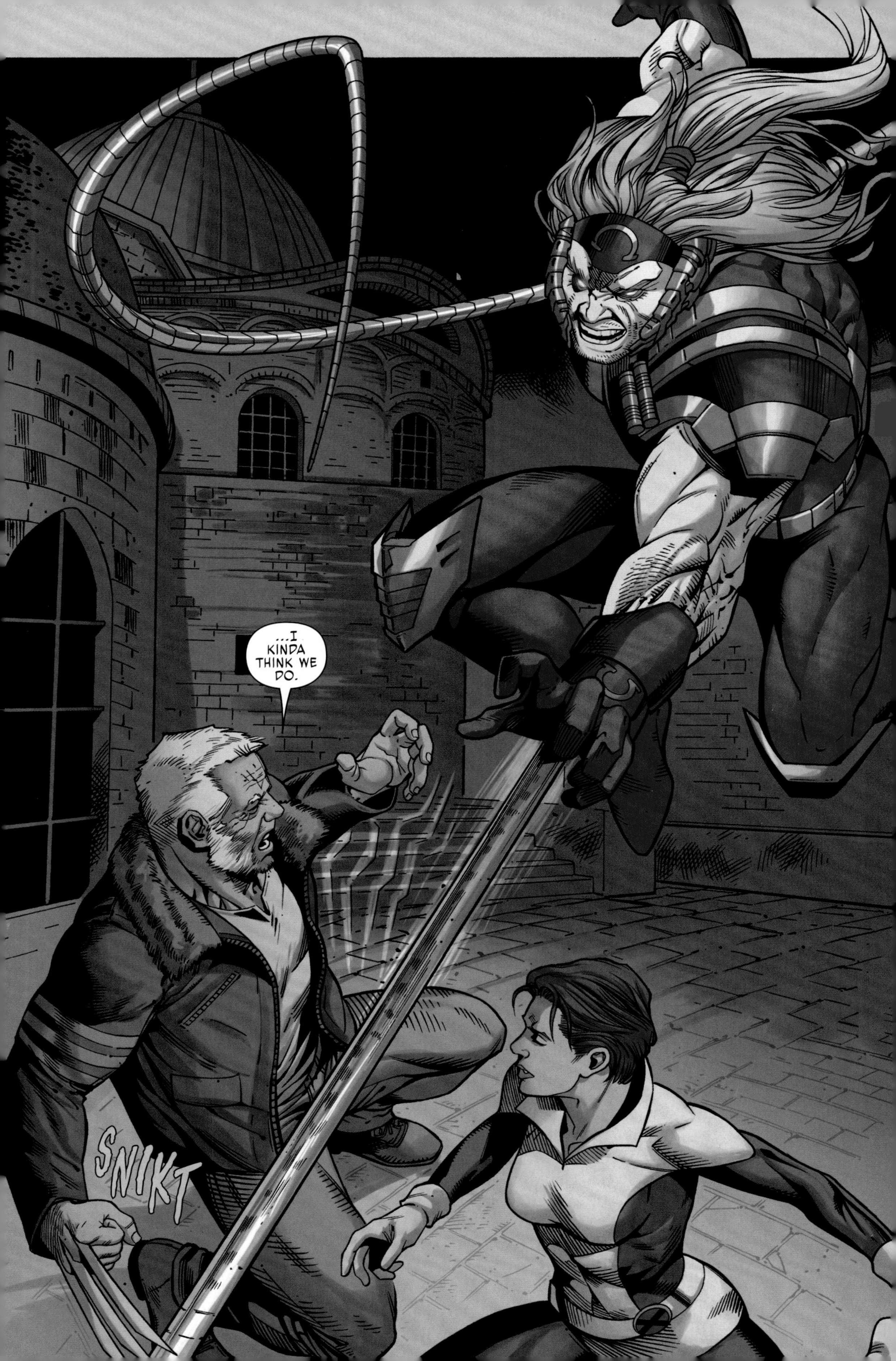
...I KINDA THINK WE DO.
SNIKT

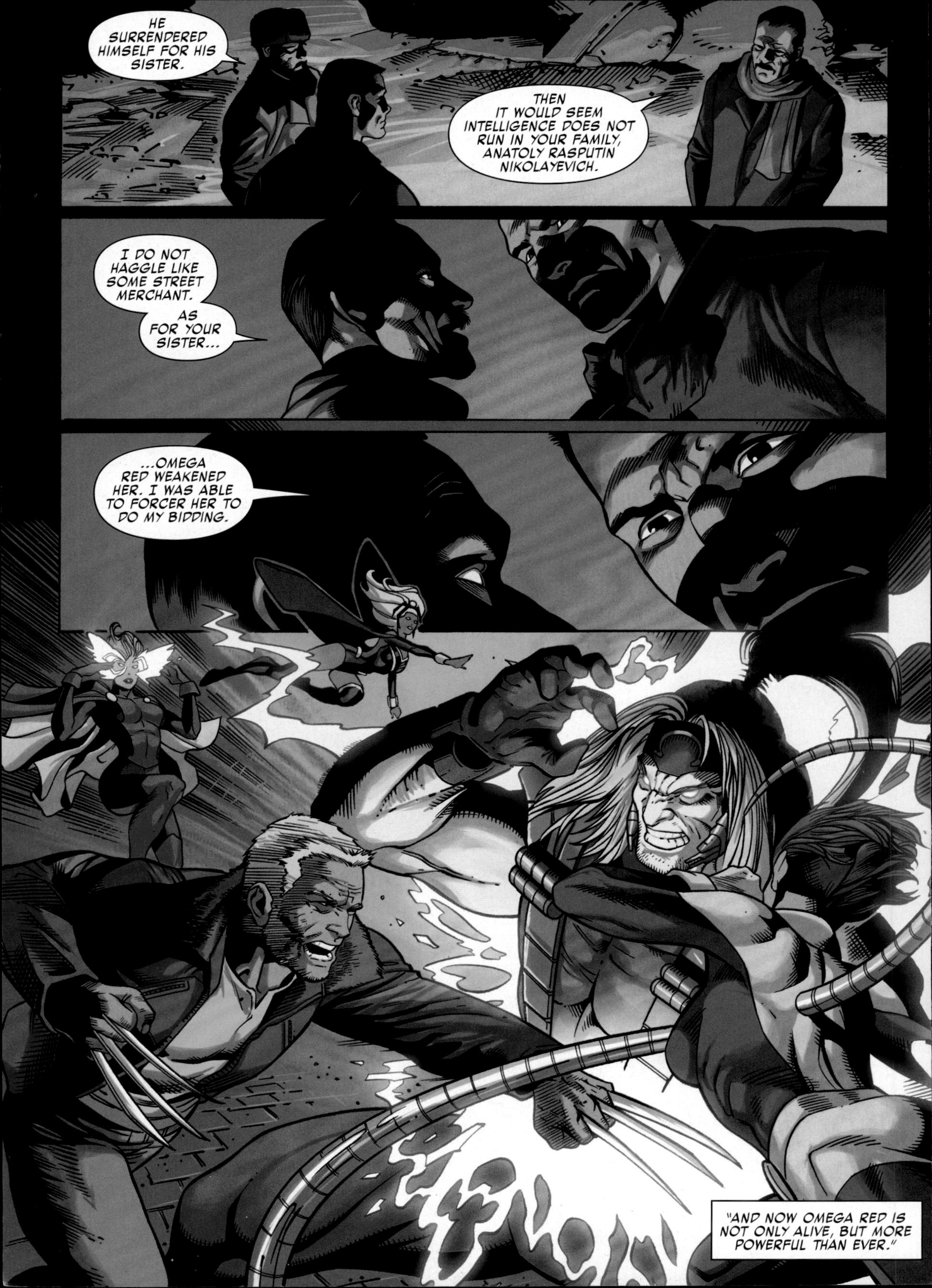
HE SURRENDERED HIMSELF FOR HIS SISTER.
THEN IT WOULD SEEM INTELLIGENCE DOES NOT RUN IN YOUR FAMILY, ANATOLY RASPUTIN NIKOLAYEVICH.
I DO NOT HAGGLE LIKE SOME STREET MERCHANT.
AS FOR YOUR SISTER...
...OMEGA RED WEAKENED HER. I WAS ABLE TO FORCER HER TO DO MY BIDDING.
"AND NOW OMEGA RED IS NOT ONLY ALIVE, BUT MORE POWERFUL THAN EVER."

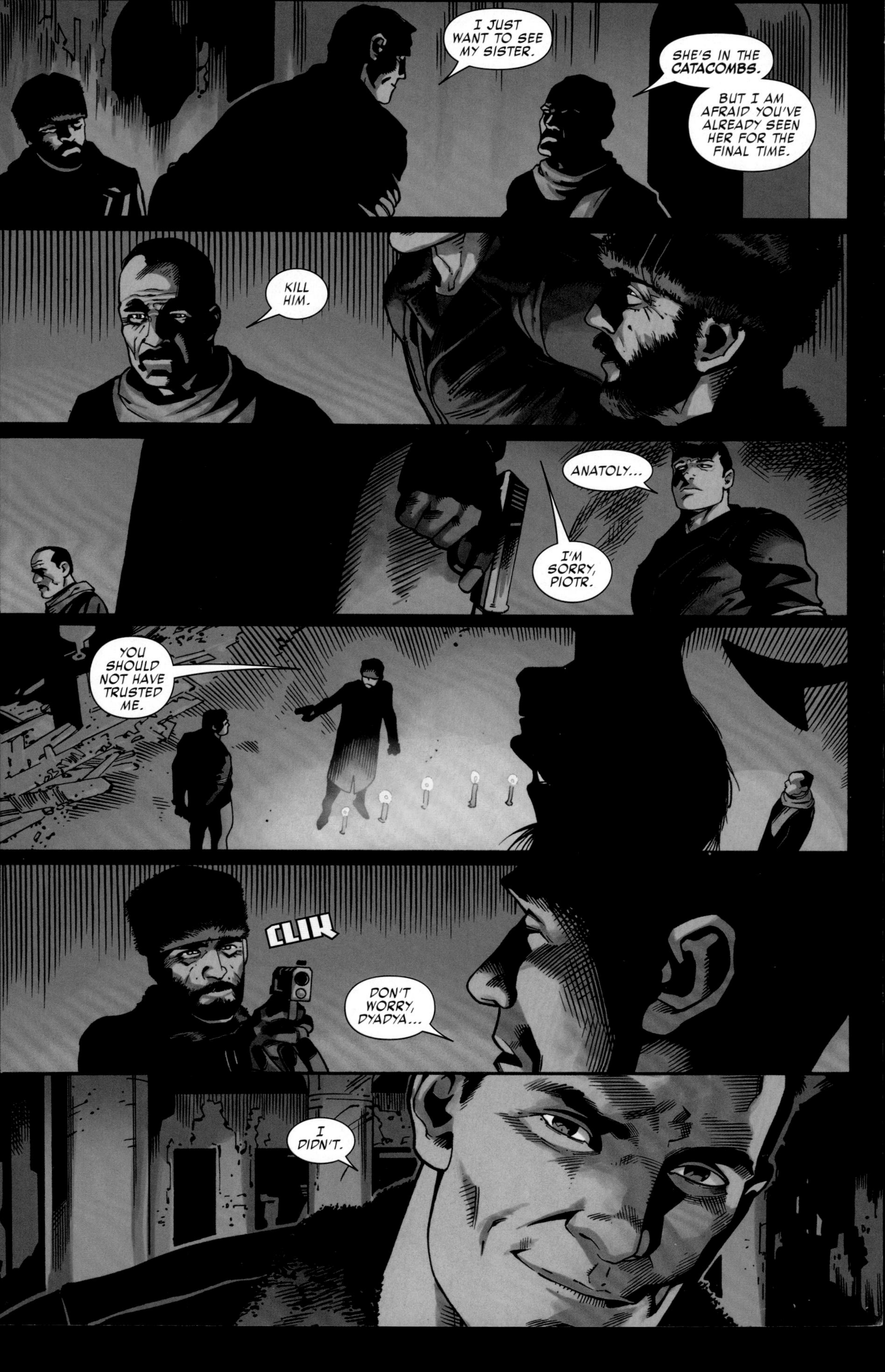
I JUST WANT TO SEE MY SISTER.
SHE'S IN THE CATACOMBS.
BUT I AM AFRAID YOU'VE ALREADY SEEN HER FOR THE FINAL TIME.
KILL HIM.
ANATOLY...
I'M SORRY, PIOTR.
YOU SHOULD NOT HAVE TRUSTED ME.
CLIK
DON'T WORRY, DYADYA...
I DIDN'T.

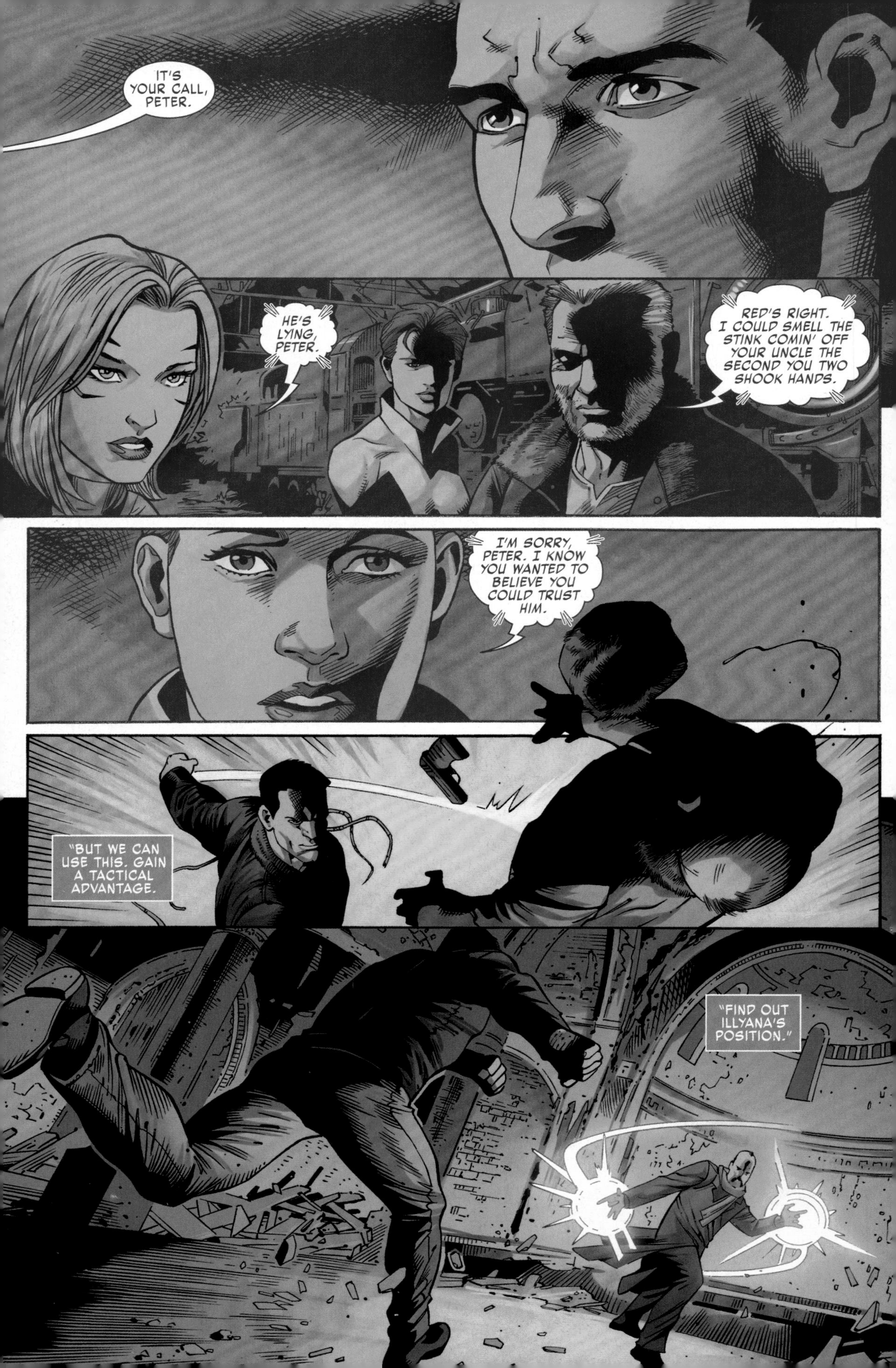
IT'S YOUR CALL, PETER.
HE'S LYING, PETER.
RED'S RIGHT. I COULD SMELL THE STINK COMIN' OFF YOUR UNCLE THE SECOND YOU TWO SHOOK HANDS.
I'M SORRY, PETER. I KNOW YOU WANTED TO BELIEVE YOU COULD TRUST HIM.
"BUT WE CAN USE THIS. GAIN A TACTICAL ADVANTAGE.
"FIND OUT ILLYANA'S POSITION."

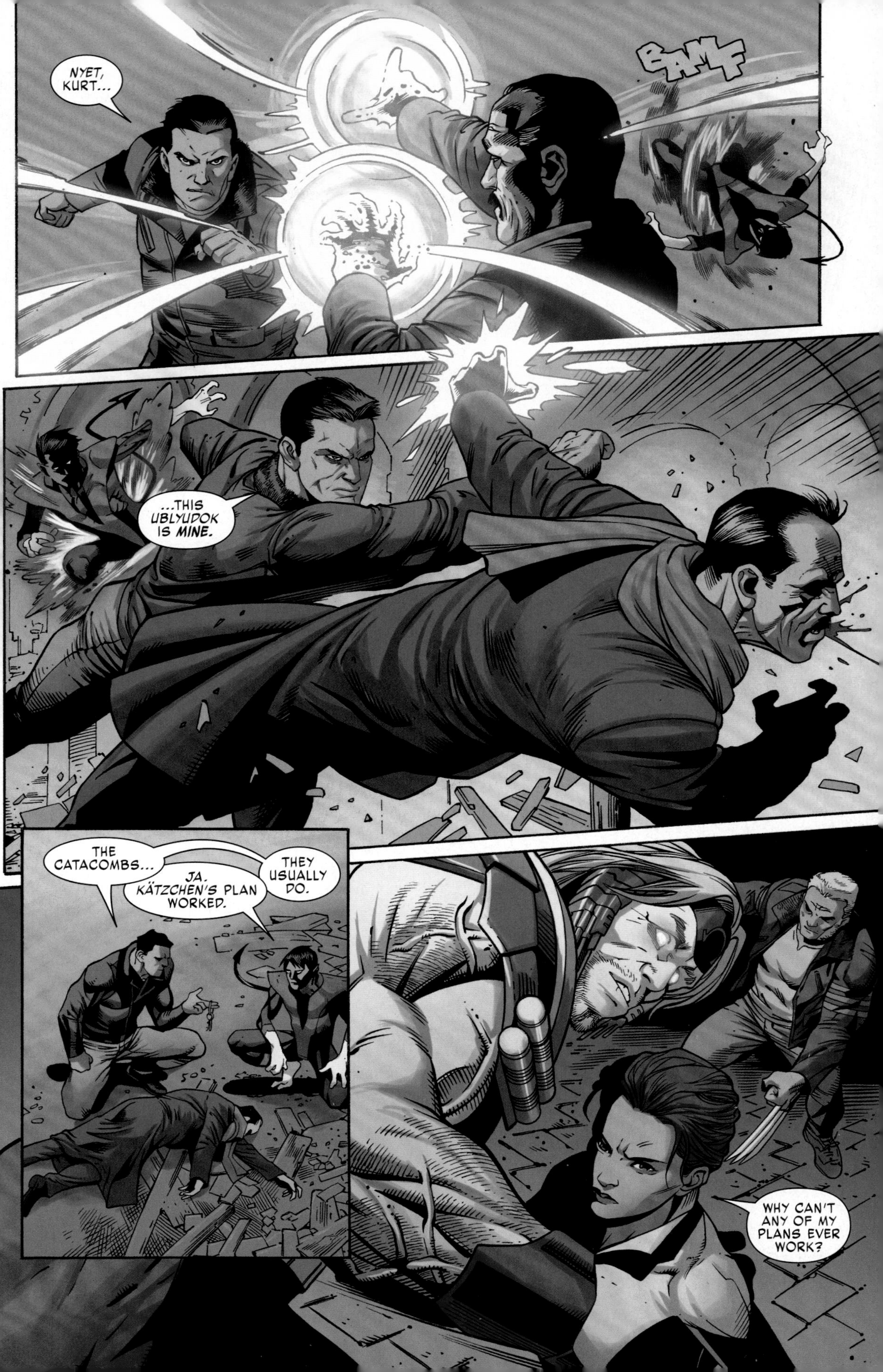
NYET, KURT...
BAMF
...THIS UBLYUDOK IS MINE.
THE CATACOMBS...
JA. KÄTZCHEN'S PLAN WORKED.
THEY USUALLY DO.
WHY CAN'T ANY OF MY PLANS EVER WORK?

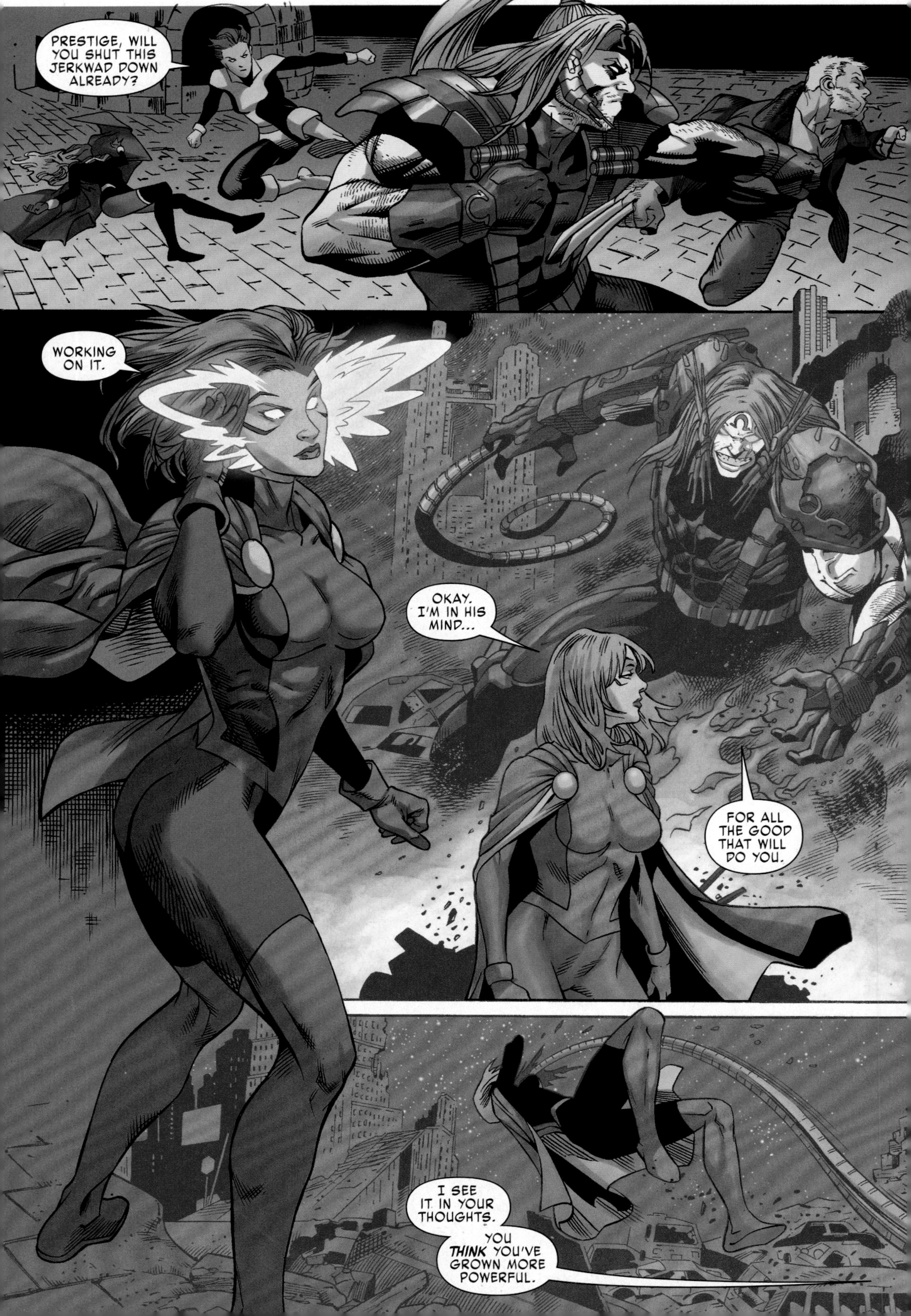

PRESTIGE, WILL YOU SHUT THIS JERKWAD DOWN ALREADY?
WORKING ON IT.
OKAY. I'M IN HIS MIND...
FOR ALL THE GOOD THAT WILL DO YOU.
I SEE IT IN YOUR THOUGHTS.
YOU *THINK* YOU'VE GROWN MORE POWERFUL.

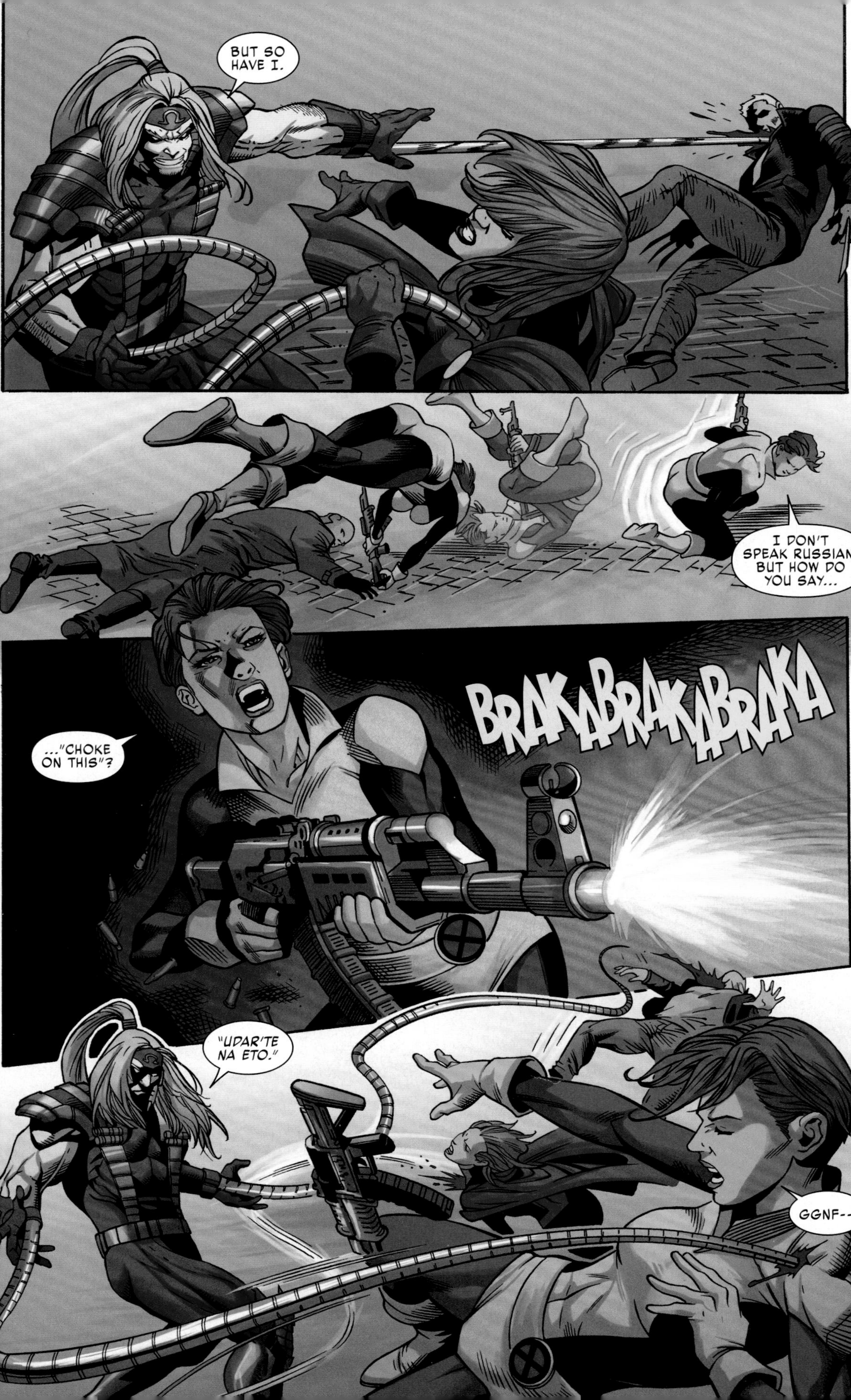
BUT SO HAVE I.
I DON'T SPEAK RUSSIAN, BUT HOW DO YOU SAY...
..."CHOKE ON THIS"?
BRAKABRAKABRAKA
"UDAR'TE NA ETO."
GGNF--

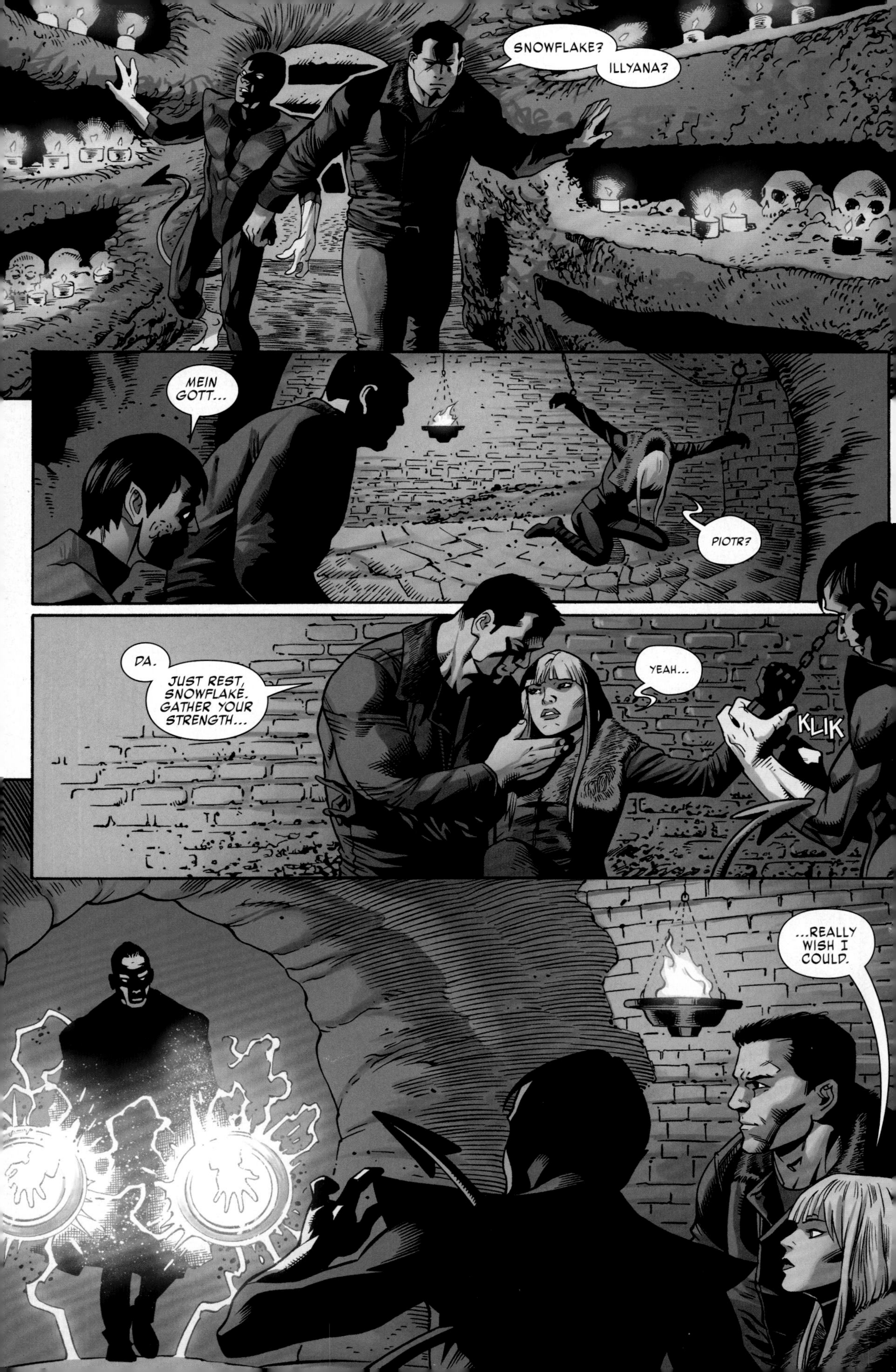
SNOWFLAKE?
ILLYANA?
MEIN GOTT...
PIOTR?
DA.
JUST REST, SNOWFLAKE. GATHER YOUR STRENGTH...
YEAH...
KLIK
...REALLY WISH I COULD.

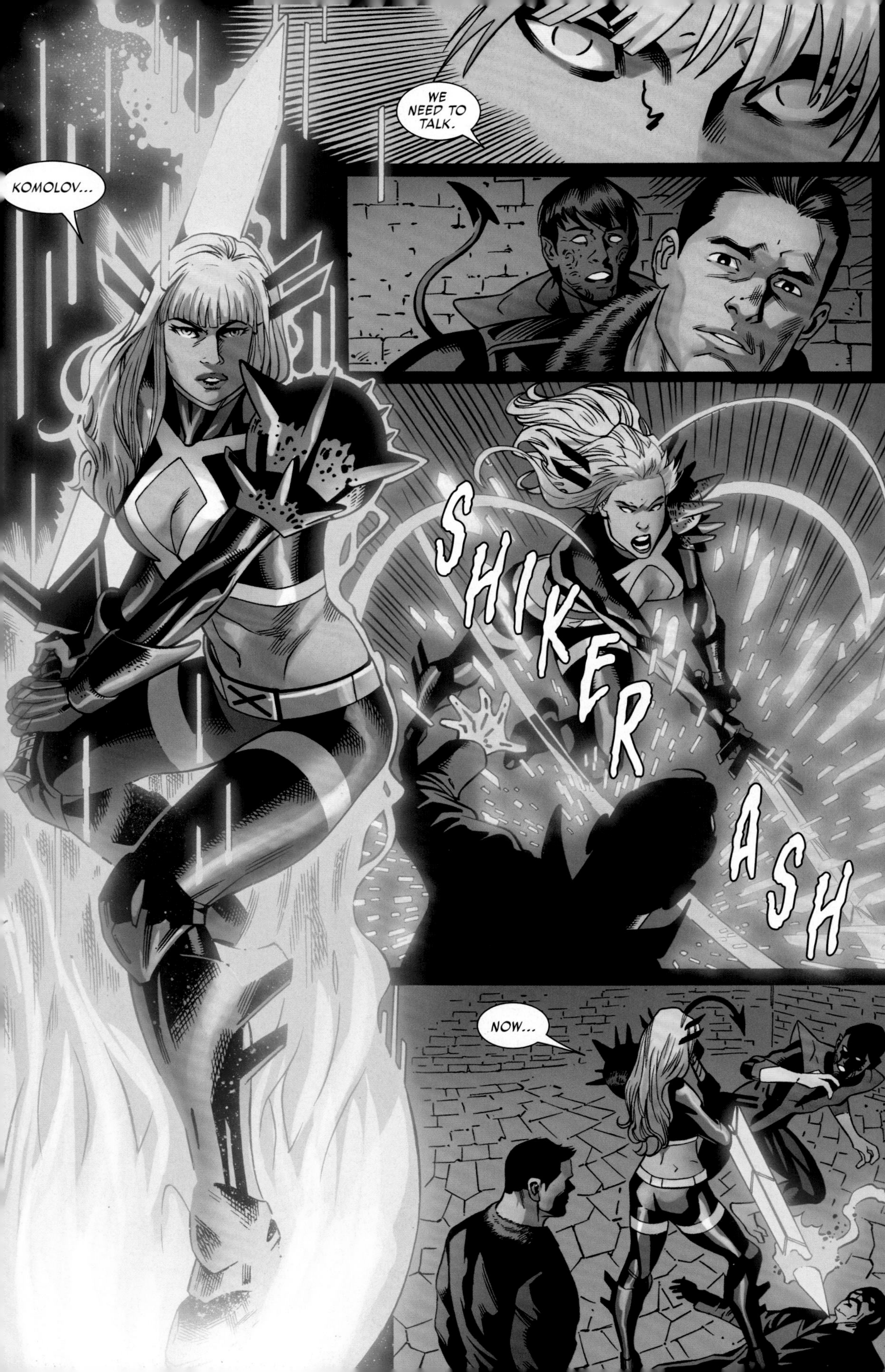

WE NEED TO TALK.
KOMOLOV...
SHIKERRASH
NOW...

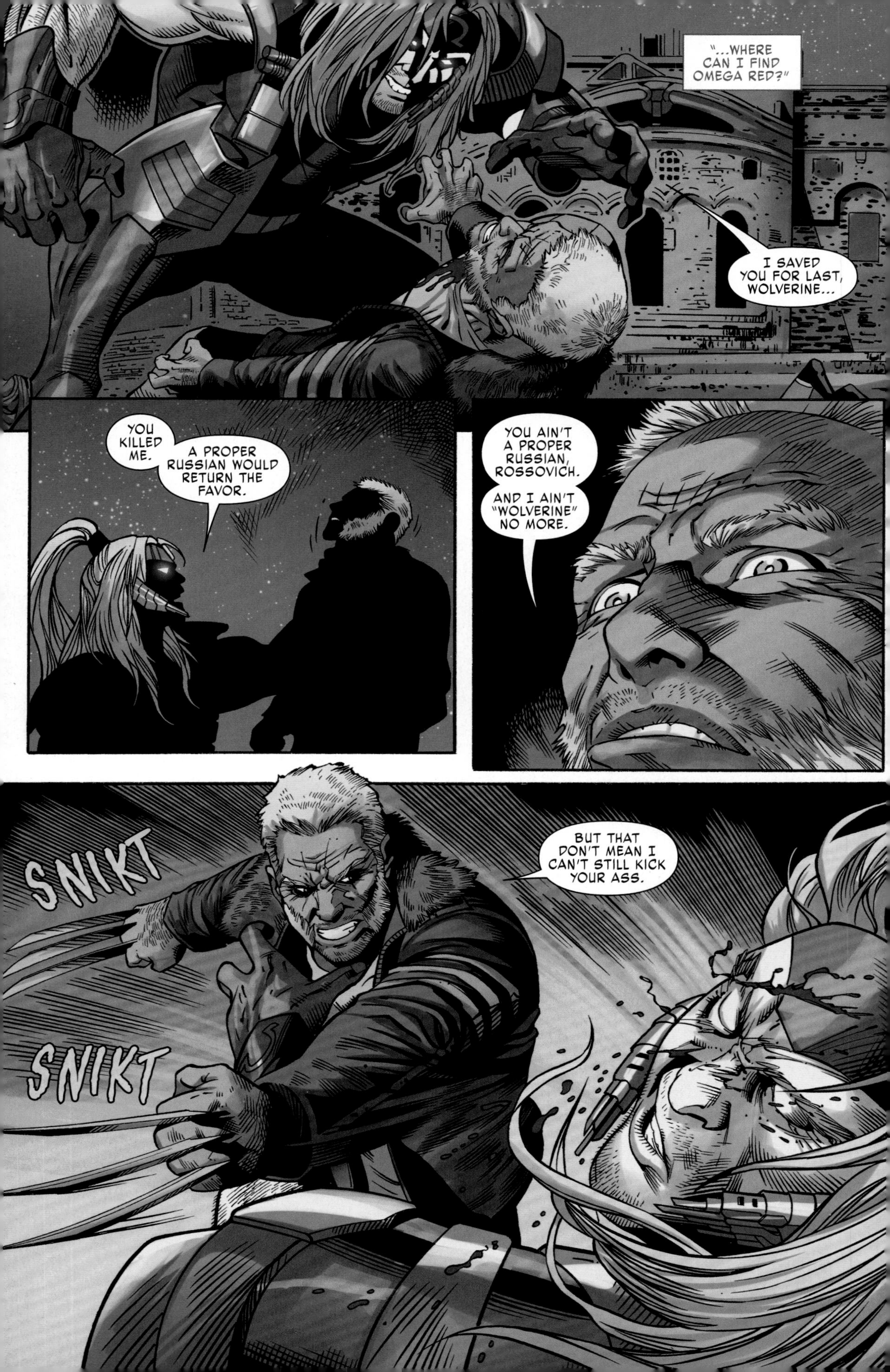
"...WHERE CAN I FIND OMEGA RED?"
I SAVED YOU FOR LAST, WOLVERINE...
YOU KILLED ME.
A PROPER RUSSIAN WOULD RETURN THE FAVOR.
YOU AIN'T A PROPER RUSSIAN, ROSSOVICH.
AND I AIN'T "WOLVERINE" NO MORE.
SNIKT
BUT THAT DON'T MEAN I CAN'T STILL KICK YOUR ASS.
SNIKT

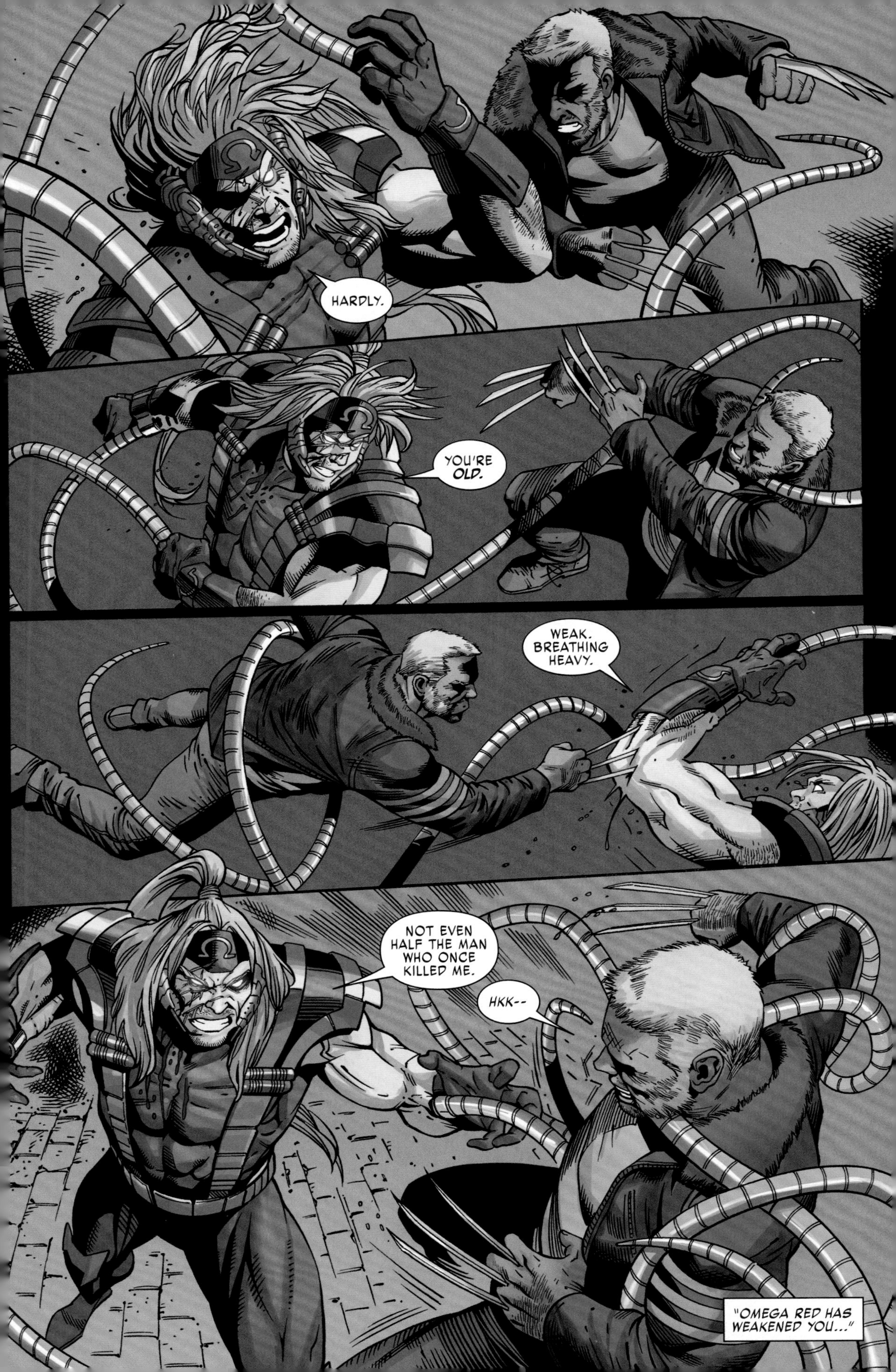
HARDLY.
YOU'RE OLD.
WEAK. BREATHING HEAVY.
NOT EVEN HALF THE MAN WHO ONCE KILLED ME.
HKK--
"OMEGA RED HAS WEAKENED YOU..."

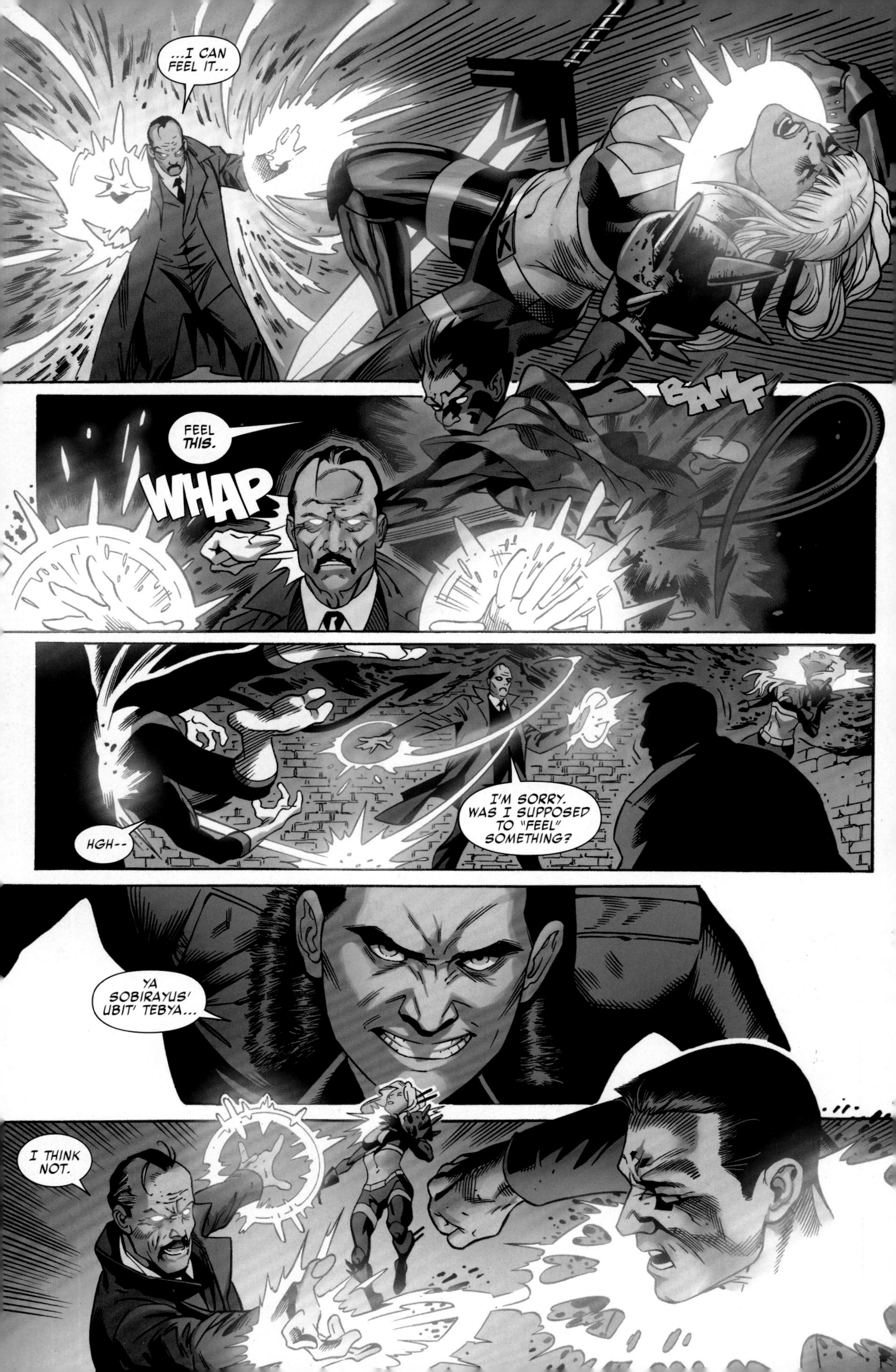
...I CAN FEEL IT...
BAMF
FEEL THIS.
WHAP
HGH--
I'M SORRY. WAS I SUPPOSED TO "FEEL" SOMETHING?
YA SOBIRAYUS' UBIT' TEBYA...
I THINK NOT.

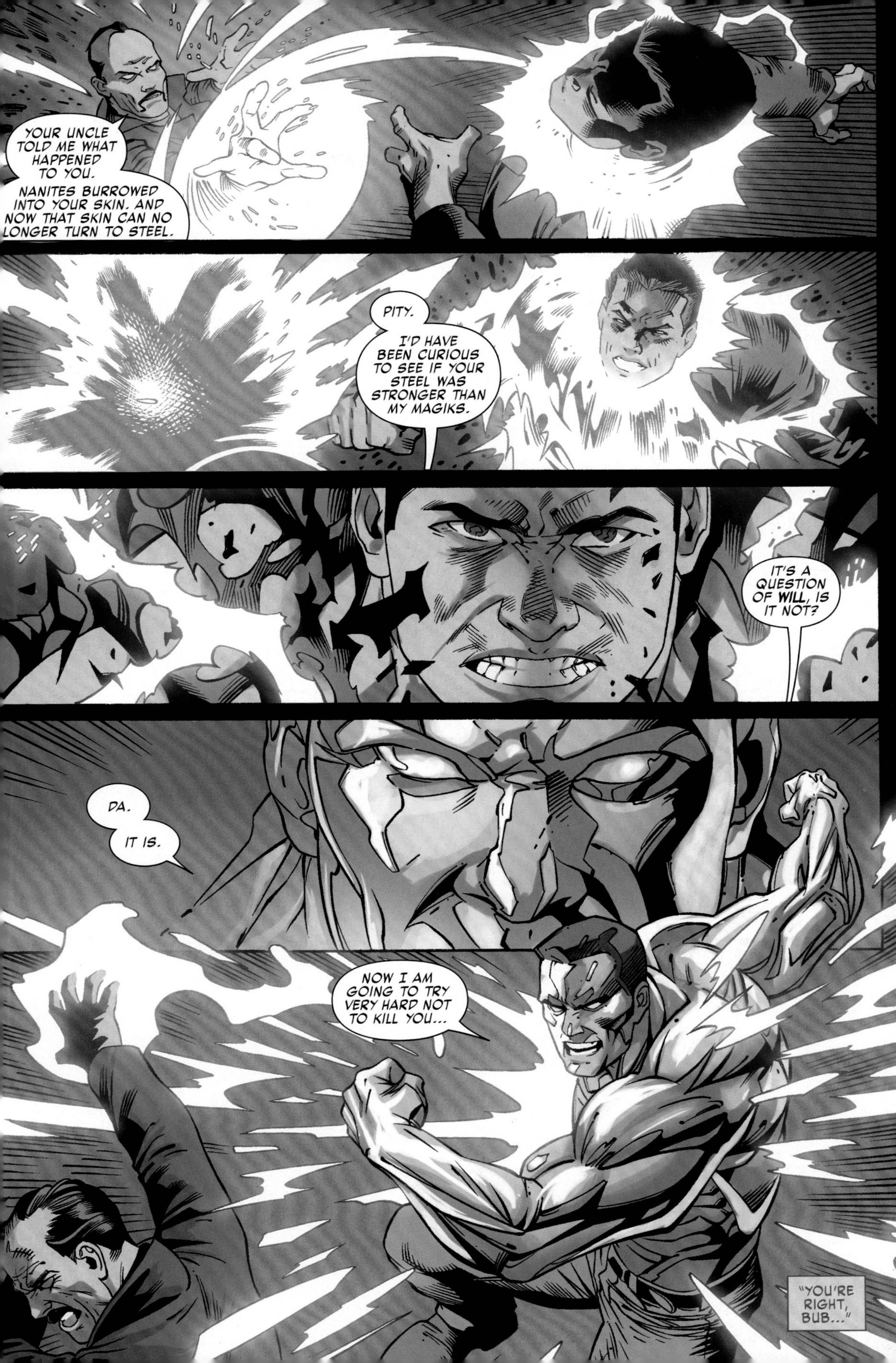
YOUR UNCLE TOLD ME WHAT HAPPENED TO YOU.
NANITES BURROWED INTO YOUR SKIN. AND NOW THAT SKIN CAN NO LONGER TURN TO STEEL.
PITY.
I'D HAVE BEEN CURIOUS TO SEE IF YOUR STEEL WAS STRONGER THAN MY MAGIKS.
IT'S A QUESTION OF WILL, IS IT NOT?
DA.
IT IS.
NOW I AM GOING TO TRY VERY HARD NOT TO KILL YOU...
"YOU'RE RIGHT, BUB..."

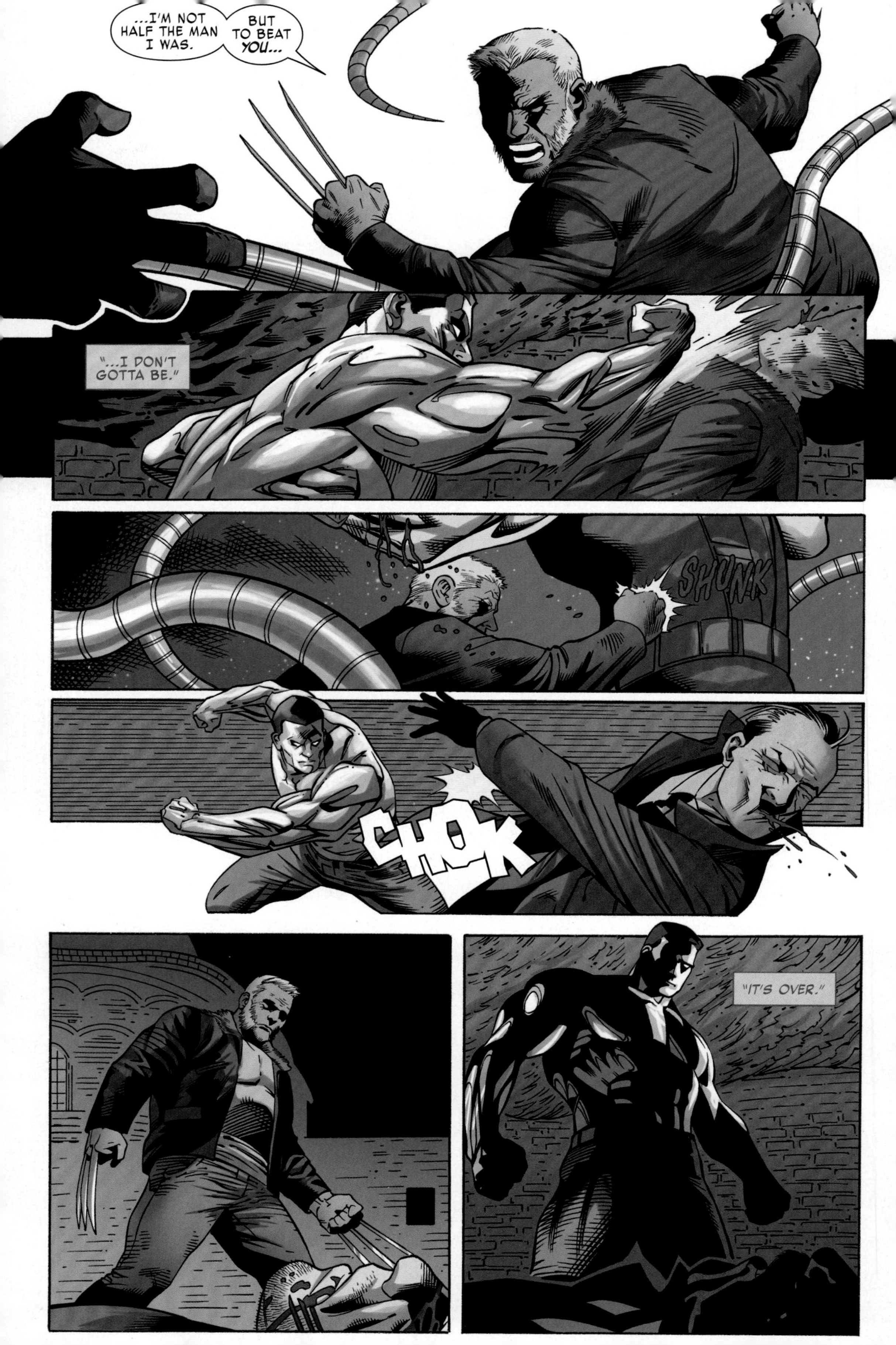
...I'M NOT HALF THE MAN I WAS.
BUT TO BEAT YOU...
"...I DON'T GOTTA BE."
SHUNK
CHOK
"IT'S OVER."

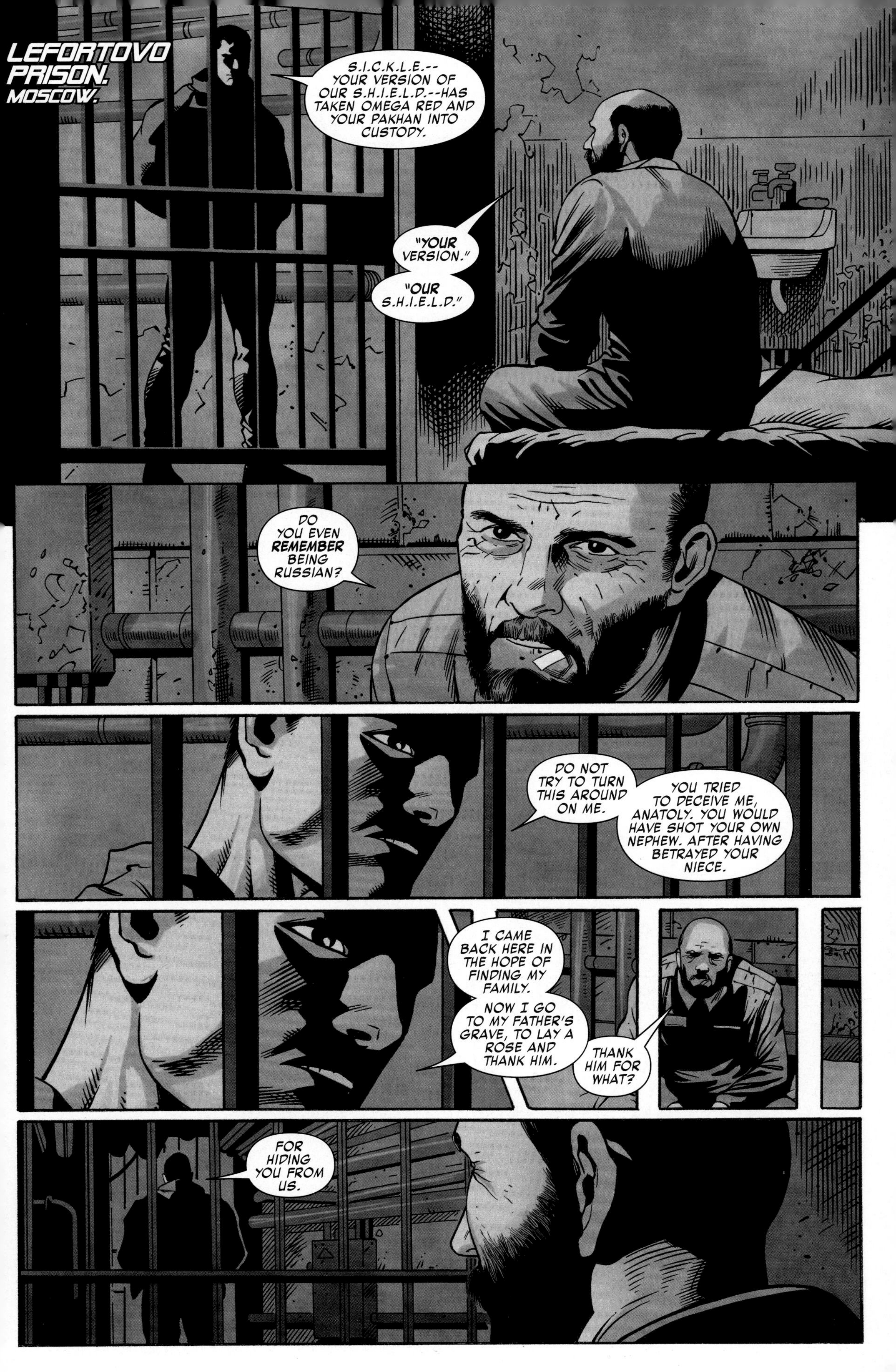
LEFORTOVO PRISON. MOSCOW.
S.I.C.K.L.E.--YOUR VERSION OF OUR S.H.I.E.L.D.--HAS TAKEN OMEGA RED AND YOUR PAKHAN INTO CUSTODY.
"YOUR VERSION."
"OUR S.H.I.E.L.D."
DO YOU EVEN REMEMBER BEING RUSSIAN?
DO NOT TRY TO TURN THIS AROUND ON ME.
YOU TRIED TO DECEIVE ME, ANATOLY. YOU WOULD HAVE SHOT YOUR OWN NEPHEW. AFTER HAVING BETRAYED YOUR NIECE.
I CAME BACK HERE IN THE HOPE OF FINDING MY FAMILY.
NOW I GO TO MY FATHER'S GRAVE, TO LAY A ROSE AND THANK HIM.
THANK HIM FOR WHAT?
FOR HIDING YOU FROM US.

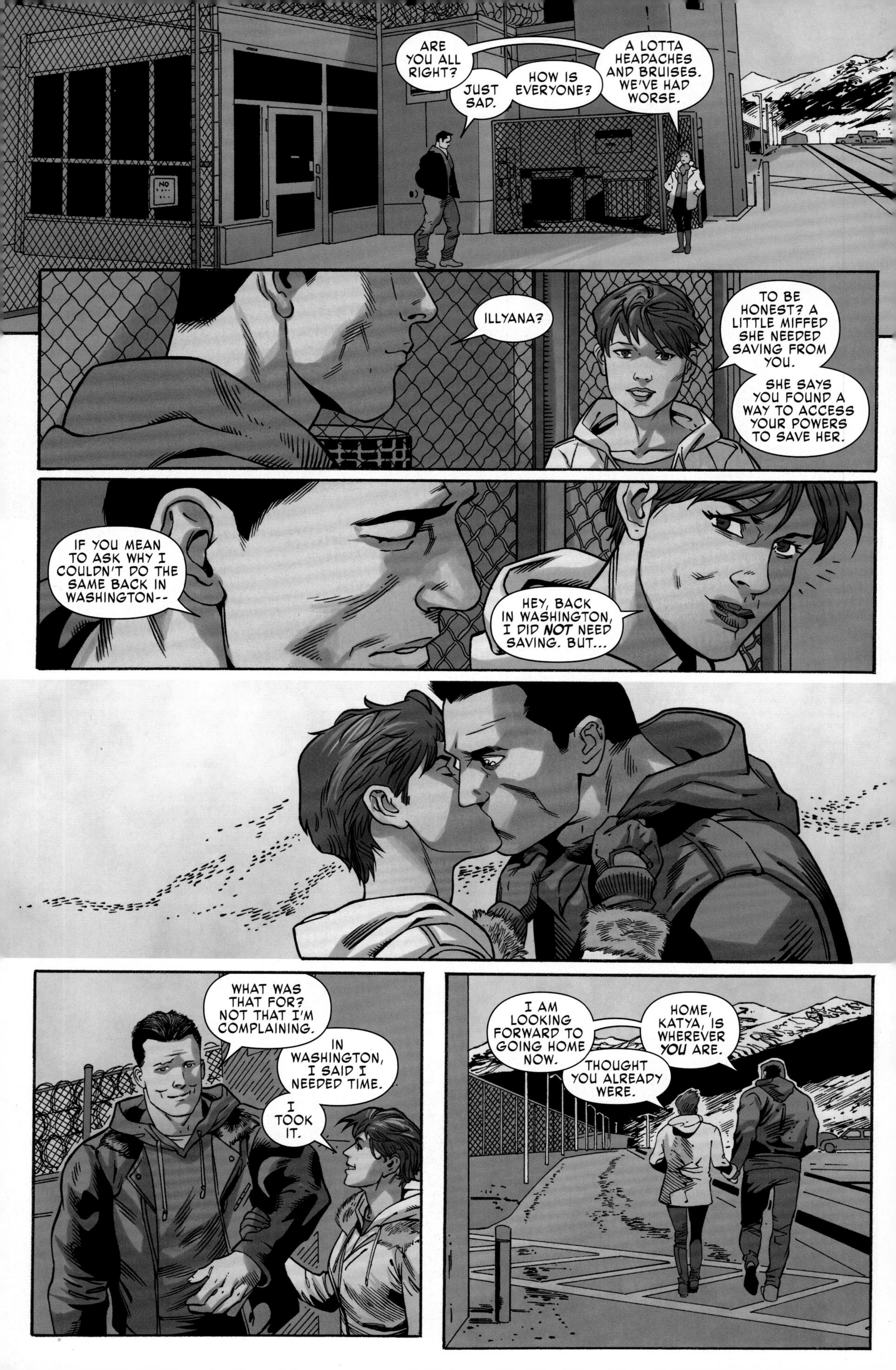
ARE YOU ALL RIGHT?
JUST SAD.
HOW IS EVERYONE?
A LOTTA HEADACHES AND BRUISES. WE'VE HAD WORSE.
NO
ILLYANA?
TO BE HONEST? A LITTLE MIFFED SHE NEEDED SAVING FROM YOU.
SHE SAYS YOU FOUND A WAY TO ACCESS YOUR POWERS TO SAVE HER.
IF YOU MEAN TO ASK WHY I COULDN'T DO THE SAME BACK IN WASHINGTON--
HEY, BACK IN WASHINGTON, I DID ***NOT*** NEED SAVING. BUT...
WHAT WAS THAT FOR? NOT THAT I'M COMPLAINING.
IN WASHINGTON, I SAID I NEEDED TIME.
I TOOK IT.
I AM LOOKING FORWARD TO GOING HOME NOW.
HOME, KATYA, IS WHEREVER ***YOU*** ARE.
THOUGHT YOU ALREADY WERE.

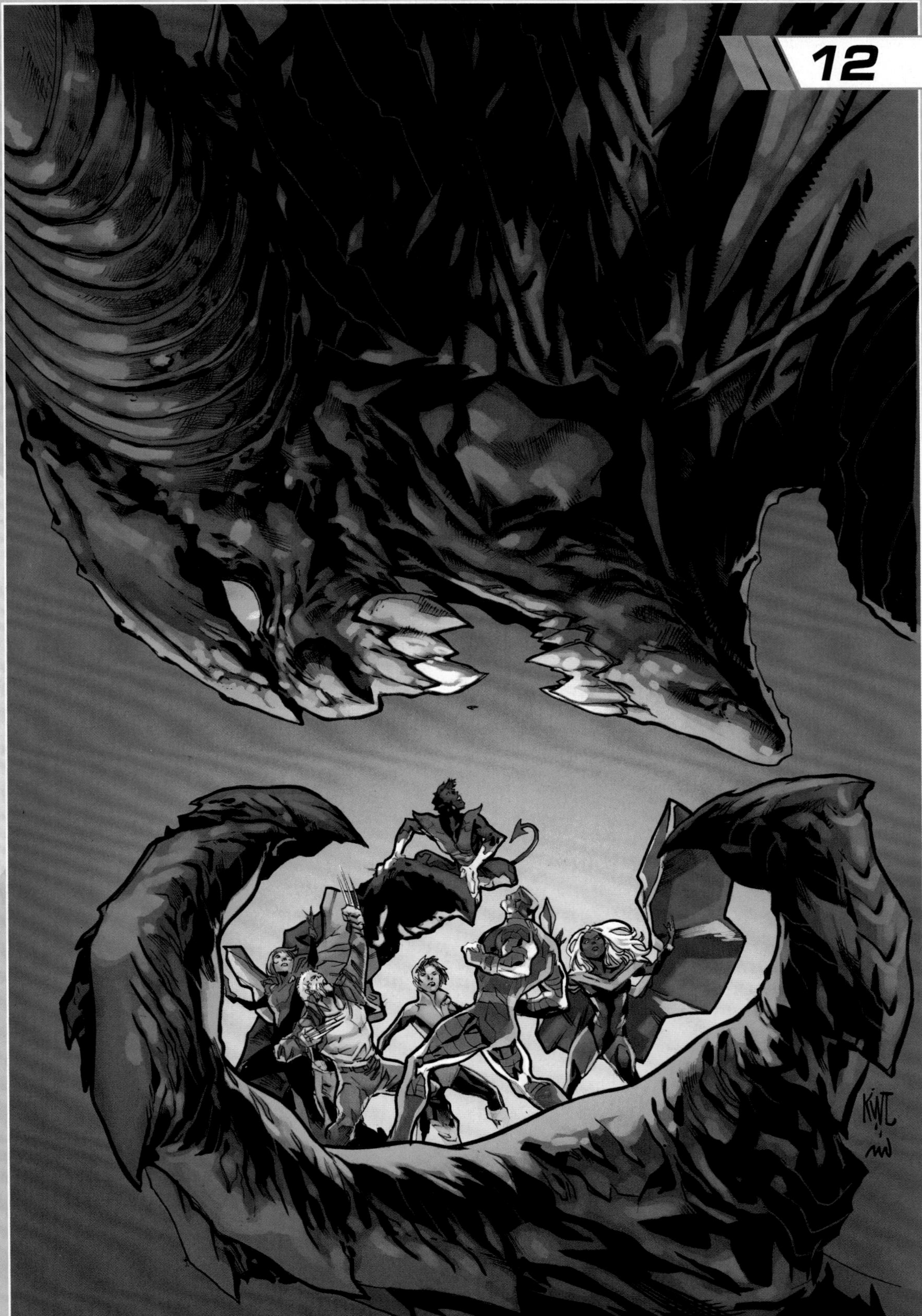
12

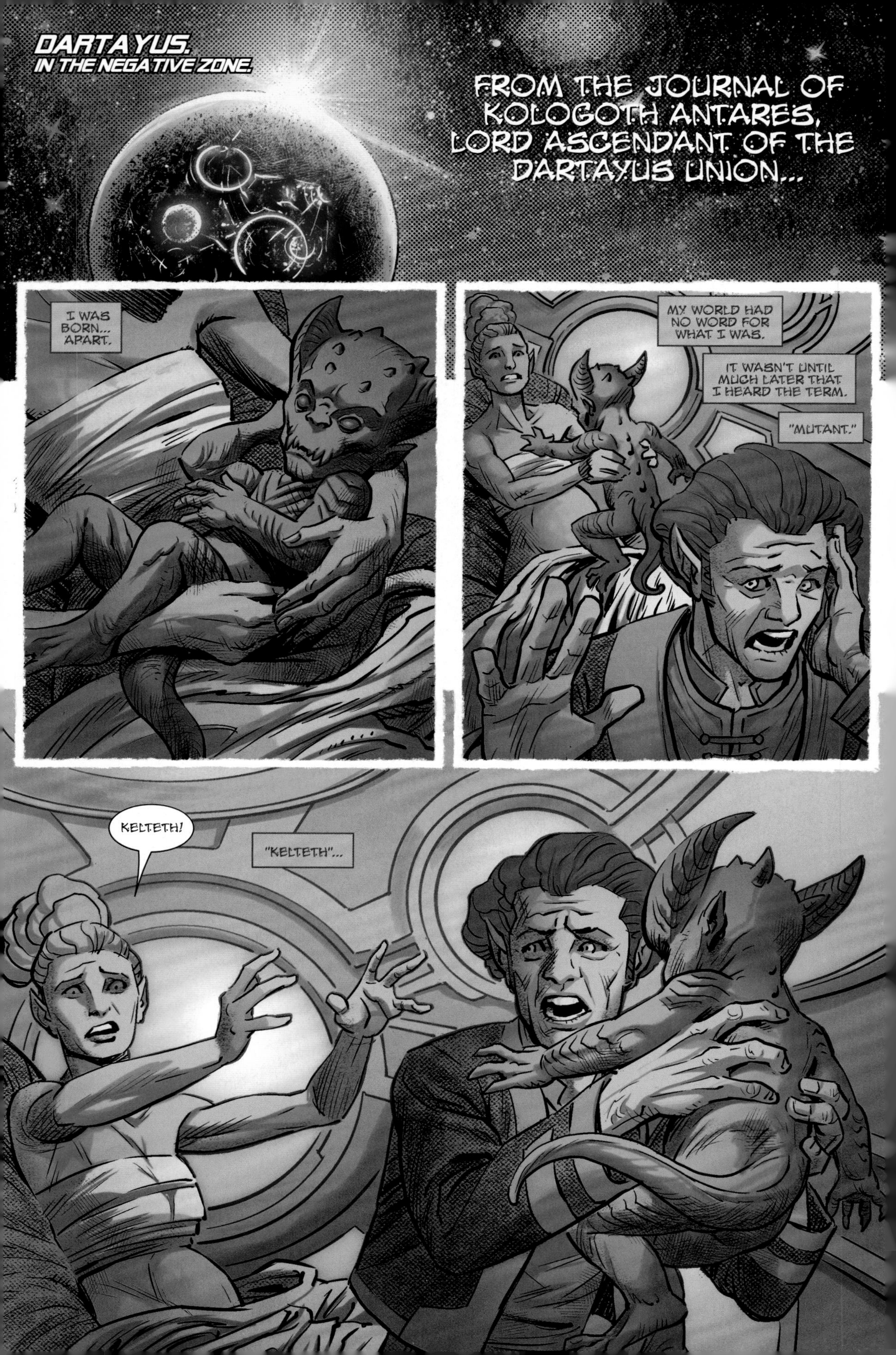
DARTAYUS.
IN THE NEGATIVE ZONE.
FROM THE JOURNAL OF KOLOGOTH ANTARES, LORD ASCENDANT OF THE DARTAYUS UNION...
I WAS BORN... APART.
MY WORLD HAD NO WORD FOR WHAT I WAS.
IT WASN'T UNTIL MUCH LATER THAT I HEARD THE TERM.
"MUTANT."
KELTETH!
"KELTETH"...

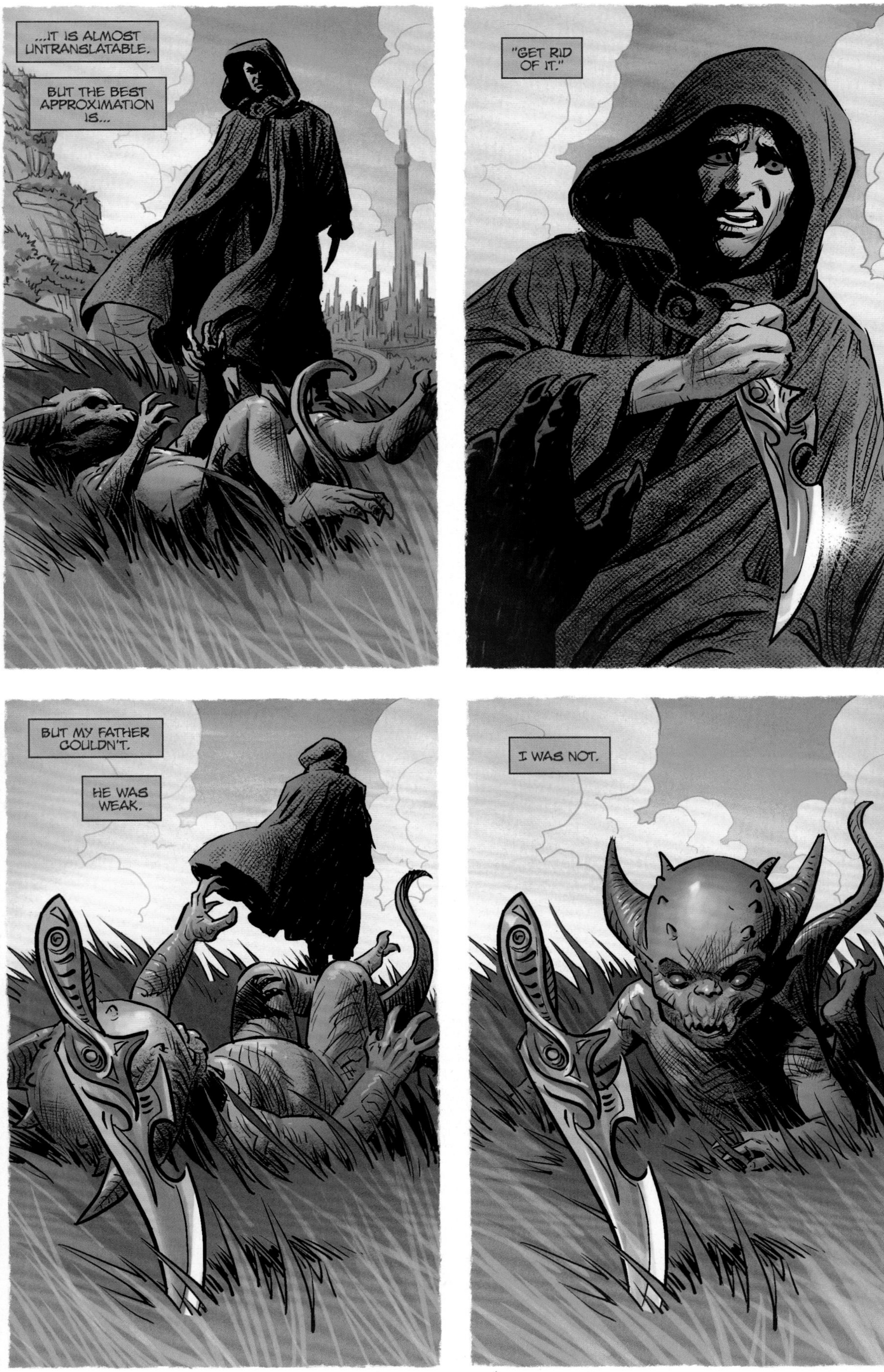
...IT IS ALMOST UNTRANSLATABLE.
BUT THE BEST APPROXIMATION IS...
"GET RID OF IT."
BUT MY FATHER COULDN'T.
HE WAS WEAK.
I WAS NOT.

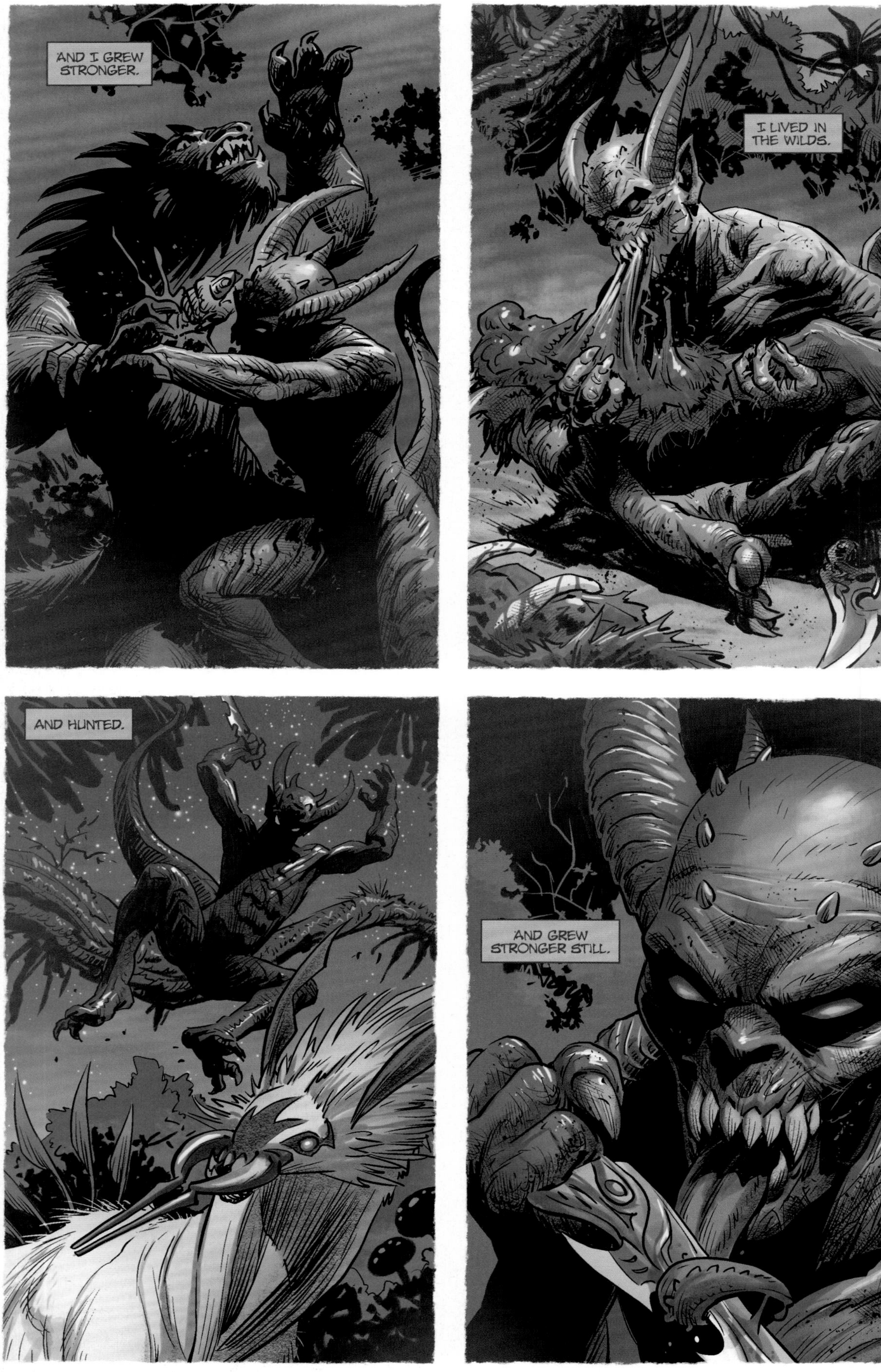
AND I GREW STRONGER.
I LIVED IN THE WILDS.
AND HUNTED.
AND GREW STRONGER STILL.

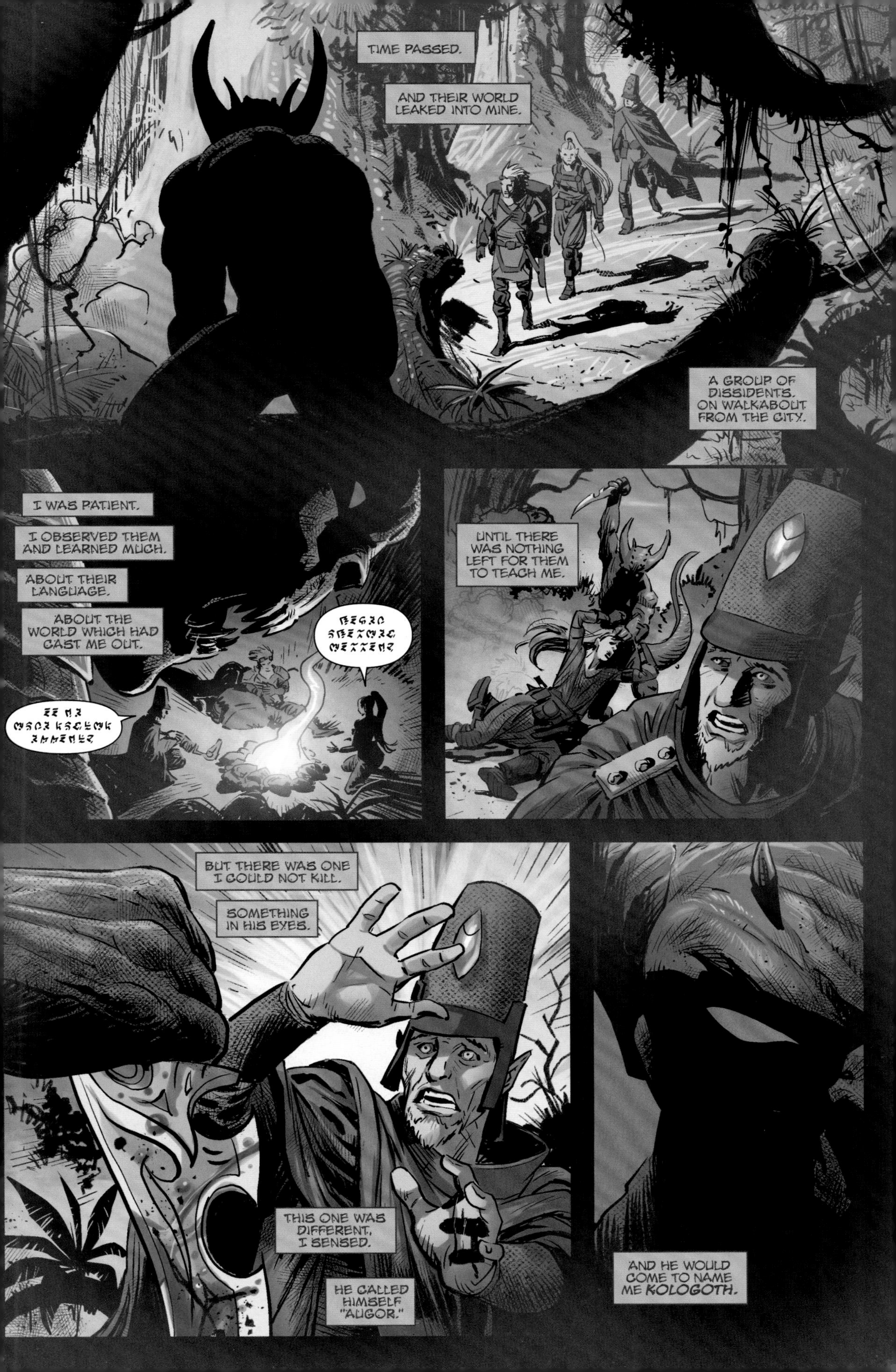
TIME PASSED.
AND THEIR WORLD LEAKED INTO MINE.
A GROUP OF DISSIDENTS, ON WALKABOUT FROM THE CITY.
I WAS PATIENT.
I OBSERVED THEM AND LEARNED MUCH.
ABOUT THEIR LANGUAGE.
ABOUT THE WORLD WHICH HAD CAST ME OUT.
UNTIL THERE WAS NOTHING LEFT FOR THEM TO TEACH ME.
BUT THERE WAS ONE I COULD NOT KILL.
SOMETHING IN HIS EYES.
THIS ONE WAS DIFFERENT, I SENSED.
HE CALLED HIMSELF "AUGOR."
AND HE WOULD COME TO NAME ME KOLOGOTH.

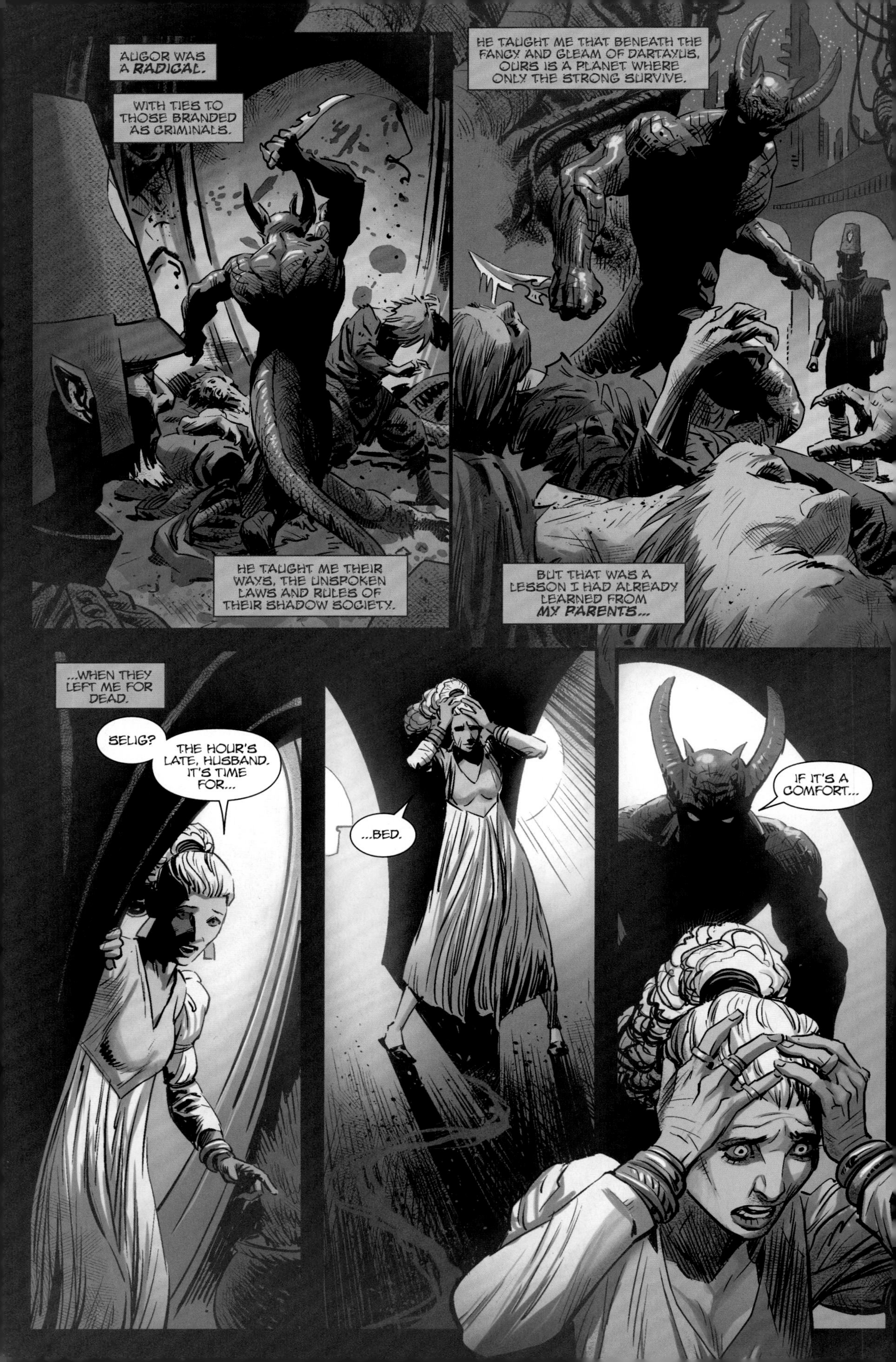
AUGOR WAS A RADICAL.
WITH TIES TO THOSE BRANDED AS CRIMINALS.
HE TAUGHT ME THEIR WAYS, THE UNSPOKEN LAWS AND RULES OF THEIR SHADOW SOCIETY.
HE TAUGHT ME THAT BENEATH THE FANCY AND GLEAM OF DARTAYUS, OURS IS A PLANET WHERE ONLY THE STRONG SURVIVE.
BUT THAT WAS A LESSON I HAD ALREADY LEARNED FROM MY PARENTS...
...WHEN THEY LEFT ME FOR DEAD.
SELIG?
THE HOUR'S LATE, HUSBAND. IT'S TIME FOR...
...BED.
IF IT'S A COMFORT...

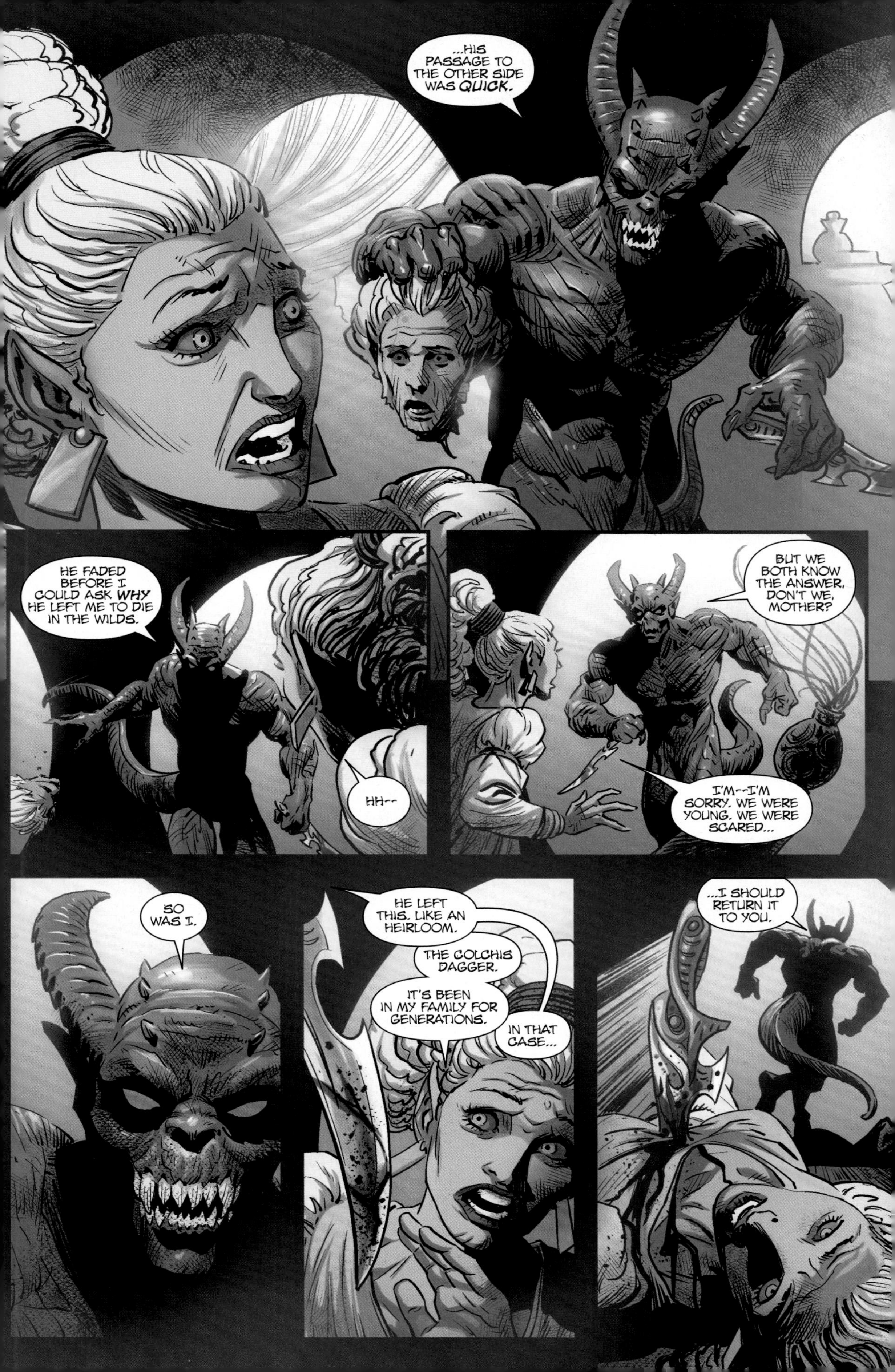
...HIS PASSAGE TO THE OTHER SIDE WAS QUICK.
HE FADED BEFORE I COULD ASK WHY HE LEFT ME TO DIE IN THE WILDS.
HH--
BUT WE BOTH KNOW THE ANSWER, DON'T WE, MOTHER?
I'M--I'M SORRY. WE WERE YOUNG. WE WERE SCARED...
SO WAS I.
HE LEFT THIS. LIKE AN HEIRLOOM.
THE COLCHIS DAGGER.
IT'S BEEN IN MY FAMILY FOR GENERATIONS.
IN THAT CASE...
...I SHOULD RETURN IT TO YOU.

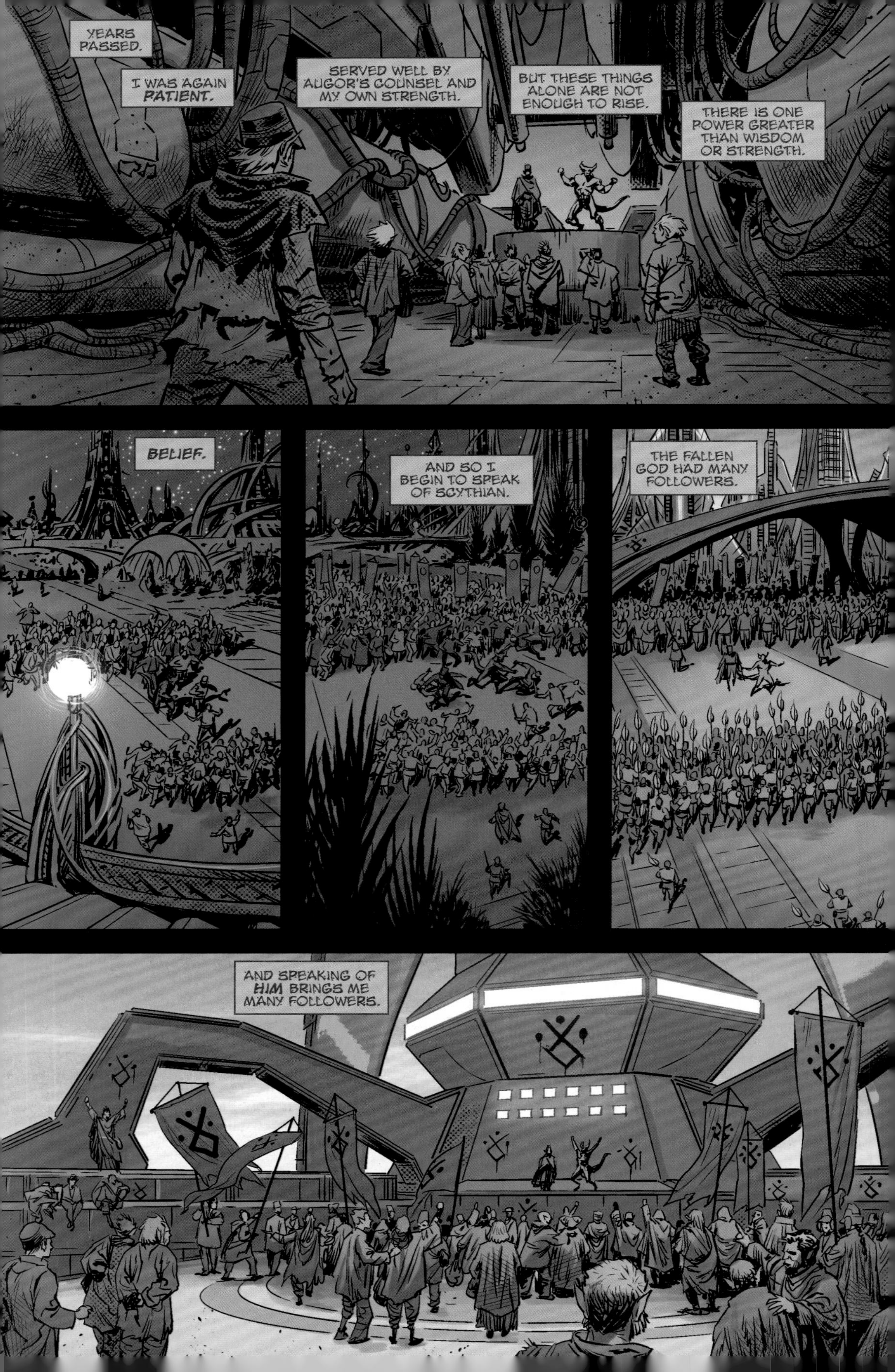
YEARS PASSED.
I WAS AGAIN PATIENT.
SERVED WELL BY AUGOR'S COUNSEL AND MY OWN STRENGTH.
BUT THESE THINGS ALONE ARE NOT ENOUGH TO RISE.
THERE IS ONE POWER GREATER THAN WISDOM OR STRENGTH.
BELIEF.
AND SO I BEGIN TO SPEAK OF SCYTHIAN.
THE FALLEN GOD HAD MANY FOLLOWERS.
AND SPEAKING OF HIM BRINGS ME MANY FOLLOWERS.

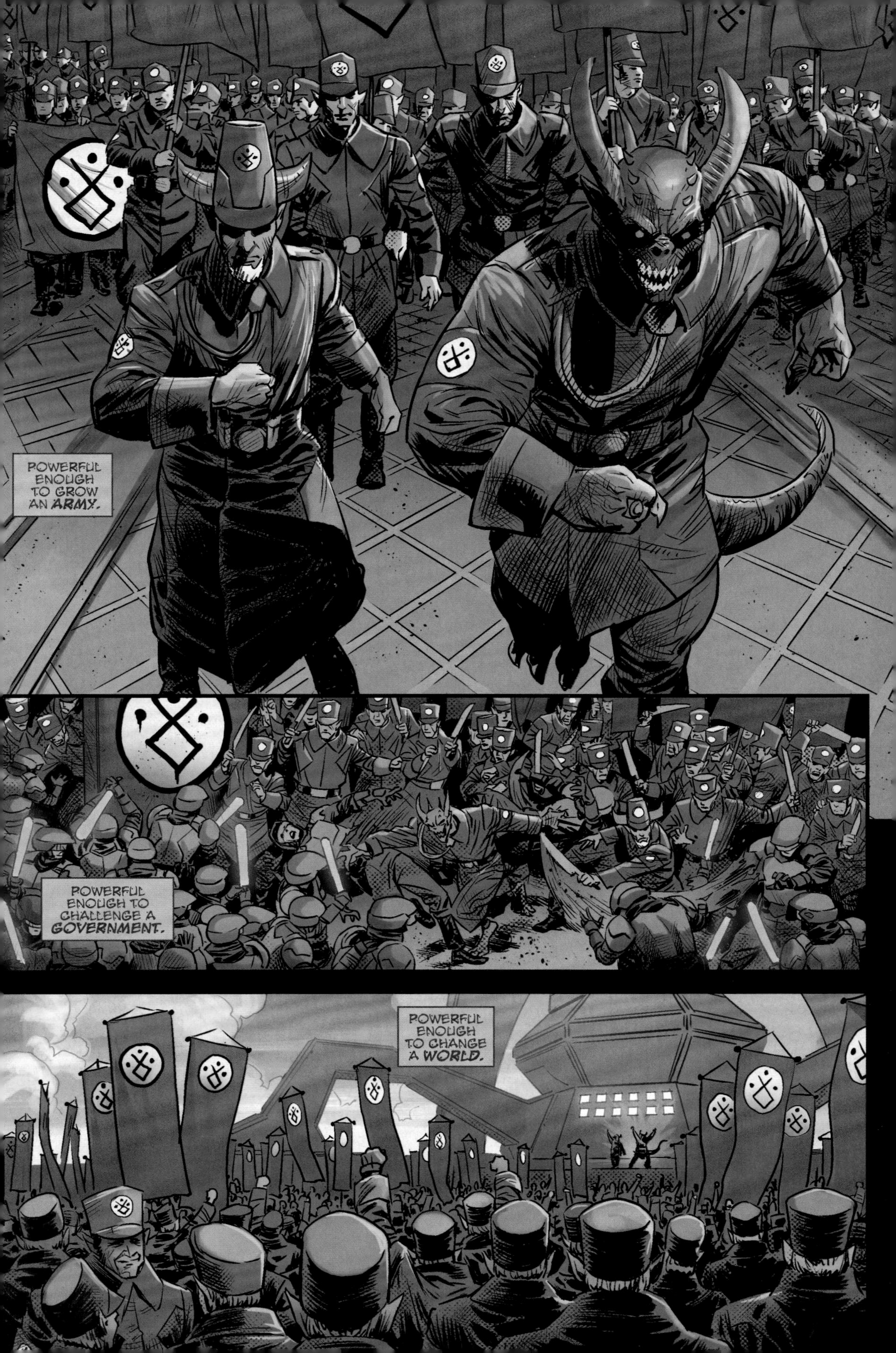
POWERFUL ENOUGH TO GROW AN ARMY.
POWERFUL ENOUGH TO CHALLENGE A GOVERNMENT.
POWERFUL ENOUGH TO CHANGE A WORLD.

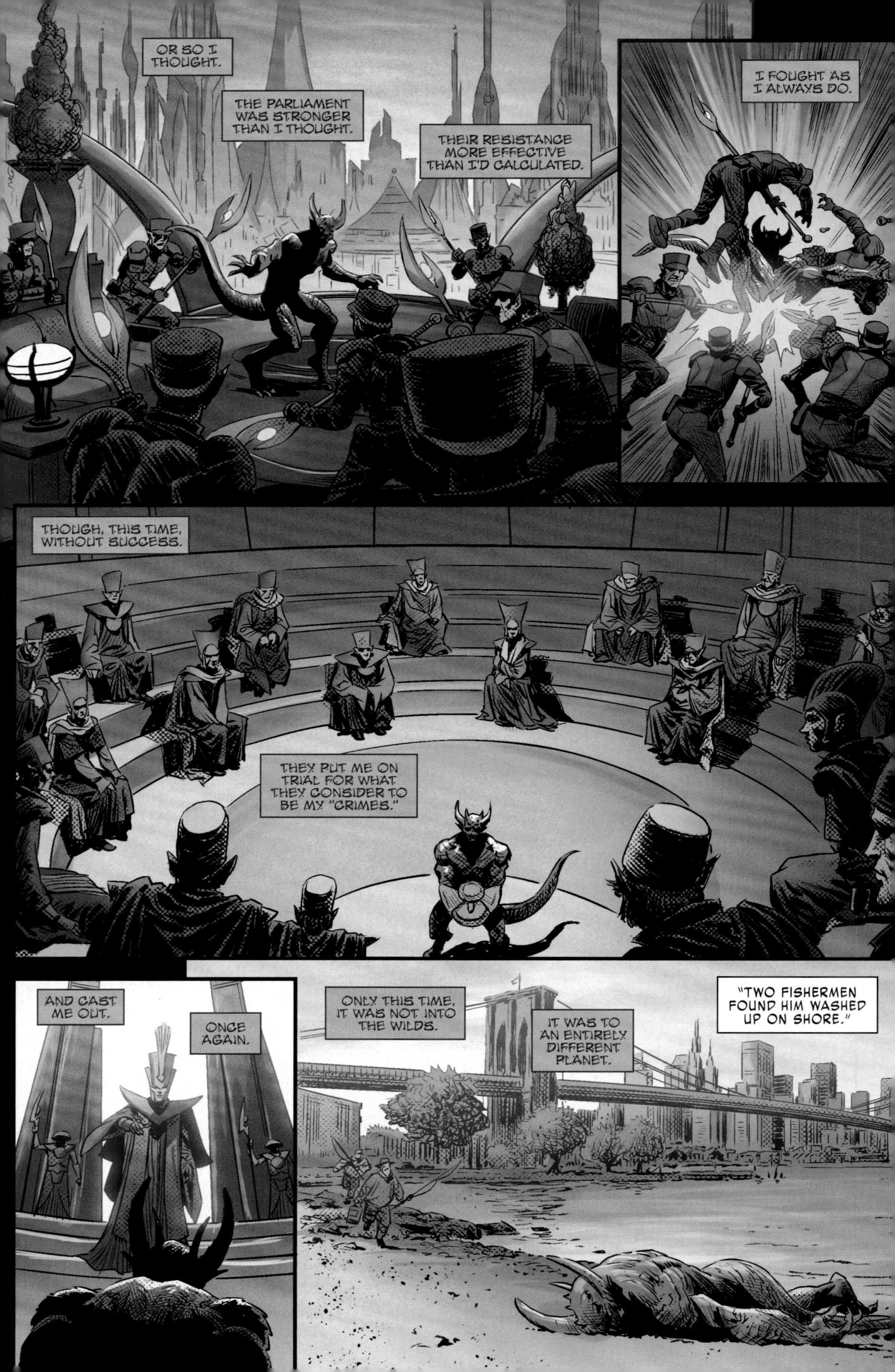
OR SO I THOUGHT.
THE PARLIAMENT WAS STRONGER THAN I THOUGHT.
THEIR RESISTANCE MORE EFFECTIVE THAN I'D CALCULATED.
I FOUGHT AS I ALWAYS DO.
THOUGH, THIS TIME, WITHOUT SUCCESS.
THEY PUT ME ON TRIAL FOR WHAT THEY CONSIDER TO BE MY "CRIMES."
AND CAST ME OUT.
ONCE AGAIN.
ONLY THIS TIME, IT WAS NOT INTO THE WILDS.
IT WAS TO AN ENTIRELY DIFFERENT PLANET.
"TWO FISHERMEN FOUND HIM WASHED UP ON SHORE."

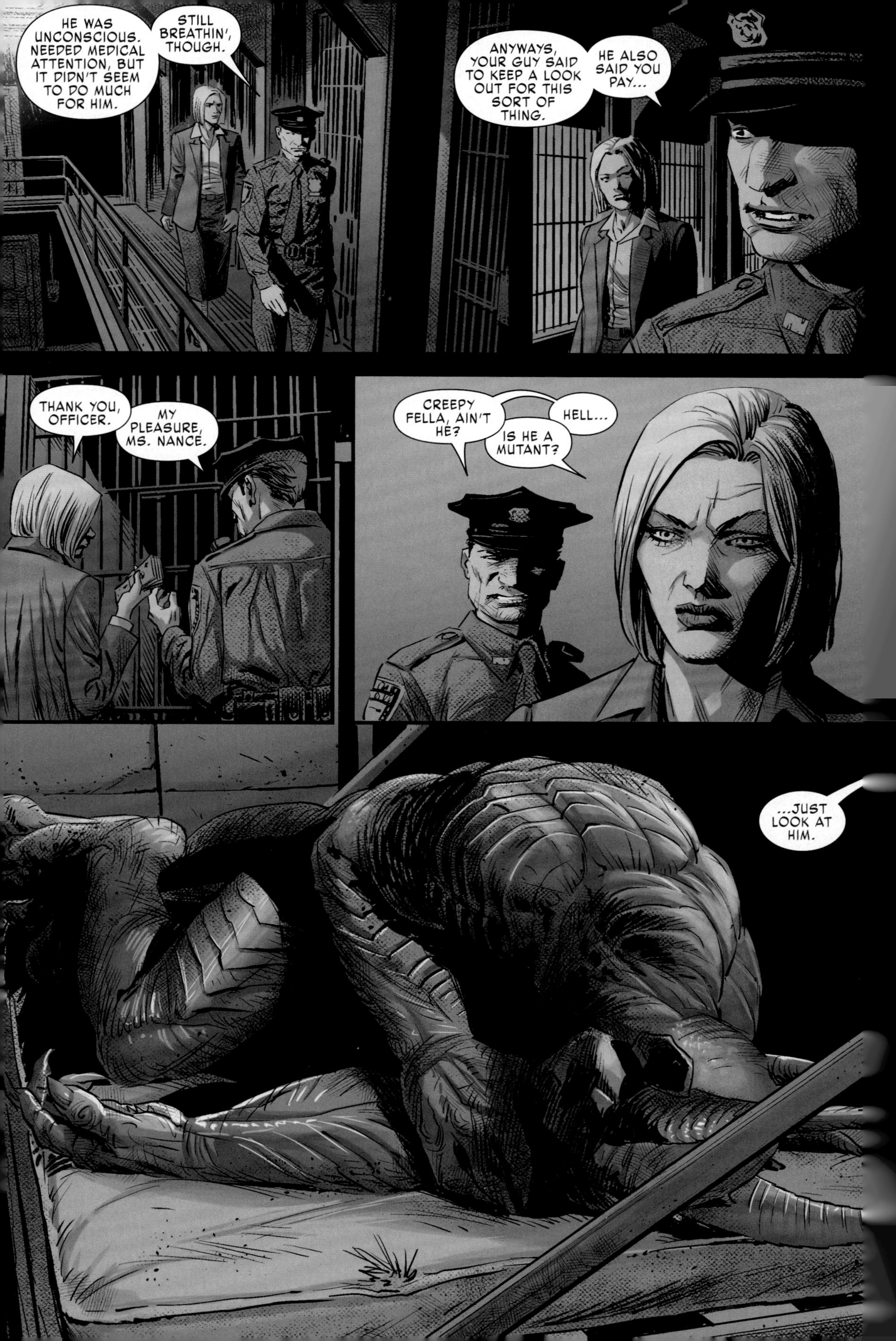

HE WAS UNCONSCIOUS. NEEDED MEDICAL ATTENTION, BUT IT DIDN'T SEEM TO DO MUCH FOR HIM.
STILL BREATHIN', THOUGH.
ANYWAYS, YOUR GUY SAID TO KEEP A LOOK OUT FOR THIS SORT OF THING.
HE ALSO SAID YOU PAY...
THANK YOU, OFFICER.
MY PLEASURE, MS. NANCE.
CREEPY FELLA, AIN'T HE?
IS HE A MUTANT?
HELL...
...JUST LOOK AT HIM.

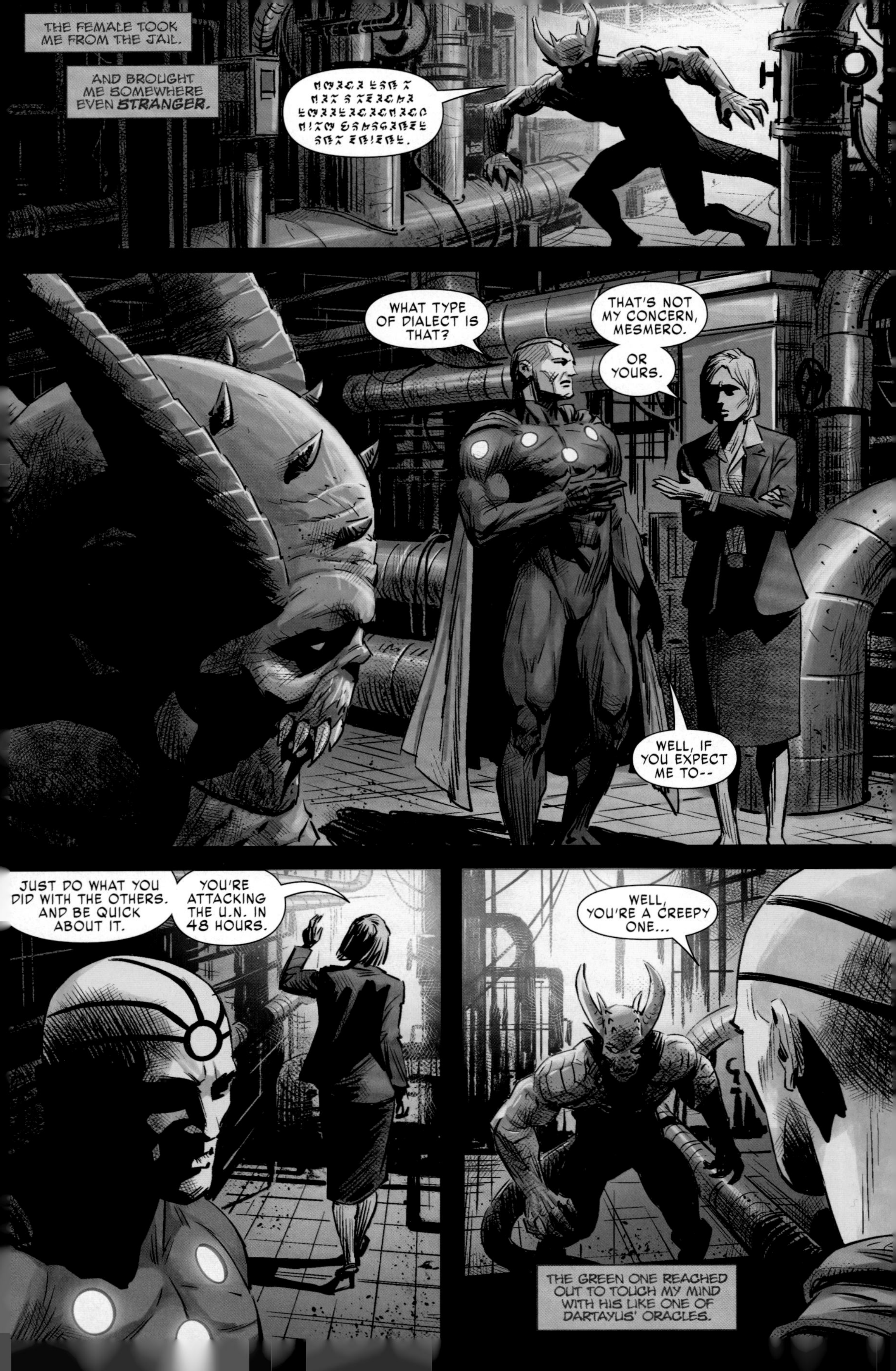
THE FEMALE TOOK ME FROM THE JAIL.
AND BROUGHT ME SOMEWHERE EVEN STRANGER.
WHAT TYPE OF DIALECT IS THAT?
THAT'S NOT MY CONCERN, MESMERO.
OR YOURS.
WELL, IF YOU EXPECT ME TO--
JUST DO WHAT YOU DID WITH THE OTHERS. AND BE QUICK ABOUT IT.
YOU'RE ATTACKING THE U.N. IN 48 HOURS.
WELL, YOU'RE A CREEPY ONE...
THE GREEN ONE REACHED OUT TO TOUCH MY MIND WITH HIS LIKE ONE OF DARTAYUS' ORACLES.

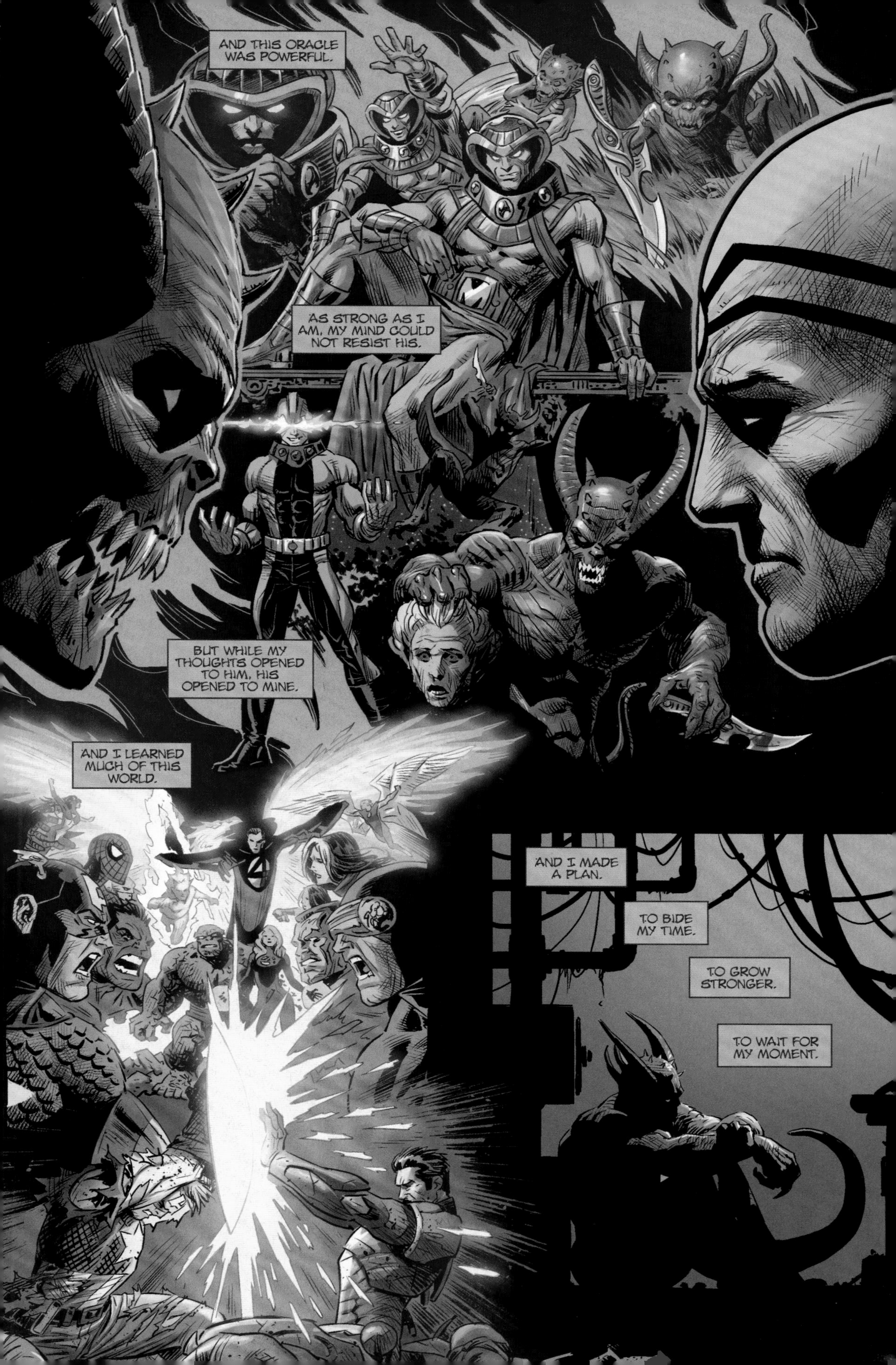
AND THIS ORACLE WAS POWERFUL.
'AS STRONG AS I AM, MY MIND COULD NOT RESIST HIS.
BUT WHILE MY THOUGHTS OPENED TO HIM, HIS OPENED TO MINE.
'AND I LEARNED MUCH OF THIS WORLD.
'AND I MADE A PLAN.
TO BIDE MY TIME.
TO GROW STRONGER.
TO WAIT FOR MY MOMENT.

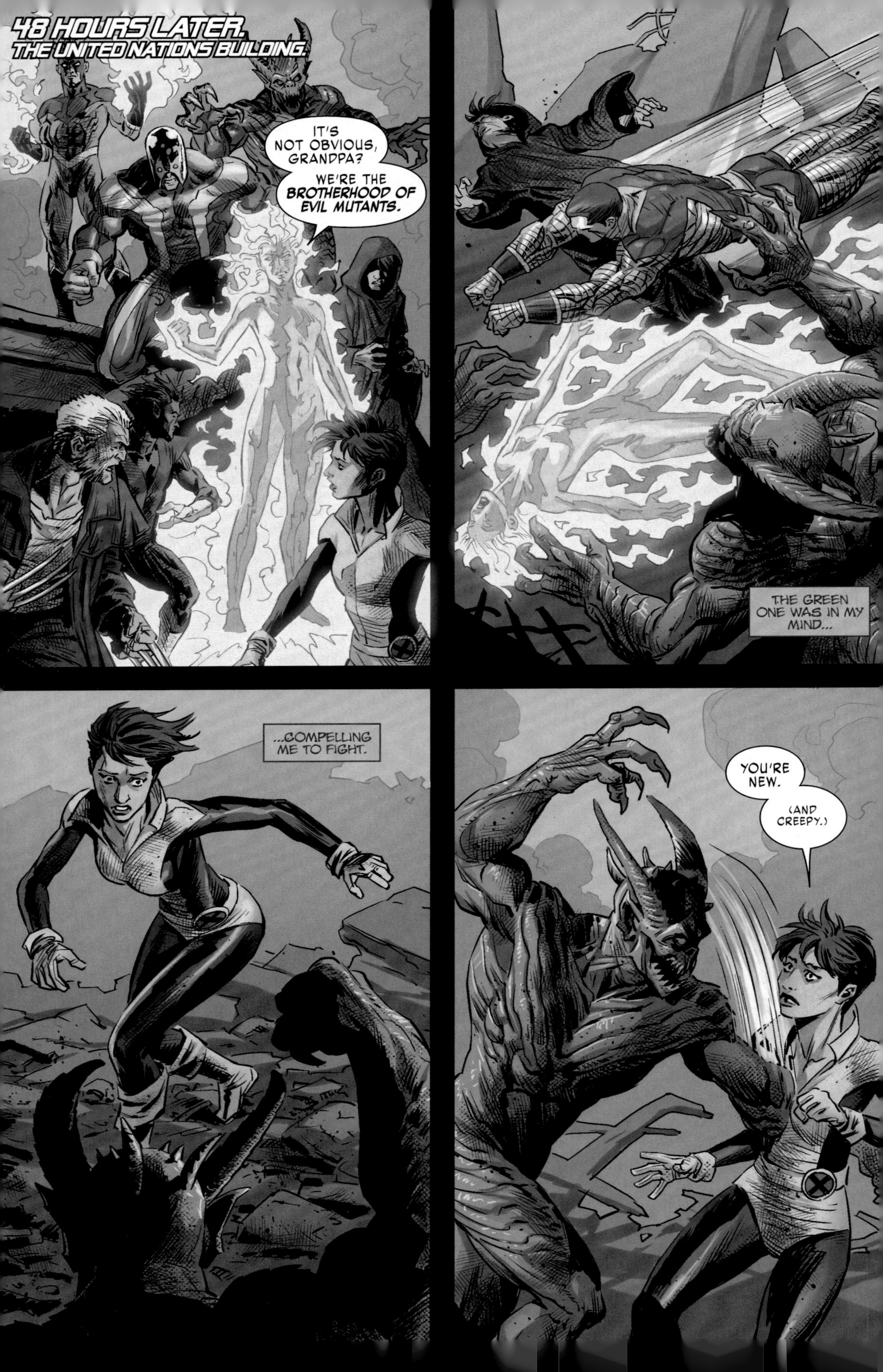

48 HOURS LATER.
THE UNITED NATIONS BUILDING.
IT'S NOT OBVIOUS, GRANDPA?
WE'RE THE BROTHERHOOD OF EVIL MUTANTS.
THE GREEN ONE WAS IN MY MIND...
...COMPELLING ME TO FIGHT.
YOU'RE NEW.
(AND CREEPY.)

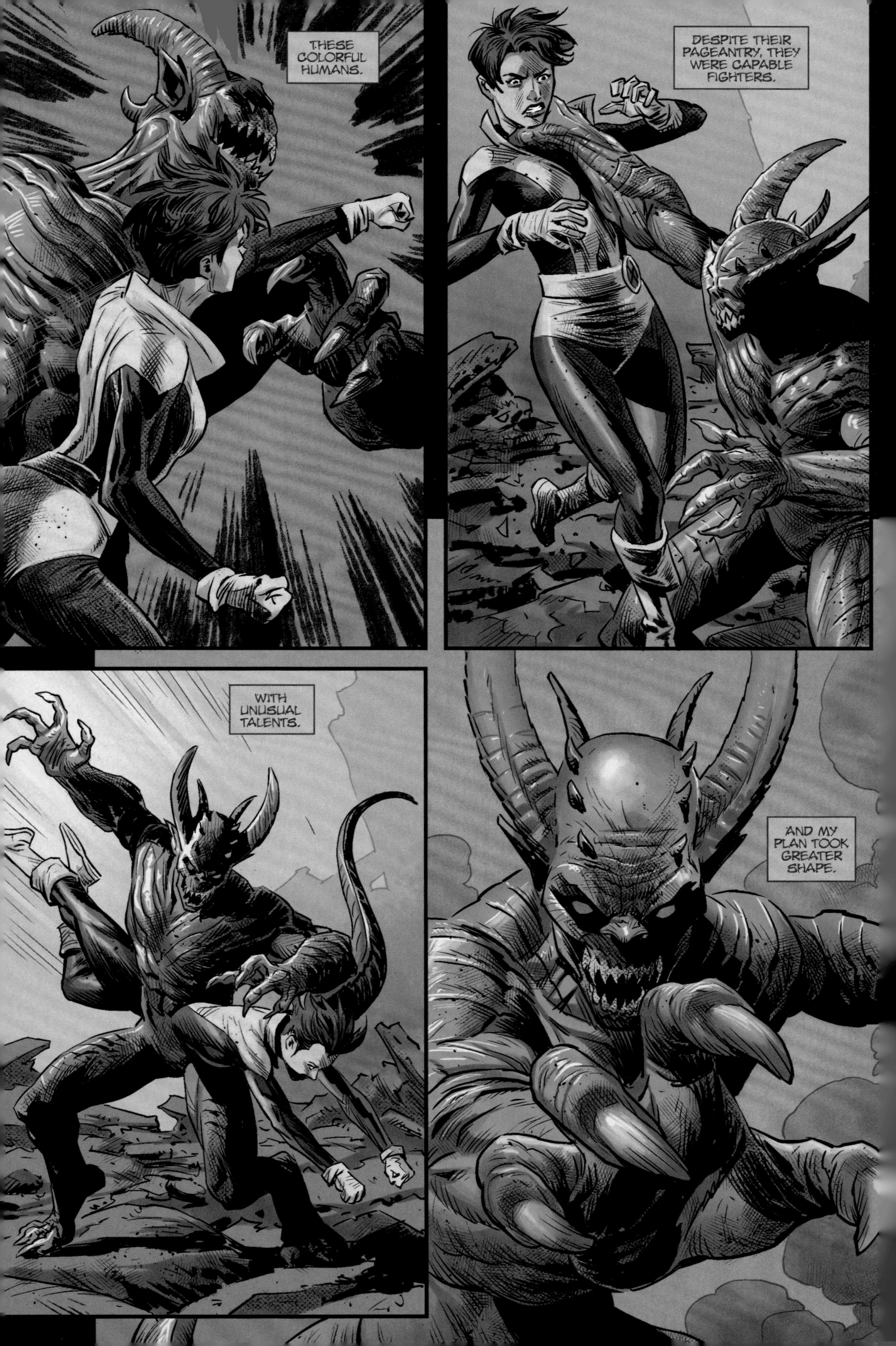
THESE COLORFUL HUMANS.
DESPITE THEIR PAGEANTRY, THEY WERE CAPABLE FIGHTERS.
WITH UNUSUAL TALENTS.
AND MY PLAN TOOK GREATER SHAPE.

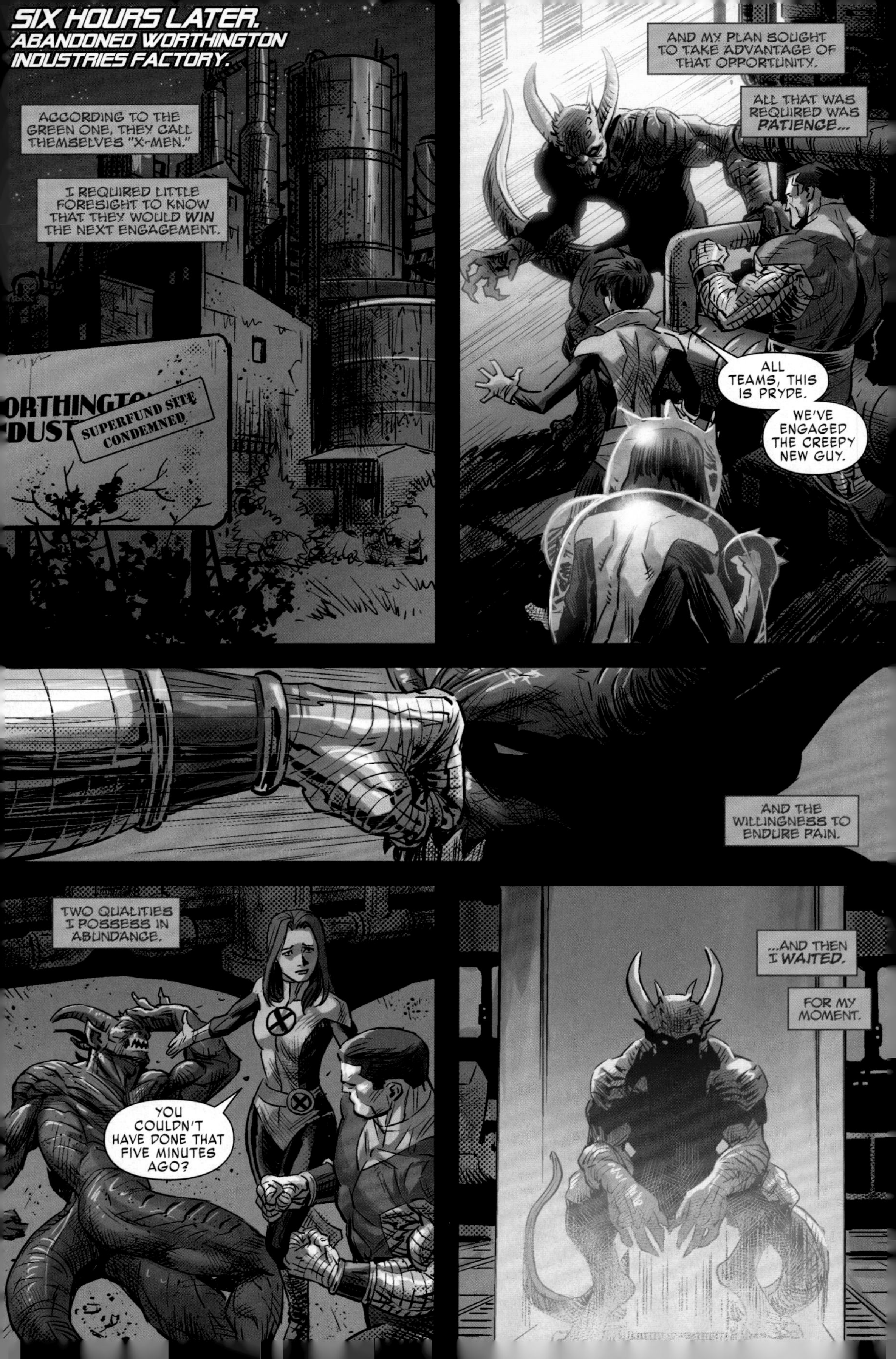
SIX HOURS LATER. ABANDONED WORTHINGTON INDUSTRIES FACTORY.
ACCORDING TO THE GREEN ONE, THEY CALL THEMSELVES "X-MEN."
I REQUIRED LITTLE FORESIGHT TO KNOW THAT THEY WOULD WIN THE NEXT ENGAGEMENT.
SUPERFUND SITE CONDEMNED
AND MY PLAN SOUGHT TO TAKE ADVANTAGE OF THAT OPPORTUNITY.
ALL THAT WAS REQUIRED WAS PATIENCE...
ALL TEAMS, THIS IS PRYDE.
WE'VE ENGAGED THE CREEPY NEW GUY.
AND THE WILLINGNESS TO ENDURE PAIN.
TWO QUALITIES I POSSESS IN ABUNDANCE.
YOU COULDN'T HAVE DONE THAT FIVE MINUTES AGO?
...AND THEN I WAITED.
FOR MY MOMENT.

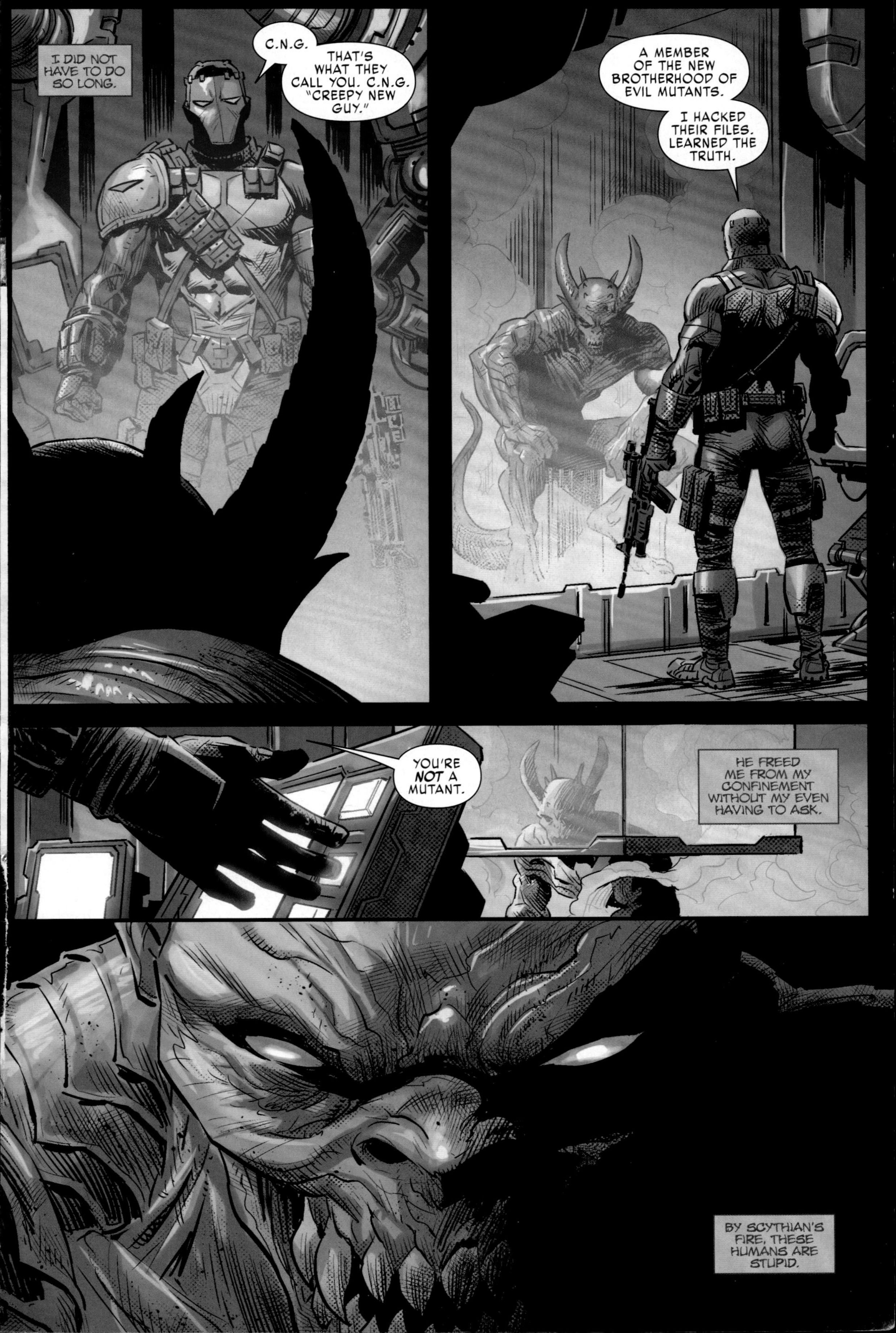

I DID NOT HAVE TO DO SO LONG.
C.N.G.
THAT'S WHAT THEY CALL YOU. C.N.G. "CREEPY NEW GUY."
A MEMBER OF THE NEW BROTHERHOOD OF EVIL MUTANTS.
I HACKED THEIR FILES. LEARNED THE TRUTH.
YOU'RE NOT A MUTANT.
HE FREED ME FROM MY CONFINEMENT WITHOUT MY EVEN HAVING TO ASK.
BY SCYTHIAN'S FIRE, THESE HUMANS ARE STUPID.

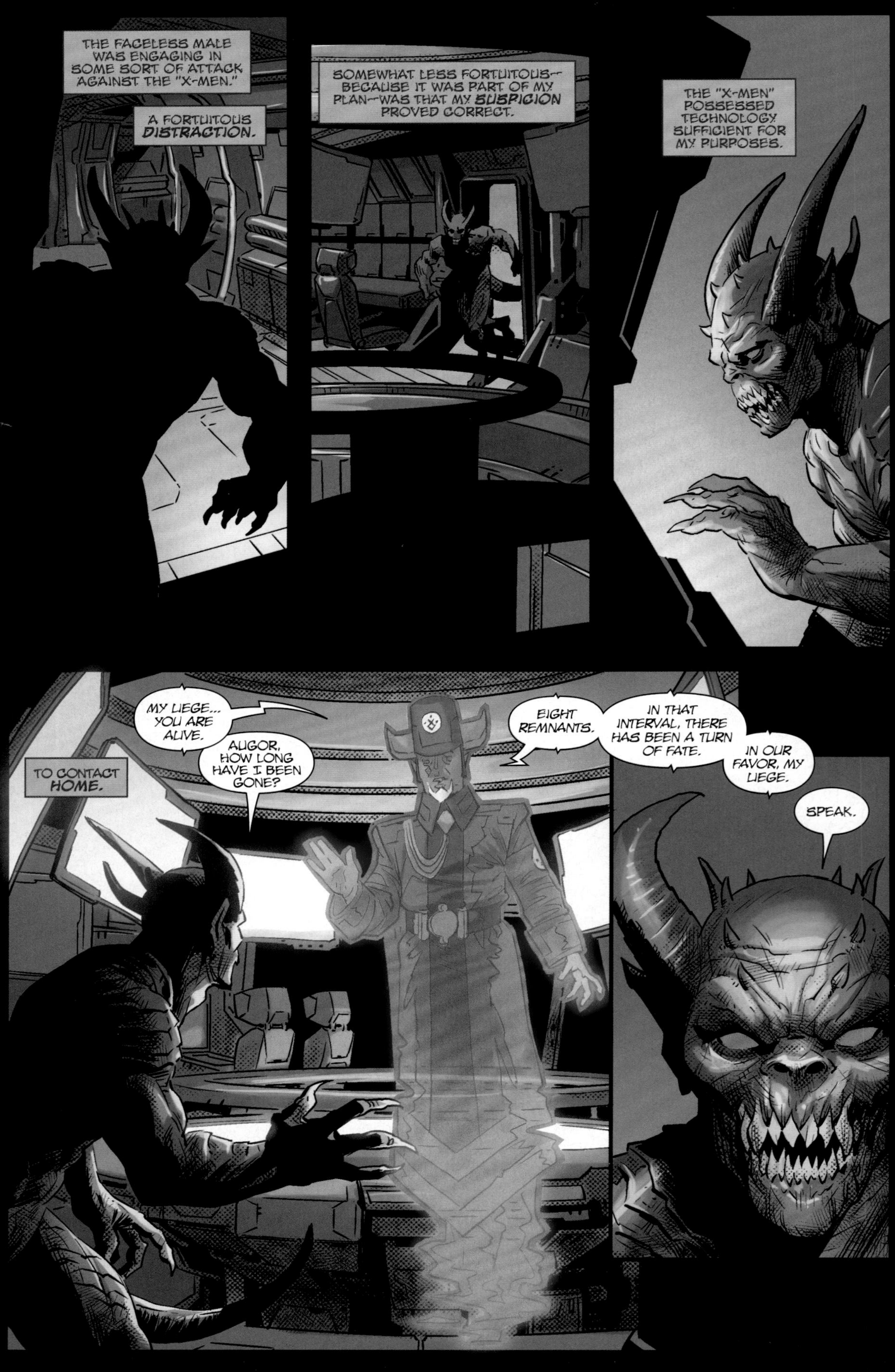

THE FACELESS MALE WAS ENGAGING IN SOME SORT OF ATTACK AGAINST THE "X-MEN."
A FORTUITOUS DISTRACTION.
SOMEWHAT LESS FORTUITOUS-- BECAUSE IT WAS PART OF MY PLAN--WAS THAT MY SUSPICION PROVED CORRECT.
THE "X-MEN" POSSESSED TECHNOLOGY SUFFICIENT FOR MY PURPOSES.
TO CONTACT HOME.
MY LIEGE... YOU ARE ALIVE.
AUGOR, HOW LONG HAVE I BEEN GONE?
EIGHT REMNANTS.
IN THAT INTERVAL, THERE HAS BEEN A TURN OF FATE.
IN OUR FAVOR, MY LIEGE.
SPEAK.

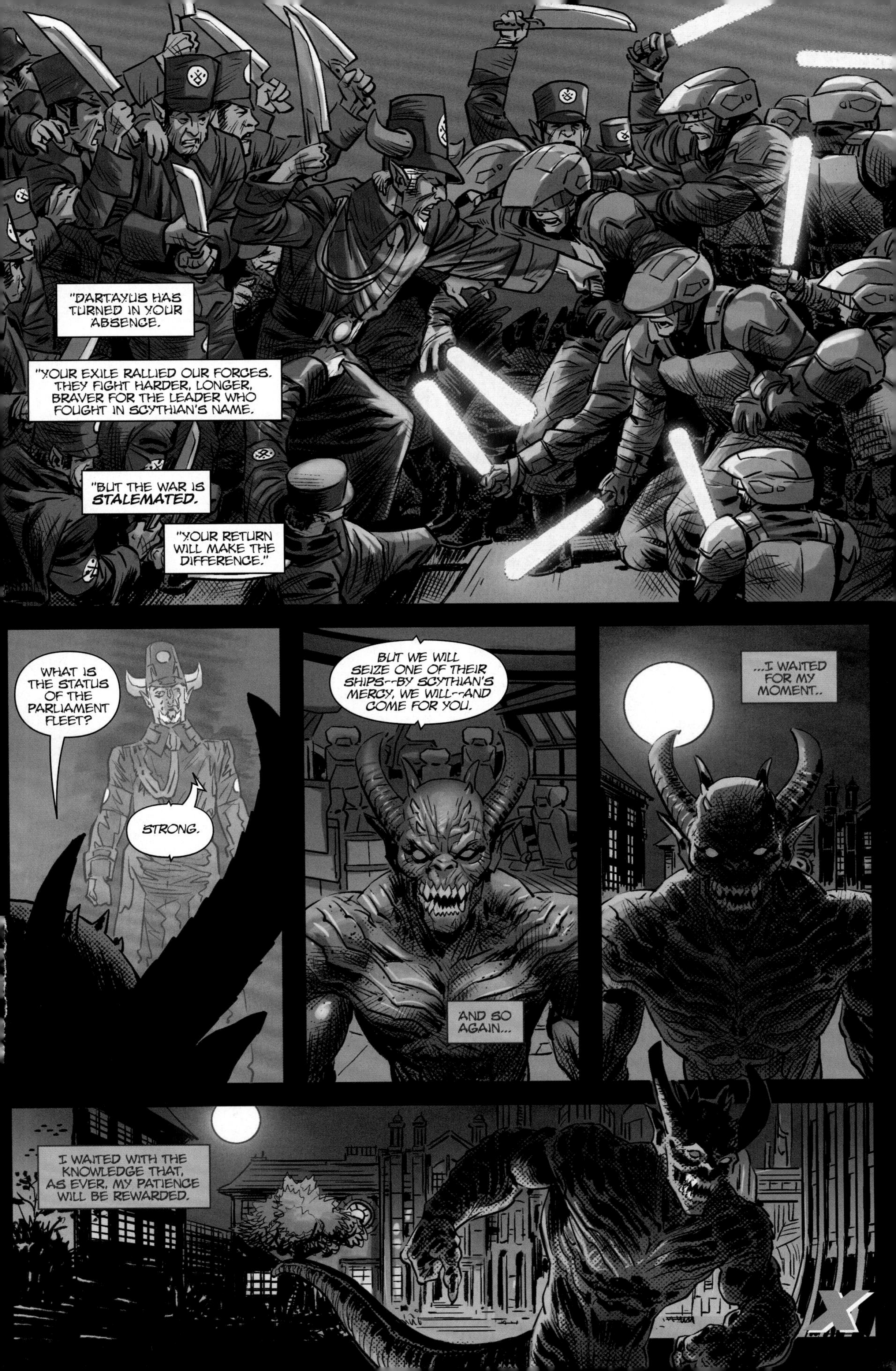
"DARTAYUS HAS TURNED IN YOUR ABSENCE.
"YOUR EXILE RALLIED OUR FORCES. THEY FIGHT HARDER, LONGER, BRAVER FOR THE LEADER WHO FOUGHT IN SCYTHIAN'S NAME.
"BUT THE WAR IS STALEMATED.
"YOUR RETURN WILL MAKE THE DIFFERENCE."
WHAT IS THE STATUS OF THE PARLIAMENT FLEET?
STRONG.
BUT WE WILL SEIZE ONE OF THEIR SHIPS--BY SCYTHIAN'S MERCY, WE WILL--AND COME FOR YOU.
AND SO AGAIN...
...I WAITED FOR MY MOMENT..
I WAITED WITH THE KNOWLEDGE THAT, AS EVER, MY PATIENCE WILL BE REWARDED.

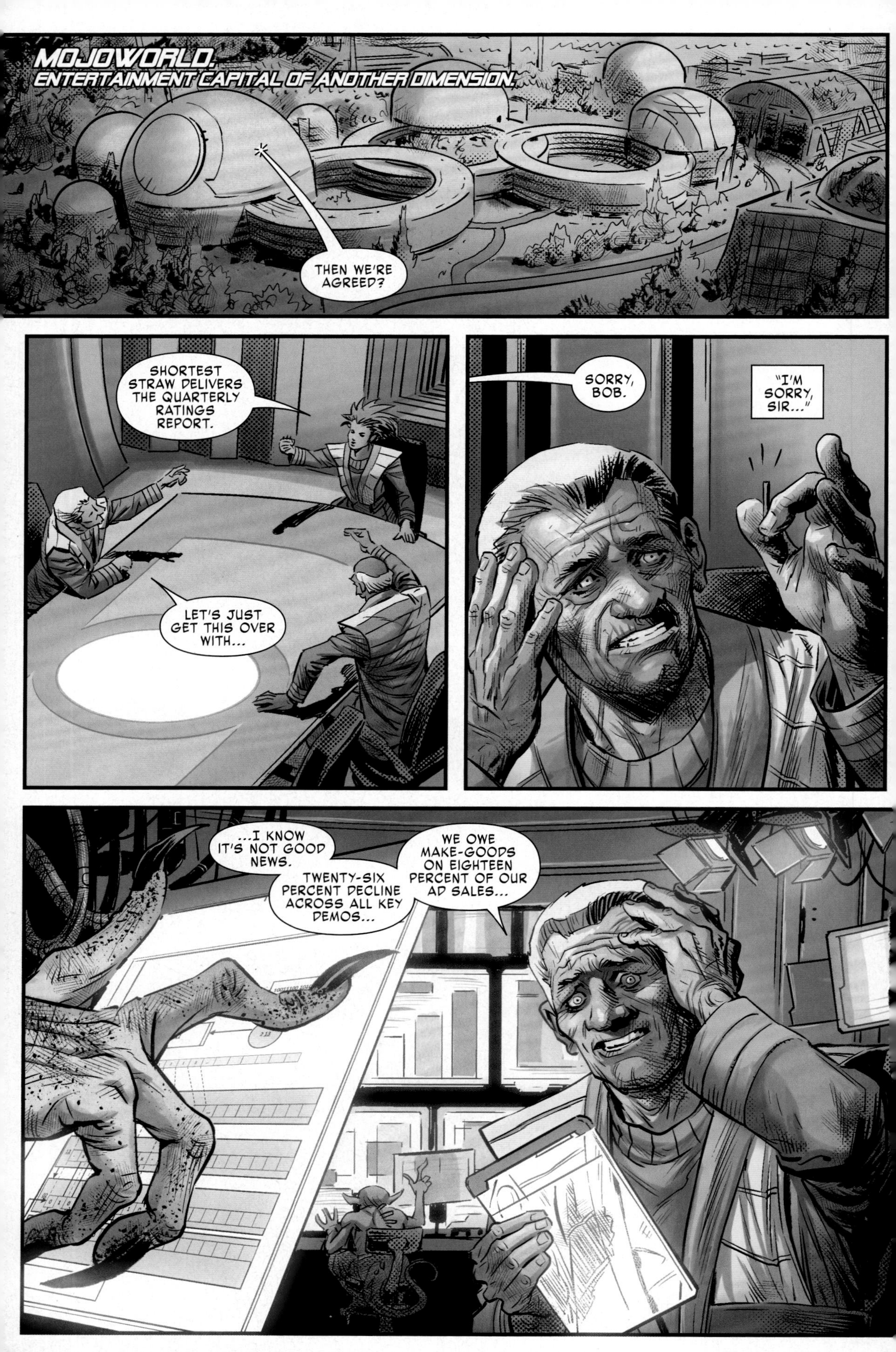
MOJOWORLD.
ENTERTAINMENT CAPITAL OF ANOTHER DIMENSION.
THEN WE'RE AGREED?
SHORTEST STRAW DELIVERS THE QUARTERLY RATINGS REPORT.
LET'S JUST GET THIS OVER WITH...
SORRY, BOB.
"I'M SORRY, SIR..."
...I KNOW IT'S NOT GOOD NEWS.
TWENTY-SIX PERCENT DECLINE ACROSS ALL KEY DEMOS...
WE OWE MAKE-GOODS ON EIGHTEEN PERCENT OF OUR AD SALES...

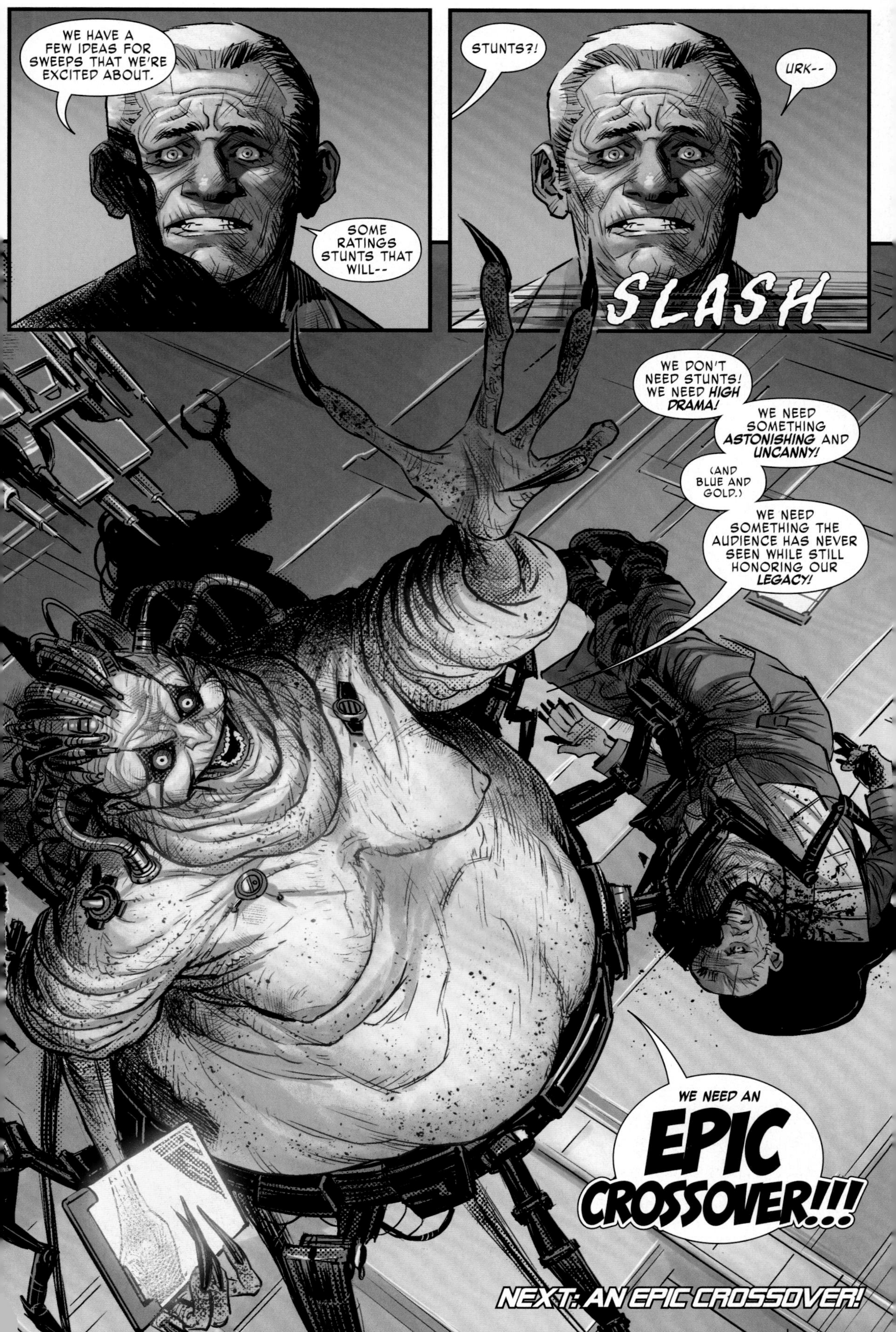
WE HAVE A FEW IDEAS FOR SWEEPS THAT WE'RE EXCITED ABOUT.
SOME RATINGS STUNTS THAT WILL--
STUNTS?!
URK--
SLASH
WE DON'T NEED STUNTS! WE NEED HIGH DRAMA!
WE NEED SOMETHING ASTONISHING AND UNCANNY!
(AND BLUE AND GOLD.)
WE NEED SOMETHING THE AUDIENCE HAS NEVER SEEN WHILE STILL HONORING OUR LEGACY!
WE NEED AN EPIC CROSSOVER!!!
NEXT: AN EPIC CROSSOVER!

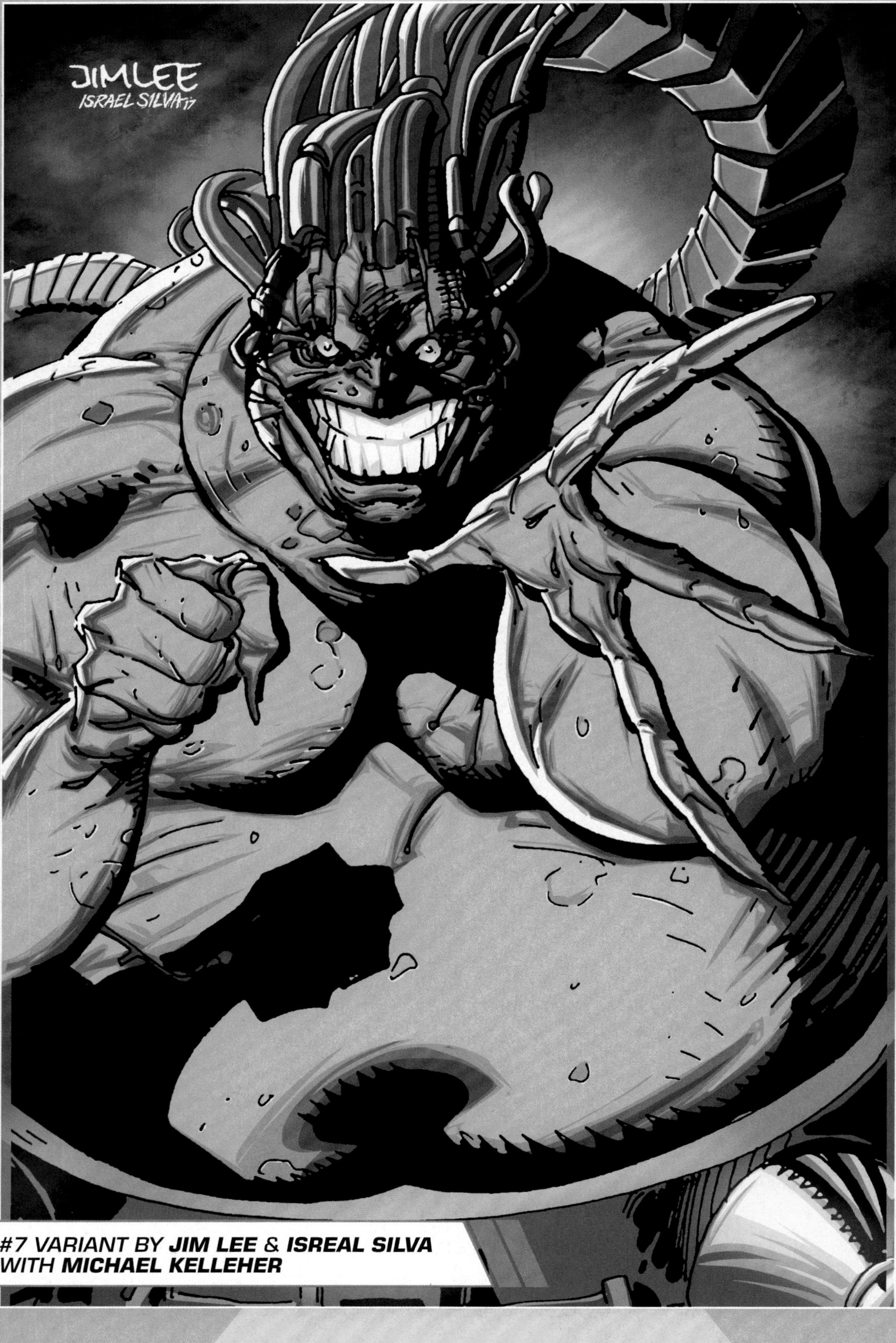
JIMLEE
ISRAEL SILVA '17

#7 VARIANT BY **JIM LEE** & **ISREAL SILVA**
WITH **MICHAEL KELLEHER**

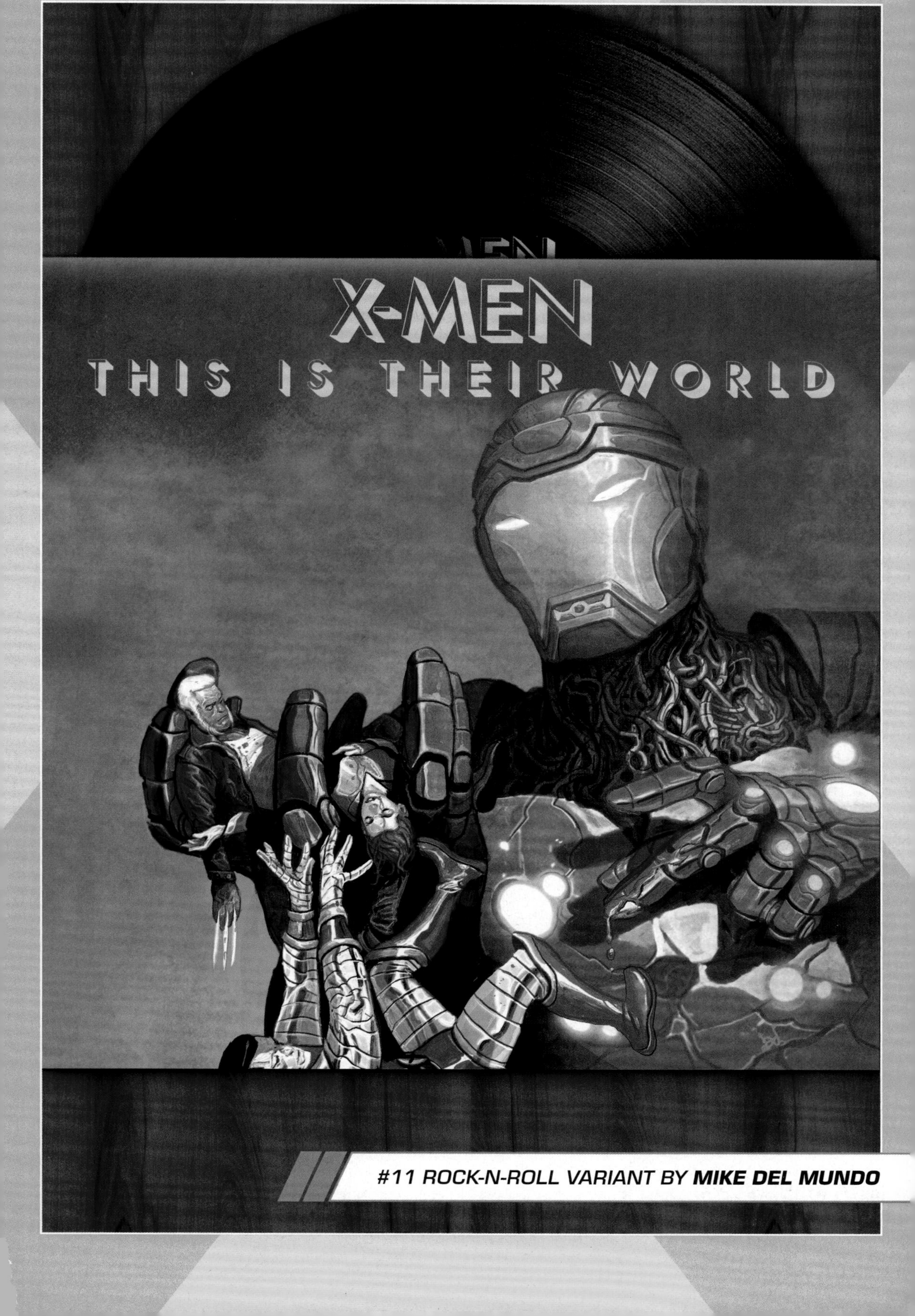
X-MEN
THIS IS THEIR WORLD

#11 ROCK-N-ROLL VARIANT BY **MIKE DEL MUNDO**

#11 VENOMIZED VILLIANS VARIANT
BY **CLAYTON CRAIN**

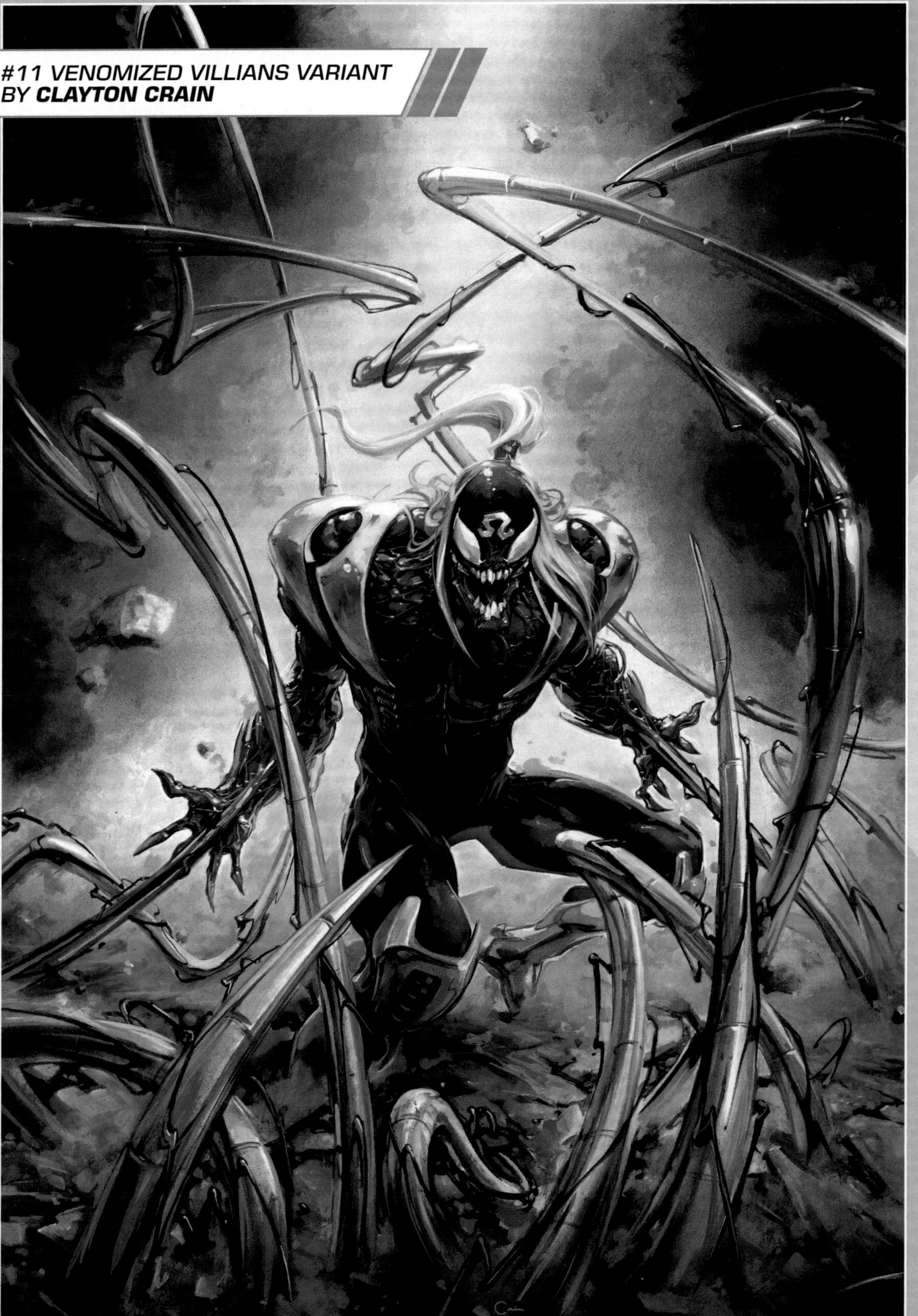

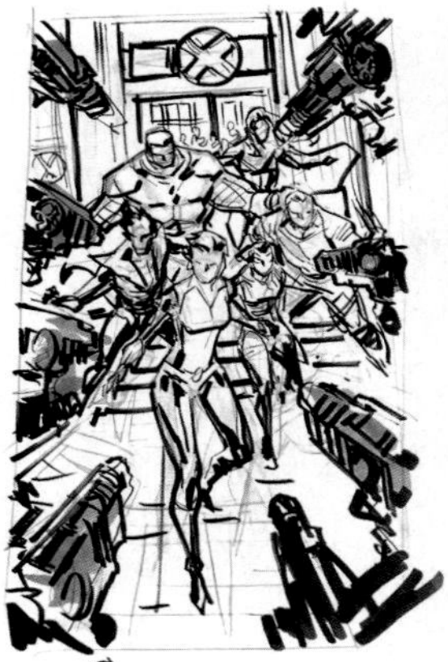

A

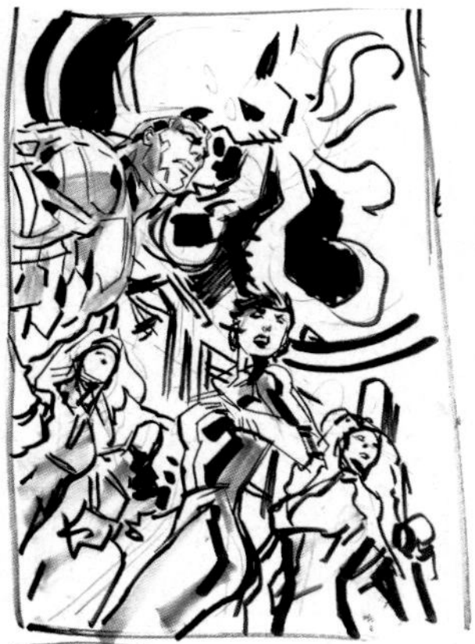

B

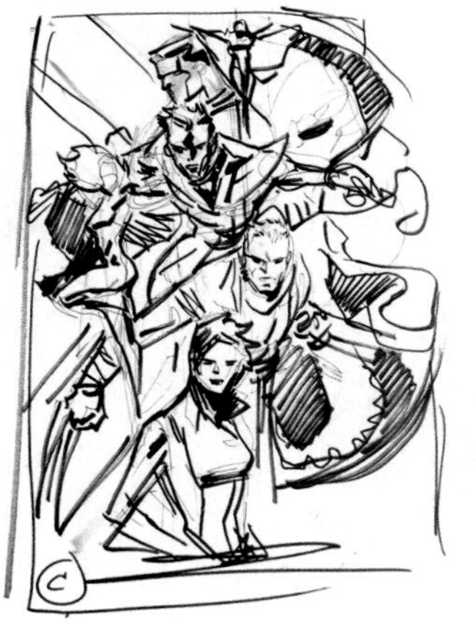

C

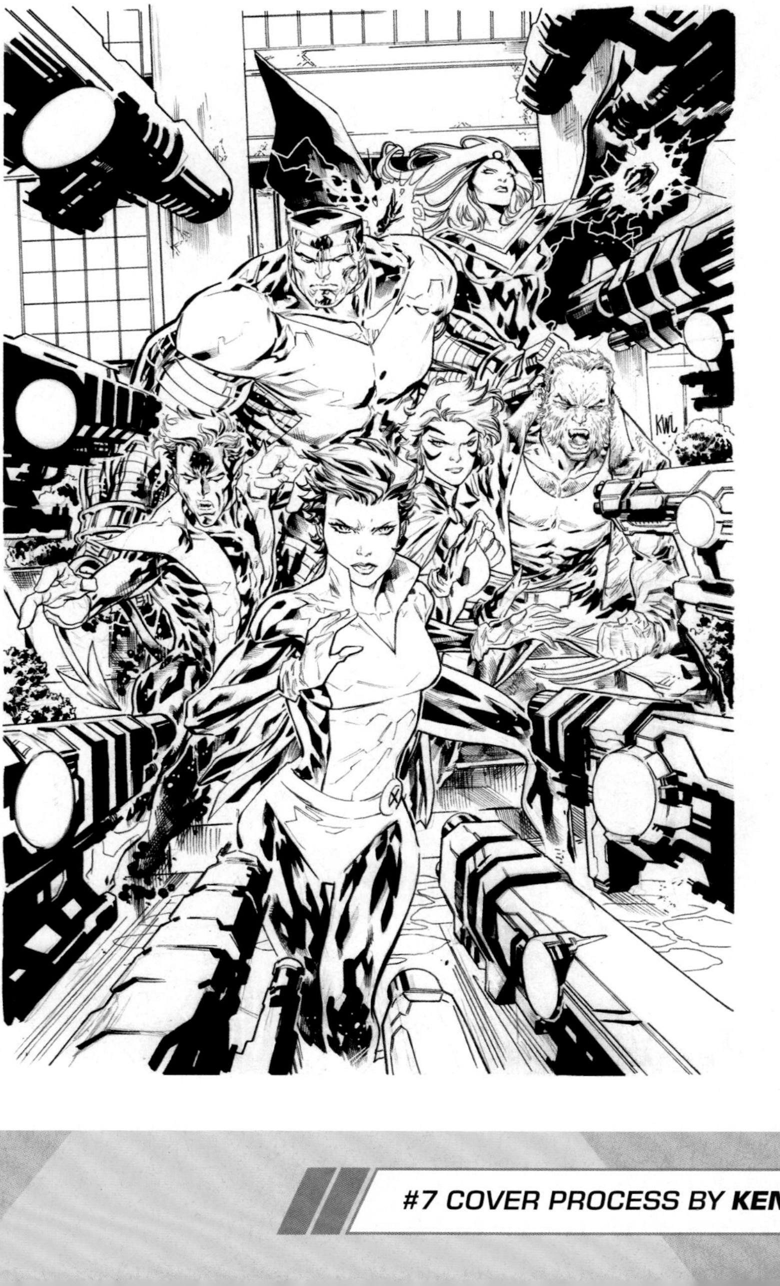

#7 COVER PROCESS BY **KEN LASHLEY**

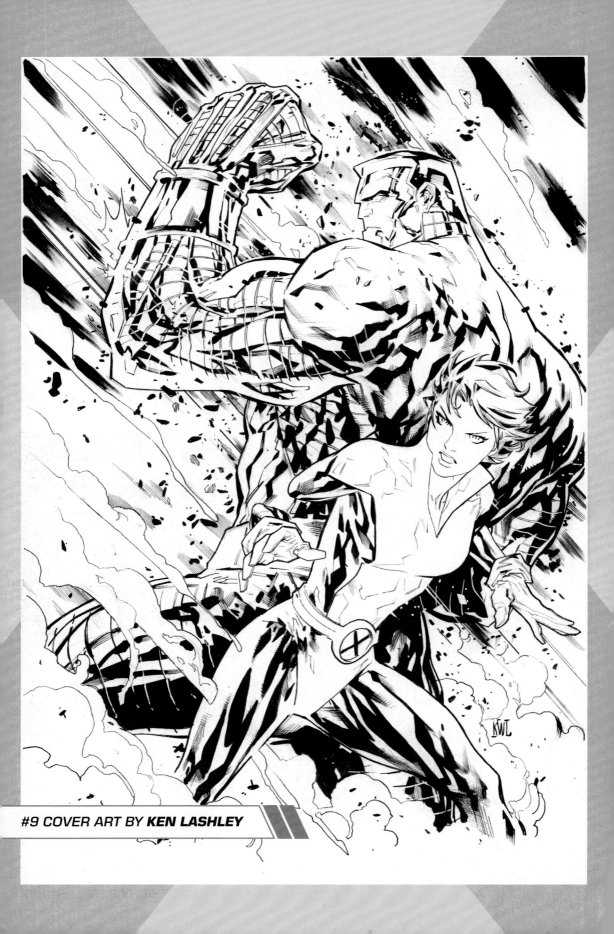

#9 COVER ART BY **KEN LASHLEY**

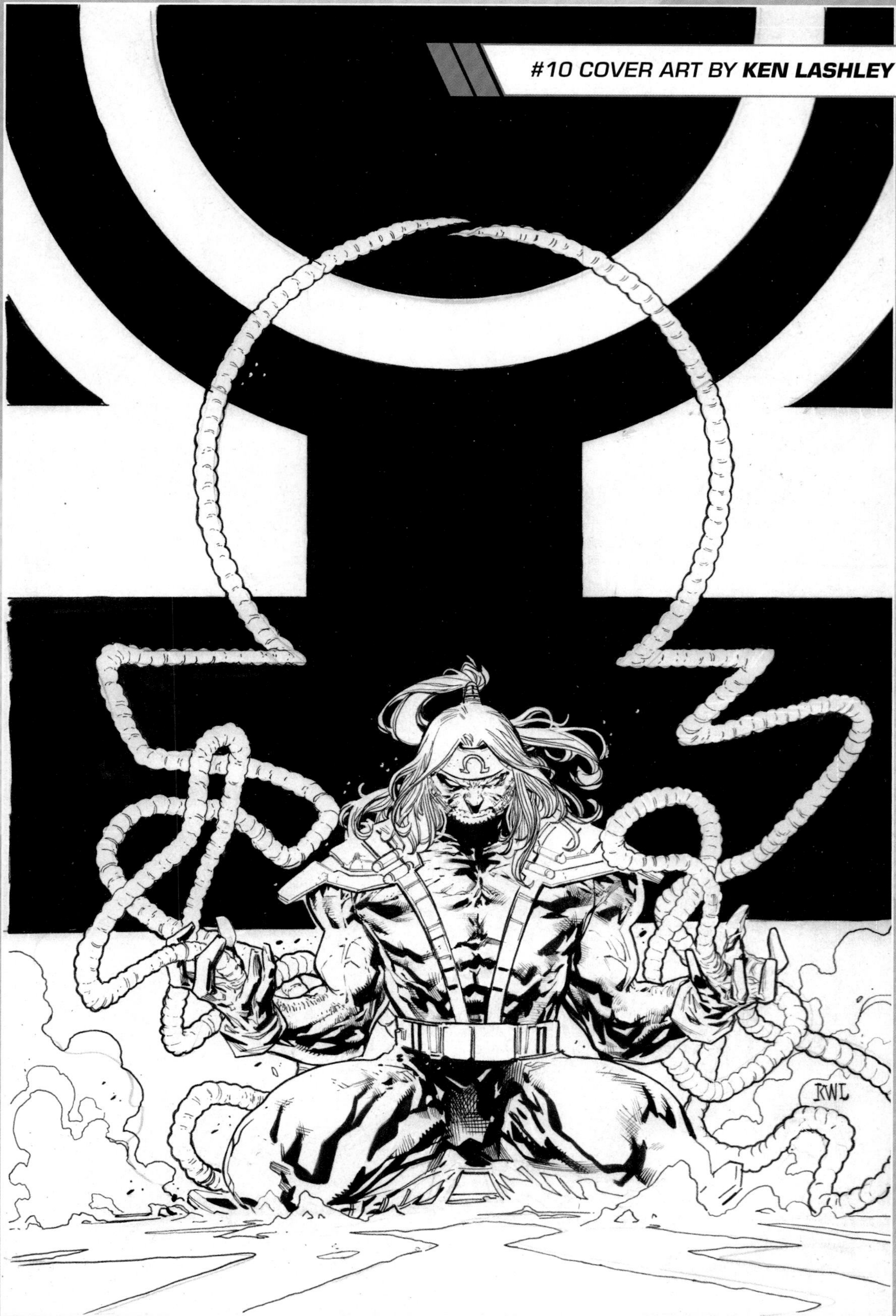

#10 COVER ART BY **KEN LASHLEY**

#12 COVER ART BY **KEN LASHLEY**

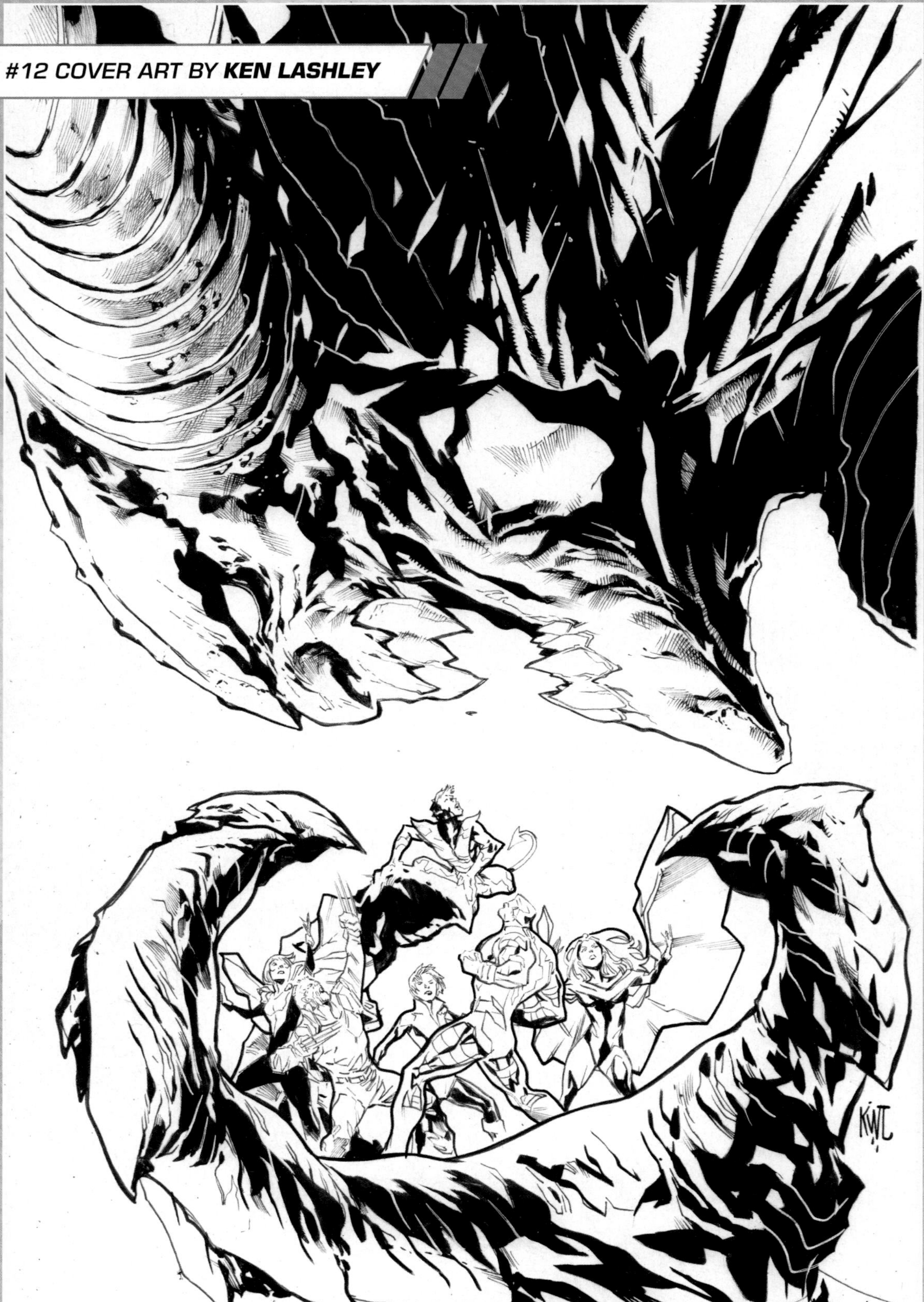